Michael J. Miller

The Hijacked Elephant

Every major theological event in Christianity found in the New Testament is the fulfillment of the archetypical high holy days found in the Old Testament.

The second coming of Christ is no exception.

If the shoe fits, wear it.

Also by Michael J. Miller
The Blind Man's Elephant

Copyright © 2008, 2009
The Hijacked Elephant, Michael J. Miller

All rights reserved under International and Pan-American Copyright Conventions. No part of this book may be reproduced in any form or by any means whatsoever without prior written permission of the publisher except in the case of brief quotations embodied in critical articles, reviews or books when properly credited.

ISBN: 978-976-8212-34-4

A redshoebooks publication www.redshoe.com

Cover design: Blue-Concepts GmbH
www.blue-concepts.com

The red shoe and redshoebooks bookmark graphics are trademarks of redshoebooks.

Dedication

"...for wide is the gate and broad is the way that leads to destruction, and there are a multitude who go in by it."

This book is for all those who don't run with the herd.

Table of Contents

	Page
Acknowledgements	9
Preface	13
Chapter One Where do we go to see the elephant?	21
Chapter Two Archetypes: The Duality of Days	57
Chapter Three Passover, Days of Unleavened Bread	83
Chapter Four Pentecost, the First Fruits & Christianity	119
Chapter Five Christ's Return, Trumpets, Civil New Year	145
Chapter Six Christ & the Duality of Atonement	199
Chapter Seven The Duality of the Autumn Harvest	227
Chapter Eight The Last Great Day	245
In Conclusion	261
Appendix One Lists	271
Appendix Two Endnotes	279

The Hijacked Elephant

Acknowledgements

First of all, I would like to thank the person or persons who've put a lot of effort into creating www.eliyah.com. While I do not know those involved personally, the resource has saved me countless hours of time between the covers of my own books whose fonts have surreptitiously shrunk and blurred over the decades. Command+ is a wonderful device. The tools therein provided made my work much more efficient and productive. It is a worthwhile website for anyone wishing to seek answers for themselves. I recommend you check it out. And when you do, I should point out that I use the common names in the Biblical record for the LORD, God and Jesus as the readers already have enough of it getting their minds around the discoveries presented in this book.

I'd also like to thank Matthew Henry for his studious and exhaustive commentary on the Biblical record. However, seeing as how he was born in 1662 in England, I may encounter a bit of difficulty in doing so. My primary reason in using Mr. Henry's fine commentary is that one, it is well expressed; and two, it was published in 1706. As such his explanations and studied opinions, coupled with his being a bit of a non-conformist, have the advantage of being seen through late 17th and early 18th century eyes. For a bit of perspective, 1706 was the year Benjamin Franklin was born, and the year that the kingdoms of England and Scotland became Great Britain. And I'm very grateful that my friends in Scotland at Bruichladdich are independent still, pun intended, providing their fair share to the angels.

For much the same reason, I would be referring to Matthew Henry now, not Bruichladdich, I'd like to thank the trio of Robert Jamieson, A.R. Fausset and David Brown [JFB] for their commentary first published in 1871 less than a year before Darwin's 6th edition of *Origin of the Species*. Generally, their commentary is considered conservative in its theology, which is to say they were not so much influenced by popular notions of the day, but more by objective scholarship. This is why it is so useful in our time. Looking at what commonly passes today for "conservative religious thought," actually is noticeably liberal when compared to the first century writings of the apostles as I have endeavored to show in both *The Blind Man's Elephant* and this book. Jamieson, Fausset and Brown's input, therefore, presents us with a singularly different perspective. Both commentaries are much quoted in the book.

A bit more contemporarily, I wish to thank Dr. Ernest L. Martin for his book, *Restoring the Original Bible*, which was an inspiration in providing me the philosophical basis for the origin of my books, namely that we need to attentively rely on the original document's integrity as the basis for our theological research and for delineating the similarities of organization between the two testaments. Also, it's imperative to let the Biblical record interpret itself, which it always does when give the opportunity. This foundational research principle I learned in my first theology class with Dr. Martin. It has proven a steadfast companion now for decades.

Doc, as we referred to Dr. Martin, was always a source of inspiration and a vast repository of information. Eager students packed his lectures, and it was always SRO for students who were too late to officially register for one of his classes. I've never witnessed this with any other professor in more than seven years of university classes. I often wondered where he found the time and the resources for his seemingly endless information stream on so many subjects, not to mention the humorous wit he used to communicate his knowledge.

Acknowledgements

Initially, Doc was my professor, then my mentor and later my friend. He always had time to chat about various subjects when I dropped by his office. While he is missed, his widow, Ramona, carries on his work along with David Sielaff. If you'd like to read some of Doc's books, you can find them at www.askelm.com. If you are a history buff, then I highly recommend Doc's book *The Temples That Jerusalem Forgot*. As always, Doc is a very engrossing read.

I would be remiss as well if I didn't thank John, the apostle who had the final responsibility for assembling the New Testament canon we have today and for the wisdom and instruction imparted in 1 John 2:27.

It goes without saying that I must give grateful thanks to my wife who has supported my time writing especially as it requires a fair bit of solitude. Her patience, understanding and technical assistance are well appreciated. Of course, it greatly helps that I have promised her a return trip to Venice when I finished writing this book. As it advises in the book of Proverbs, "…rejoice with the wife of your youth." She likes to rejoice in Venice. I think it has something to do with gondolas, gelatos and musical evenings in St. Mark's Square.

As you will discover in reading *The Hijacked Elephant*, I liberally quote from the original documents that you may better get a feel for their cohesiveness of plot. Many times one quote follows another, one being from the New Testament, the other from the Old and vice versa. To assist in the flow of the reading, rather than you having to flip to the endnotes to determine whether or not it is new or old covenant, I have used an asterisk after the initial quotation mark, "*…, to denote the beginning of an Old Testament quote. The New Testament quotes are not so indicated. If you wish to determine the exact location of the quote in the Biblical record, as always, they are found in the endnotes. Please take time to read the endnotes as they contain timely and important supplemental information.

This will help you more readily see that the subject at hand, while often thought of as being definitely New Testament in its application, say the apocalypse, is plainly evident in the Old Testament too. The reverse holds true as well. All this goes back to one of my original points. The Biblical record is one book written to the same people; thus, it is one story from Genesis to Revelation.

I would highly recommend reading the surrounding verses or the entire chapter of the Biblical record quoted in the book. Very likely, you will come across something in particular that really grabs your attention. In doing so, you may discover the starting point for your own journey in the theological landscape of the Biblical record.

Preface

Every major theological event in Christianity found in the New Testament is the fulfillment of the archetypical high holy days found in the Old Testament.

The second coming of Christ is no exception.

If you are a Christian reading this, or a descendant of Judah, no doubt you will have a reaction that borders on incredulity. However, if you are truly strong in your faith, enough so that you don't run with the herd, by the time you finish the amazing journey in this book, you will discover the veracity of this claim for yourself. Incredulity will have morphed into startling fact.

You'll discover that the path the apostles walked with Christ nearly two thousand years ago is much different than what we commonly believe it to be today.

The Biblical record, the Bible, is one complete entity written to the same people. However, the relationships of its main characters remain significantly changed in relation to each other at this point in time. The Old and the New Testaments are vitally joined together. It is not that the Old Testament is for the Jews and the New Testament for the gentiles. This error in understanding has led Christianity off the path to really understanding the world we inhabit. It has lead to gross misinterpretations of canon that detrimentally impacts our lives, and continues to do so. For all our modern day sophistication, we are blind to our own historical ignorance.

The Hijacked Elephant, shows that the events of the Old Testament are tied to those of the New Testament just as a shoelace ties together both sides of a shoe. To our great surprise, we discover that both testaments fit together perfectly; Christ being the common denominator of both. If you are a "Doubting Thomas" at this point, I can't say as I blame you. To our customary way of thinking, this is a rather outlandish claim. But, the truth is stranger than the fiction that Christianity has become over the past two millennia, as you will discover in reading *The Hijacked Elephant*.

Many of you may be familiar with the 1993 movie "Six Degrees of Separation." It's about the principle that each of us is only six degrees of separation away from knowing everyone in the world. It's been called the Small World experiment initially conducted by Michael Gurevich in the 1960's. In researching theological topics, I get the feeling that the same principle applies to the knowledge available to us in the Biblical record. So often, I start off in one direction and end up someplace I didn't expect just by following the leads of one chapter or verse or even a single word.

As a result, when someone asks me about reading the Biblical record, and where should they start, more and more I think my answer should be, "It doesn't matter. Start with whatever interests you. Then just follow wherever it takes you. Eventually, you'll discover it's all very closely connected and you end up finding everything." Of course, this unstructured, eclectic "right-brain" method of discovery may be a bit too amorphous for many people.

Over the decades of wandering about the peaks, valleys and steeply walled box canyons of this seemingly incoherent theological terrain, lost paths have been rediscovered that link the most unexpected and intriguing places. Perhaps the biggest discovery is that Christ is pivotal to the events in both the Old and New Testaments. This will probably shock folks on both sides of the aisle. Nevertheless, the Bible is one book written for the same people. In a metaphorical sense, Christ is that shoelace that ties them both together.

When all the right-brain pieces are assimilated, the pieces are bound into a lucid, "left-brain" order. We come into possession of a theological image complete with plot points for us to follow. Where a cliff confronted, footholds were found. Where a dead-end perplexed, an abandoned path was discovered. Where there was nonsense, rationale appears. All things considered, however, this book is definitely a right-brain look at Christianity. So you will need to be in your right mind to consider the information presented here.

Even so, it seems obstacles are ubiquitous. The modern order of the books we see in contemporary versions of the Biblical record are not in the order found in the original canon. Subsequently our task is made harder by another degree of separation. For a listing of the original order, please see Appendix One: Lists. In fact, the title, *The Hijacked Elephant*, is a reflection upon the fact that modern day Christianity has become a blind man's elephant because the original got mugged and hijacked along the way. Instead of being in a direct relationship with the truth, we are increasingly separated by degrees.

Nevertheless, some diligent sleuthing can put us back on track. I believe that by time you finish reading *The Hijacked Elephant*, you will come to see just how far we have become separated. And you'll wonder why you haven't noticed it before. Rather than irrelevant pieces of a puzzle strewn between two covers, in the end, we find that the Biblical record is much like a screenplay or non-fiction book. It's one story. The leading man and the supporting cast of characters that we find in the first chapter are there in the last chapter. Genesis and Revelation are tied together by its characters, as is the entire plot found in the Biblical record. It's quite an amazing story.

While our story ebbs and flows through seven key events, or waypoints in *The Hijacked Elephant*, with all its character's dramatic circumstances changing physically and spiritually, it makes for a heart-pounding experience because unlike other books, your life, your actions and your ancestors are part of the story. We discover that the original documents that comprise the Biblical record are like an ancient version of a GPS, in our case, God's Plan for uS. Contained in it are our itinerary, waypoints and our destination. Travel time, however, is measured in terms of millennia. Without this knowledge, we wander aimlessly, lost in ever changing theological scenery, long since having abandoned the waypoints established for us thousands of years ago.

Shakespeare was correct when his cynical character Jacques stated in <u>As You Like It</u>, "All the world's a stage...and one man in his time plays many parts...." He was much more insightful than he realized. Life on this temporary summer stock theater stage is not about the physical experiencing the spiritual, but the spiritual experiencing the physical. It is this duality, the spiritual and the physical, that lies at the core of our story. This duality first experienced on the physical level points us to the larger spiritual events that began unfolding on the world's stage about 2000 years ago.

When we come to see the big picture through this prism, the entire scope of the story, its beginning and its ending, and what happens to the characters in-between, suddenly our perspective of life's landscape flips. The world is no longer seen in grainy

Preface

black and white, but rather in full color high def. It all begins to make sense.

Another point I'd like to address is why it is so important that we stick to the first century canon for our text. For the uninitiated, the Biblical record is not the result of casual and serendipitous processes. As I mention throughout the book, both the Tanakh, a Hebrew acronym for the Law [**T**orah], the Prophets [**N**evi'im] and the Writings [**K**etuvim], which is the Hebrew Bible or Old Testament, and the New Testament are a complete, unified text. There are no other books that could merit consideration for inclusion any more than a writer could seriously claim his writing merited insertion into Shakespeare's Hamlet or Macbeth. The Old Testament was put together under very stringent guidelines. The Levitical priesthood led by Ezra after the Babylonian captivity was very meticulous in handing down the final canonization including every "jot and tittle" to each successive generation.

The New Testament canon was put together only by those who actually walked and talked and were taught by Christ. They were his disciples and apostles. While Paul's writings make up the bulk of the New Testament, Peter, James, and by the end of the first century, John put all the writings together into a coherent and *complete* document for those of us who would come after their deaths specifically for the avoidance of error by ever increasing degrees of separation.

While those who are not familiar with the contents of the Biblical record often consciously dismiss the divine nature of the text, discernment shows this is more a matter of ignorance rather than knowledge.[1] Our faith, then, is to be based on evidence. If you wish to read a very thorough and intriguing examination of the canonization process, please get a copy of *Restoring the*

Original Bible by Ernest L. Martin.[2]

In this book, I have quoted the original sources quite heavily so you can get it straight from the "elephant's mouth" so to speak. If you have an aversion to reading anything in the Biblical record, this book is not for you. But if you have an open mind, and have a bit of holy curiosity as Einstein phrased it, I can guarantee you will be surprised, perhaps even shocked at what you will find.

I have used the King James Version [KJV] in all the quotes. Personally, I still prefer this version to other versions, as I am most familiar with it. While there are some mistranslations in this version, they are known and documented. And as an English literary document, the KJV is still held in the highest regard. However, I have, for ease of reading, updated the thees, the thous, and the saiths, etc. Occasionally, an old English word is not well understood in which case I have gone back to the original Hebrew or Greek and replaced it with the modern word or words. For example, the old English word, *quicken* means to make alive. After its first use, I use *to make alive* in its place being sure it is correct in context. In all cases, the KJV quote is end noted. I've used *italics* for clarification or emphasis of the text throughout the book. Unless noted otherwise, all *italics* are the author's.

For those of you who've read *The Blind Man's Elephant*, you will have noticed that I refer to the Biblical record rather than using the word Bible. I do so here as well. I've done this intentionally in that many people have a knee-jerk reaction to the word for better or worse. In some ways, I can readily understand this as the Bible has been used, or more correctly, misused and misrepresented for just about every purpose under the Sun. To invoke it as an authority automatically pigeonholes one's cognitive abilities in certain circles while in others it may elicit a worshipful primitive awe.

Either reaction is unfair to both the text and to the diligent dedication in which it has been preserved for us not only as a theological document, but as a historical one as well. Thus, my intent is to the let Biblical record speak for itself. And it can do this quite well when given the chance. I have done this for reasons not altogether altruistic. If someone wishes to argue a point, then their argument must be with the original text and hopefully, not my understanding of it.

Feedback makes books living entities. As always, if you have any sincere questions and comments, please let me know. Our web address is www.redshoe.com. You can send your queries to me there.

Michael J. Miller
March 2009

Chapter One
Where do we go to see the elephant?

"The blind have no fear of the dark, yet neither can they see the light."

For those of you who read *The Blind Man's Elephant*, you will recall the book's underlying theme was one of going on an adventure. It was an adventure to climb unscaled peaks that lie within each of us. Our goal was to reach the summit by putting aside the fears that restrain us from discovering once again the breathtaking joy of truth, the light that is our Father's Word.

But where do we go from there? Where does the path take us from that summit? The path takes us on the first step of the rest of our lives, but with a much different perspective on life than we had prior to climbing the mountain. The person who returns from the summit is not the person who began the journey. For it is not the mountains that we conquer, but ourselves as Sir Edmund Hillary so notably pointed out.

The Hijacked Elephant will lay out for us the big picture of our journey. It will show us where as a people, we've been and where we still are heading. It is not for the timid or weak in spirit roaming through life with a "herd mentality." It is for those who seek the light of understanding. There is a definite path that has been set out for us beginning thousands of years into our past and vanishing into our horizon at least a thousand years distant into our future. Yet while we should be very much aware of this path, most are swept along life's journey with nary a hint of what's going on, much less why.

We have in our possession a very detailed account that tells us where exactly we are in the flow of history. In it, there are seven signposts that point us in the proper direction. Identifying them, we can gauge our progress. We can know what the future holds for us in general terms. Knowing this, we can measure our daily lives to make sure we, our children and perhaps grandchildren are on course to reach our next waypoint in life's journey. By passing this information along to each generation, we help them remain true to their destiny.

By losing this information, however, along with our identity, each successive generation has become increasingly lost. Of all the directions available to us, we don't know which one to take. And even if the correct information bumps into us along the way, most have no means to verify its worthiness. And while this may seem a bold statement, this is the state of Christianity today.

Depending on the source you go to, there are more than 30,000 different Christian denominations or versions, if you will, pointing out the direction we should be taking. Which one should we follow? Or are any of them the correct path for us to take? We have strayed, chasing, as John Godrey Saxe put it in his poem, "an elephant not one of them had seen." Thankfully, "the elephant" remembers. Recall from *The Blind Man's Elephant*, the clear view from the summit is that which was delivered to us by those who saw the elephant. In it, we discovered many key points of understanding on various topics as well as the primary sub-plot that runs through the entirety of the Biblical record as discussed in chapter six.

In the case of the New Testament, it was the apostles and disciples who walked and talked and ate with Christ that provided further insight and understanding for us. They, and their "Old

Testament" [*Tanakh*] predecessors, are keepers and identifiers of the waypoints we need to follow. And they all came from the same family tree. The entirety of the Old and New Testaments, which together make up our Christian Bible, are exactly what they need to be. There are no extraneous books or writings that could just as easily have been a part of the canon.

Our only means to verify the unique waypoints are to go back to those who first recorded them. We need the original documents. And that's what we will do in this book. We will go back to the original source to discover once again, we have strayed far from the path set out by our forefathers.

In going back to the original source, we are going to discover some rather unsettling and for many, some very intimidating facts. But this is the consequence of Christianity unwittingly substituting fables in place of the truth for millennia.

Because these mythical traditions have grown large over two thousand years or so, they are particularly odious. Why? They have led us astray causing us to stumble from the elected path. We have lost sight of our identity, our heritage and the real meaning of Christ's first coming. We are walking on a perfidious path. Christ was "not sent except to the *lost sheep of the House of Israel*." That's what Christ said. And he said that to a gentile woman. He told her it wasn't good and honorable to "take the children's [*House of Israel's*] bread and cast it to the dogs [gentiles]." Christ wasn't sent to be the savior of the gentiles of the world.

The crucial point to understanding the Biblical record is in knowing this. It is the $E=mc^2$ that unlocks the door to truthful spiritual awareness. Being unaware of this vital cornerstone has caused us to build our faith on the theological sands of deceit. If you learn nothing else from this book, learn this.

We hear a myriad of Christian denominations talk about the saved or "raptured 144,000." Yet why is it we never hear them say the 144,000 are comprised of 12,000 from each *of the nations of Israel*? Who even knows that Israel is comprised of twelve nations today? Israel is not just the Jews. "And I heard the number of them that were sealed: and there were sealed a hundred and forty four thousand of *all the [twelve] tribes of the children of Israel*" as we read in the Book of Revelation chapter seven. What happened to all the gentiles? Some claim that the 144,000 in chapter fourteen are the gentile group opposed to the chapter seven group. This is but another error induced because we don't know who we are. There is only one group sealed. And they are the children of Israel who stand on Mt. Sion, Jerusalem, with Christ. This will become very clear over the course of the book.

There is a reason why Christ began his ministry in Galilee, the historic land of the *House of Israel* rather than in the land of Judea even though he was, genealogically, a direct physical descendant of King David of Judah. Do you know why?

There is a reason why the gentiles in the land of Galilee turn out to be the sons of Israel as mentioned in chapter forty-nine of Genesis which identifies what should befall them in the last days. Do you know why?

There is a reason why the apostle Paul, the apostle to the *gentiles*, a descendant of the nation of Benjamin, one of the twelve sons of Israel, in the New Testament wrote to the *gentile* Corinthians that "Moreover brethren, I would not have you ignorant, how that *all our brothers* were under the cloud and *all* passed through the sea; and *all were baptized unto Moses* in the cloud and in the sea; and *all* ate the same spiritual meat; and *all* drank the same spiritual drink: for they drank of that *spiritual Rock* that followed them: and *that Rock was Christ.*"[3] Did you know that Christ, our LORD was literally there with Moses and all the children of Israel?

If you didn't know any of this, you're not alone. In fact, it would be surprising if you did know this. By the time you finish reading this book, however, you will plainly see that the Biblical record interprets itself. And it will show us that the single biggest step off the path of Christianity, as it was delivered to us in the original documents from the first century, is in not knowing who we are.

The indigenous Christian nations of the world today are the House of Israel.[4] Because Christianity in general has erroneously thought we are an amalgamated mish-mash of some gentiles who happen to believe in Christ, we have been deluded for millennia as to our true identity, our true purpose, our birthright and our obligation in the world.

No doubt this will strike you as rather absurd. This concept is alien to our normal Christian perception. And I would feel the same way had I come across this for the first time here. But as stated, the process of deception and lies began while the apostles Peter, James, John and Paul were alive. These lies have evolved theologically over the past two thousand years. As such, the lies have crept into Christian theology like a cancer. Unnoticed, they have slowly eroded our spiritual health. And like a deadly terminal cancer, if we remain unaware, our ignorance will kill us. For the time being, the choice is ours. Sooner or later, there is an apocalyptic price to be paid, we are told, for continuing in our ignorance and apathy.

The main reason, as just stated, for the evolution of Christianity into 30,000 or so versions from the original, stems from the fact that we have lost sight of who we are. Christians in the first century knew exactly who they were. But even tiny steps off that path began to occur by 60 CE [*Christian Era*] or so, eventually leading us so far a field that we don't have a clue as to which direction to look or that we even need to for that matter. Truth be known, we are up to our eyeballs in ignorance. And that's not a good place for us to be. But we don't have to stay this course. Each of us has the opportunity to change it.

To do so, the only tangible, credible source we can turn to is the original words set out in the canon by those who held a sacred trust. Therefore, the Biblical record, once again, is our trusted guide. We need to let the Biblical record interpret itself, as it does, rather than imprint our personal preferences on the interpretation thereof. This takes a certain amount of fortitude as we discovered on our adventure in reaching the summit in *The Blind Man's Elephant*. Yet our reward was a clearer view of that first century elephant. This book is the next adventure in our journey.

In the Biblical record, we find the principle of duality. Life itself has this duality. We have life in the flesh, but we also have a spirit of life within us. We are alive both in the flesh and in the spirit. In mankind's case, it is the spirit of man. It is this spirit that is the significance of the first man Adam's, and all mankind's, creation.

In the case of creatures before Adam, and since, they too have a duality of spirit and flesh. But when they die, both their flesh and spirit return to the dust of the Earth.[5] Mankind's spirit does not return to the dust of the Earth as does our flesh or bodies. In this, man has no preeminence over any fleshly beast. Our preeminence that places us above the animal kingdom is man's spirit. It is this spirit that returns, at the death of the body, to God who gave it. This does not mean we have an immortal soul. It means mankind has the potential for immortality that creatures do not.

This principle of duality manifests itself in prophecies too. One example, which occurred rather recently historically speaking, directly relates to the Genesis Birthright[6] and is found in the second chapter of Daniel, "*You [*king of Babylon*] saw until a **stone** was cut out without hands [*that is, not by the power of man*]…which struck the image upon his feet of iron and clay and broke them into pieces." As we saw in *The Blind Man's Elephant*, this was a reference to the end of the great image that lasted from the reign of Nebuchadnezzar of Babylon more than 2500 years into Daniel's future ending with the Ottoman or Turkish Empire. It was the British, primarily, who defeated Germany and their Ottoman allies in World War One. Think Lawrence of Arabia. As we'll discover, the British Empire was that stone mentioned by Daniel.

At the end of World War One in 1918, the land areas including both Jerusalem and the ancient site of Babylon were lost by the Ottomans and became known as British Palestine. The British, specifically Winston Churchill, drew up a portion of this area into current day Iraq. You can read all about it in Christopher Catherwood's, "Churchill's Folly: How Winston Churchill Created Modern Iraq." Iraq, of course, continues to be somewhat of a folly for the west, but not without reason. Iraq's significance in world events will remain for the foreseeable future because it is the site of ancient Babylon.

Now when we check out the description of the sons of Israel in the "last days," we discover that the **stone** of Israel is mentioned in the prophetical chapter Genesis forty-nine, verses twenty-two to twenty-six concerning Joseph, one of the twelve sons of Israel who are nations today. Joseph became the kingly line of the House of Israel after the death of King Solomon. [*See Appendix One: Lists*] The first king of the House of Israel was Jeroboam, a descendant of Ephraim as likely are the current royal household. The kingly line of the House of Judah remained with Judah.

The scholarly Matthew Henry's Commentary says this about Joseph in context, "The state of honor and usefulness to which he [*Joseph*] was subsequently advanced: Thence (from this strange method of providence) he became the shepherd and **stone**, the feeder and supporter, of God's Israel...." Who is it that made Joseph this stone, a stone cut out not by the power of man? "*But his bow abode in strength, and the arm of his hands were made strong by the hands of the mighty [God] of Jacob [Israel]." 7

Now rather interestingly, in the history of Israel the heritage of Joseph is described through his two sons, the brothers Ephraim and Manasseh. Manasseh is the elder brother. Therefore the kingly line would be expected to pass through Manasseh. However, the patriarch Israel, in chapter forty-eight of Genesis, specifically went to his son Joseph and told him, "*And now your two sons, Ephraim and Manasseh...are mine as Rueben and Simeon, they shall be mine." Reuben and Simeon were the natural first and second born sons of Israel. Israel is explaining that Joseph's sons, Ephraim and Manasseh, also in the last days shall be considered as the first and second born sons of Israel.

When it came time for Israel to pass along the birthright blessings to Joseph's sons, the account in Genesis forty-eight says, "*The angel [*or messenger*] which redeemed me from all evil, bless the lads [*grandsons*]; and let my name be named on them, and the names of my fathers Abraham and Isaac…..And let them grow into a multitude in the midst of the earth. And when Joseph saw that he [*Israel*] laid his right hand upon the head of Ephraim, it displeased him; and he held his father's hand, to remove it from Ephraim's head unto Manasseh's head.

"*And Joseph said to his father, 'Not so my father: for this is the firstborn; put your right hand upon his head.' And his father refused, and said, 'I know it, my son, I know: he [*Manasseh*] shall also become a people, and he also shall be great: but truly his younger brother [*Ephraim*] shall be greater than he, and his seed shall become a multitude of nations [*or as it says in Genesis 35, a company of nations*].'"

We see two brothers, Joseph's sons becoming two distinct people, one a company of nations and the other a great nation as the first and second born of Abraham and Isaac in the last days. Of all the children of Israel as nations in *the last days*, these two shall be the greatest among their brothers.

Who are these two brothers? One would be a company or assembly of nations and the other brother a single great nation by the end of the great image at the end of World War One described by Daniel. Who fits this description in 1918? Into whose hands did the lands of the ancient Babylon and Jerusalem pass? The British. Or, the Commonwealth of the British Empire, *a company of nations*, "a fruitful bough by a well; whose branches run over the wall" as it says in Genesis. And who would be considered a single great nation, a brother to the British? The United States.

No other nations, Christian or otherwise, fit this description. As Israel said, "let my name be named on them and the names of my fathers Abraham and Isaac." And as discussed in The Genesis Birthright, the sixth chapter in *The Blind Man's Elephant*, this has huge implications for the emergence of the sixth empire and events unfolding around us today.

Historically then, more than 2500 years after Daniel wrote about the great image that was broken into pieces by a stone that struck its feet, the pivotal territory of the fifth empire, as well as the four that preceded it, passed into the hands of the British becoming known as British Palestine.

The physical or historical fulfillment of the great image being destroyed is as we read above. But there is a spiritual side to this duality as well. We read in Daniel concerning this great image, a beast with seven heads and ten horns, "*And in the days of these kings shall the God of heaven set up a kingdom which shall never be destroyed, and the kingdom shall not be left to other people, but it shall break in pieces and consume all these kingdoms, and it shall stand forever. Forasmuch as you saw that the stone was cut out of the mountain without hands and that it broke into pieces the iron, the brass, the clay, the silver and the gold...."[8]

The reference here is to the kingdom which shall never be destroyed, which began on Pentecost, and ultimately refers to the kingdom of God to be completely established on Earth at Christ's second coming, which we will discuss at length in chapter five of this book. We see the physical/spiritual duality of this prophecy in Daniel and Revelation. The physical fulfillment was the British Empire [*kingly line of the House of Israel*] in 1918. The spiritual fulfillment is the coming kingdom of God [*king of all Israel*]. One, the physical, is the shadow of the other, the spiritual just as the spirit of man is a shadow of the Spirit of God.

Together, the duality creates a whole, a wheel with each half allowing us to see the past but also to know our direction into the future. From the above example, we know the past; that the five empires of the great image of Daniel came to an end. But we also know that there is to be new beast, "whose deadly wound was healed," that is of these first five, with traits of these five, a Babylon the Great, that will come to its end at the coming of Christ establishing not a physical empire, but the spiritual kingdom of God. While the British Empire fulfilled the physical prophecy of inflicting the "deadly wound" to the image in Daniel, the kingdom of God will likewise do the same to the empires of men.

This brings us to the focal point of this book. There is the duality of certain days that must form the core of our knowledge and understanding in order to keep Christianity on the correct path. They are our waypoints, our signs in the flow of history. *All the major events of Christianity in the New Testament, past and in the future, are fulfillments of the duality of these archetypical days first provided to us in the Old Testament.*

For the past several hundred years in particular, we have observed counterfeit days that have led us away from our heritage and birthright. These days, two most popularly, have grown in strength that to question their validity today would appear to make one look rather foolish. You know, sort of like saying about four hundred years ago, the Earth orbits the Sun foolish. But these counterfeit days contain one vital flaw within them. They have no duality. The days set aside by God for the House of Israel to whom Christ said he was sent, do have this one important feature. It's just like telling counterfeit money from the real thing.

There are markers. And the Biblical physical/spiritual duality is one of them.

The two primary counterfeit days celebrated by the multitude, if you haven't already guessed, are Christmas and Easter. Before you readily dismiss this, let's take a look at them. If you're spiritually strong, you should be able to maintain an open mind. If not, you certainly will run off with the herd.

The first thing we Christians should ask ourselves is, do these two days portray Christ as strong and powerful, someone capable of being a king and savior? The obvious answer is no. These days portray Christ as a helpless baby in a manger and then dead on a cross. Make no mistake; the Roman crucifix is a symbol of death, not life. This is the spirit of the antichrist that fosters these feeble images contrary to the true nature of our Savior, as we are about to discover in the original documents of the Biblical record.

Regarding Christmas, Christ wasn't born in December. A Roman emperor, Constantine, set the 25th celebration date in the *fourth* century CE. Even though the Emperor Constantine wasn't exactly a contemporary of Christ and the apostles, his actions set in motion religious events that have snowballed pagan practices into our contemporary lives. It should be clearly noted that Peter, James, John, and Paul, who delivered to us the original documents that make up the canon, never celebrated Christmas, or the birth of Christ or anything in the least related to it. Christ was never in Christmas. It is an apostasy that has grown into a modern day "800 pound gorilla."

The original apostles did observe the days God gave to us to keep us on our path. And no, the days of celebration didn't change from the Old Testament to the New. This is merely another fable brought on by the delusion Christians are a mish-mash group of Biblically unrecognizable gentiles. What changed was the performance. No longer was there to be a physical observance of these high holy days by all Israel. Rather, they were transformed into being fulfilled spiritually by Christ on Israel's behalf, as was the intent from the very beginning when Moses first delivered them. And as we'll thoroughly discover, "Jesus Christ [is] the same yesterday, and to day, and for ever."[9] We'll read a lot more about this later in the book.

The Archbishop of Canterbury recently noted that the Nativity is a myth. But what quaint scene do we see portrayed in front of church buildings every December? And Christmas paraphernalia, no doubt including miniature nativity scenes, are available for sale in late August now in some retail stores. Of course, this stuff is available 24/7/365 on the Internet, not to mention Christmas movies showing up in spring and summer on television as well. As we'll also discover in the original documents, it's a path that has lethal consequences for Christians in a most unexpected way, from a most startling source despite the "warm and fuzzy" feelings that Christmas-time traditionally generates.

There were no wise men bearing gifts when Christ was a baby in a manger. It's a myth! It was just the shepherds. The wise men from the east showed up to visit Christ as a *young child living in a house*. That's what it says six times in seven verses in Matthew chapter two anyways. Should we trust that those first century apostles got it right? The men from the east gave their gold, frankincense and myrrh to *a king* after whom they came inquiring of Herod.

It may come as a shock to many twenty-first century Christians, but the wise men weren't first century versions of FedEx® delivering birthday presents! How far off the path have we come that we really believe these guys showed up with birthday presents? And even if they were birthday presents, which they absolutely were not, why on earth would this be cause to give each other birthday presents on someone else's birthday? It makes no sense whatsoever. We are so "stupid and foolish" in this regard. These aren't my words by the way. They are our LORD Jesus Christ's as we are about to learn from the Biblical record.

And if all the above isn't enough, throw in the pagan evergreen tree used in superstitious winter festivals, and well, we are so far from the first century Christ, some probably want to argue the point. But Christ doesn't appreciate Christmas. And remember, Christ plainly said, "I am not sent except to the lost sheep of the *House of Israel*." This being the case, let's takes a look at Jeremiah chapter ten.

In Jeremiah ten we read, "*Hear you the word which the LORD [*Christ*] speaks to you *House of Israel*." Okay, just to be clear, our LORD is addressing this specifically to whom he said *in the New Testament* he was sent. Also, the House of Judah, the Jews, was not included in this warning to Israel. As a rule, the Jews don't celebrate the mass of Christ, Christmas, even though some individually may have taken up the practice today.

Next we read, "*Thus says the LORD, Learn not the way of the heathen [*or pagan*], and be not dismayed at the signs of heaven; for the heathen are dismayed at them." First off, we are told directly not to learn the way of the heathens or pagans. Historically, that's never stopped God's people. And it's not stopping us today either.

Why were the heathens dismayed? Dismayed in Hebrew is

chathath, which means to be broken down with fear. It would be similar for us if we discovered massive asteroids headed for Earth were just days away with potential cataclysmic implications for human survival. Specifically in Jeremiah, this is a reference to the winter solstice or the day of the year in which the Sun shines least in the northern hemisphere. In the fourth century, when the polytheistic Roman Emperor Constantine declared the date to celebrate the birth of Christ, the winter solstice fell on the 25th of December. This was not a coincidence.

We all know that in autumn, the foliage begins falling from the deciduous trees. And by winter the trees are barren, their branches often covered in snow and ice. Well the heathens of old, with their limited knowledge, fearfully saw this as the Sun dying with its implied doom for them as well. And though they were dismayed, today we know this is merely the normal changing of the seasons as the Earth rotates on its axis in relation to the angle of the Sun. Yet, to these pagans, one tree was able to have power greater than the dying Sun. Therefore it must have the power of a god. This, of course, is the evergreen tree. You see lots of these little tree gods every December in supermarket parking lots fastened with little wooden stands holding them up. There must be a lot of hammering and nailing in the country's Christmas tree lots every December.

Jeremiah continues in his chapter ten account. "*For the customs [*or traditions*] of the people are vain: for a tree is cut out of the forest, the work of the hands of the workman with the axe." We call these guys lumberjacks today. And they use chainsaws rather than axes. So what trees are cut out of the forest every year in November and December? Ah, it's those evergreens, those pine trees, again. In fact, upwards of 35 million evergreen winter solstice trees a year are sold in the US alone. This does not include all the plastic trees made in China. And now, one company even boasts it's invented the world's first OLED [organic light emitting diode] Christmas tree!

What did these heathens do once they got their yuletide trees out of the forest at the winter solstice? "*They deck it with silver and with gold; they fasten it with nails and hammers, that it doesn't move [*or wobble*]." Today we use mass produced glass and plastic. If we had to decorate Christmas trees with gold and silver, well that would probably put a rather big dent in tree sales.

"*They are upright as the palm tree, but speak not; they need to be carried because they cannot walk. Be not afraid of them; for they cannot do evil, neither is it in them to do good." This can be read with a bit of a mocking tone to it. After all, what kind pathetic false god is it that people have to carry them into their homes each year? The trees can't walk, they can't talk and they are powerless. Sort of remind you of a helpless baby or being dead on a cross? They can't talk, they can't walk and they have to be carried.

So what does our LORD think about all this? "*Forasmuch as there is none like you, O LORD; you are great and your name is in might. Who would not fear you, O King of nations? For to you does it pertain: forasmuch as among all wise men of the nations, [*or wise men from the east?*] and in all their kingdoms, there is none like you."

The point is raised in Jeremiah that our LORD, our King and Savior, is mighty and great, hardly the description of a helpless infant portrayed by Christmas. Why would anyone honor a mute and stock-still evergreen tree, but not fear the King of nations?

Ignorance perhaps? Delusion certainly. And of course, we should know that a reference to the nations here is a reference to the ten nations of the House of Israel as noted by Jeremiah in verse one. So why are Christians, the House of Israel, chasing after trees every winter solstice in December rather than following the days or waypoints God did set out for us? Our LORD Jesus Christ gives us the answer himself.

"*But they are *altogether stupid and foolish*: the tree[10] is a doctrine of vanities." This is very strong language coming from Christ saying we are being stupid and foolish about all this Christmas stuff. But do we really care? I mean, even proclaimed atheists who deny Christ as the Son of God celebrate Christmas. Think about that.

Our King and Savior is telling us we are stupid and foolish concerning Christmas and trees. But will we listen? Are we willing to forsake Christmas? Do we really fear our LORD? "*The fear of the LORD is the beginning of knowledge: *fools despise wisdom and instruction*," as we are told in the first chapter of Psalms. You see, we have the opportunity for change. Which path will we choose, wisdom and instruction or continued foolishness? If we use the House of Israel's history as our paradigm, the path leading to wisdom and instruction likely will remain overgrown and lost to sight.

However, we should be careful about which path we choose. For when we continue down the same path, cutting down evergreen trees, decorating them in our homes, no longer with silver from Tarshish and gold from Uphaz, but rather with glass and plastic from China, we need to be fully aware that our LORD is, shall we say, just a tad upset. Okay, maybe it's more than a tad. Let's read it from the original documents. Please keep in mind that what you are about to read next in Jeremiah ten is *in the context of* our LORD admonishing us not to learn or take on pagan traditions especially Christmas and the tree.

"*But the LORD is the God of truth, he is the living God [*the God who is alive as opposed to a tree that is dead and has to be carried*], he is the king of eternity: at his anger the earth shall tremble [*as in a great earthquake accompanied by lots of noise and crashing*], and the nations [*House of Israel*] shall not be able to abide his anger." It might be personally worthwhile to take note of the fact that the LORD'S anger over Christmas is more than a tad sufficient in that he will *shake the entire Earth*! This is hardly the baby in a manger image of Christ we have come to embrace. But, it is the correct one.

"*Thus you shall say to them [*the House of Israel*], The gods that have not made the heavens and the earth, they shall perish from the earth, and from under the heavens. He has made the earth by his power, he has established the world by his wisdom, and has stretched out the heavens by his discretion. When he utters in his voice, there *is a multitudinous noise of waters in the heavens,* and *he causes the vapors to ascend from the ends of the earth*; he makes the lightning in the rain, he brings forth the wind out of his treasures [*storehouse*]."[11]

You see, we Christians think everything is hunky-dory. And that God is really angry with the heathens of this world, but not us. We're the good guys. He will save us from his anger. However, we would be wrong. Dead wrong might be a good way to put it. As we just read, Christ's anger is directed at Christians, the lost sheep of the House of Israel over following after false gods delivered to us by false prophets. We have become servants of corruption.[12]

Mentioned in several places, both in the Old and New Testaments as we'll read, his anger results in the subsequent events described by Jeremiah, which are more commonly known by us today as the apocalypse, the "time of Jacob's trouble," which begins with the opening of the sixth seal as described in the Book of Revelation.

How many Christians today realize there is a direct cause and effect relationship between our celebrating Christmas and the apocalypse? How many in the herd realize the apocalypse is directed towards us because we celebrate pagan winter solstice practices centered on a tree? Christ is telling us we are stupid and foolish regarding our celebration of Christmas. This would be the cause part. Because of our joyously observing pagan customs, we are told Christ will open the sixth seal, initiating the horrific apocalypse. This is the effect part. There is only one major religion that celebrates Christmas with a tree that pertains to Christ. Taking into account what we've just read in the original canon, what is the obvious course of action any Christian serious about their faith *should* be taking?

Therefore, how can Christians, who celebrate Christmas, expect to be raptured out of the apocalypse by Christ when this is the causal event of the apocalypse; and Christ is the one chastising us? We would be remiss, then, if we treat our Christian faith more like an insurance policy rather than a way of life.

While we'll discuss the time of Jacob's trouble, the apocalypse, in depth and in the context of the book of Revelation later in chapter five, let's take a sneak peek of what happens when this apocalyptic earth shaking event takes place."*For the stars of heaven and the constellations thereof shall not give their light: the sun shall be darkened in his going forth, and the moon shall not cause her light to shine. Therefore I [Christ] will shake the heavens, and the earth shall remove out of her place [a massive asteroid event?], in the wrath of the LORD of hosts, and in the day of his fierce anger."*[13]

There are proven scientific ramifications of such a massive earth shaking. "As a greenhouse gas, methane is in the big leagues, some twenty times as potent as carbon dioxide. If all the methane trapped underground were to wind up in the atmosphere, you could kiss your winter boots goodbye. 'There is so much [methane hydrate] in the ocean that if you gave *the planet a big shake* and *it came out all at once*, it would be a climate disaster far worse than anything we have with carbon dioxide,' Archer says."[14]

Could *"the vapors,"* which are gases, *ascending* from the ends of the earth as Jeremiah stated, be made of methane? Could the *"multitudinous noise of waters in the heavens"* be methane gas escaping from the seabed floor pushing ocean water with it into the atmosphere? Time will tell.[15]

Some scientists have said an event such as this would cause major, life altering climatic changes if it happened within a century or even within decades.[16] But if it occurred in one day, it would cause a species-threatening global catastrophe initiated by massive fireballs of methane gas in the atmosphere ignited by "lightning in the rain."

Whatever happens concerning this time, we know it is catastrophic, apocalyptic. As we're told by Christ in the prophetic twenty-fourth chapter of Matthew, "...except those days should be shortened, there should no flesh be saved [*alive*]: but for the elect's sake those days shall be shortened." Christ is telling us human life on Earth would be extinct if the consequences of his *"shak[ing] the heavens, and the earth... remov[ing] out of her place*, in the wrath of the LORD of hosts, and *in the day of his fierce anger*" were to run their course unabated. And unbeknown to most, if not nearly all Christians, its cause is directly linked to the Christian celebration of Christmas. If we truly take our faith seriously, then our actions need to be humbly examined with the utmost earnestness.

In the meantime, we are ignorantly led down candy cane lane while our brother Edom diligently seeks our birthright and is out to kill us, literally as we read in detail in *The Blind Man's Elephant*. And, as we'll see, the Biblical record clearly tells us it is Christ who will deliver us into Edom's hand for forty-two months for our apostasy. This, too, is part of the apocalypse. While we busily decorate our trees, we are completely oblivious to the implications of our actions. We will read the details firsthand in the coming chapters.

Our ignorance has made us blind. Our peril remains unseen. Observing these counterfeit days has made us spiritual paupers. Without a care in the world, we blissfully go along with the deception, clueless like sheep heading to the slaughter. We just don't realize that we are poor, blind and naked. We think we are blessed and rich, yet we are beset with sorrows. Who do we really serve? Plainly stated, if we have a Christmas tree in our house in December, it isn't our LORD Jesus Christ.

That is why Christ considers us stupid and foolish. We'd rather continue celebrating counterfeit days rooted in paganism, than to simply follow the plain words of our LORD. Why? Maybe it's because we really don't believe what's written in the Biblical record. Or maybe it's because we discount anything written in the Old Testament. Maybe it's because we are the weak ones; so weak in our faith, we really don't believe Christ.

To put it in today's vernacular, here's what Christ is saying to us, "Look, these pagans were scared spitless because they looked to the sky and thought the Sun was dying every year and that by honoring an evergreen tree and bringing gifts of gold and silver to place at it's feet, they thought they were able to entreat the evergreen tree to bring the Sun back to life. Obviously, their stupidity was nothing but plain foolishness. Why then are you being stupid too, you who call yourselves by my name, by doing the same things they did? It is not to honor me. You don't honor me with a dead tree used by superstitious pagans in their ignorance. Rather, you greatly anger me. But, if you insist on clinging to this foolishness and being stupid, then, I will give you something at which to be "dismayed." I *will* shake the Earth to its foundations so severely that the Sun *will* disappear from the sky, along with the moon too, so much so that every mountain and island *will* be shaken out of its place. You will be so terrified of these events that you'll call out for the rocks to fall on you to kill you. If this isn't what you really want, then this foolishness must stop." But will we stop? Will we change course?

Now lest we think this retribution upon the House of Israel, the earth shall tremble reference, is merely a historical reference in the Old Testament, think again. It is a direct reference to our future, which specifically is the opening of the sixth seal as we've just mentioned. It is a prophecy for, or more correctly in context, against modern day Christianity, the House of Israel. Let's read it in the original from the Book of Revelation.

"And I beheld when he [*Christ*] had opened the sixth seal, and lo, there was a great earthquake; the sun became black as sackcloth of hair [*clothes of mourning*], and the moon became as blood. And the stars [Greek, *aster*, from whence we get our word asteroid] of heaven fell to earth, even as a fig tree casts her untimely figs, when she is shaken of a mighty wind. And the heaven departed as scroll when it is rolled together; *and every mountain and island were moved out of their places*.

"And the kings of the earth, and the great men and the rich men, and the chief captains and the mighty men, and every bondman and every free man, hid themselves in the dens and in the rocks of the mountains and said to the mountains and rocks, Fall on us and hide us from the face of him that sits on the throne and *from the anger of the Lamb* [Christ], for *the great day of his anger is come*, who shall be able to stand?"[17] Or as it was written in Jeremiah 2600 years ago, "*...at his anger the earth shall tremble*, and the nations [*of the House of Israel*] shall not be able to abide *his fierce indignation*." Merry Christmas? I think not.

"*Thus says the LORD, Keep your judgments, and do justice: for my salvation is near to come, and my righteousness to be revealed. Blessed is the man that does this, and the son of man that lays hold on it; that keeps from polluting the sabbaths [*holy days*], and keeps his hand from doing any evil."[18]

We have another example of duality. While those of Old Testament Israel were guilty of polluting the high holy days or sabbaths physically, we are polluting the high holy days Christ is now fulfilling by observing these hijacked pagan festivals. "*But the House of Israel* rebelled against me in the wilderness: they walked not in my statutes, and they despised my judgments, which if a man do, he shall even live in them; and my sabbaths they *greatly polluted*: then I said, I would pour out my fury upon them in the wilderness, to consume them."[19]

Wilderness [Hebrew, *midbar*] means a place suitable for grazing cattle or sheep such as a pasture, and is not a reference here to a barren desert. Metaphorically, the sabbaths including the high holy days, statutes and judgments are our spiritual pastures, the word of God which gives us life. We've greatly polluted our spiritual legacy by following after pagan traditions and false holidays. And as a result, we've become spiritually blind. Nonetheless, we'll rediscover those spiritual pastures in the coming chapters.

When we don't know who we are, we can't recognize the danger signs clearly spelled out for us. Not that this is an excuse. And it won't be surprising that even upon reading this, most will probably just shrug it off somehow justifying their continued celebration of days firmly rooted in pagan ignorance. At least that's what the prophecies in the original documents tell us.

Such is our human nature. But this is the point, as Christians our nature is to be godly or spiritual rather than physically oriented. You see, we don't need the trees and we don't need the presents. They are for fearful ignorant people. The merchants who start their Christmas retailing in late summer want to us to buy what they sell. 'Tis the season to buy and sell, buy and sell. It's become Christmas paganomics. Nevertheless, we need to be aware of what the apostles originally delivered to Christianity in the first century.

The original prophetic warning about not learning the heathen customs with the evergreen tree occurred more than two and a half millennia ago. Alas, it appears the House of Israel never met an evergreen tree it didn't like. False, pagan traditions have been slowly incorporated into modern day Christianity, corrupting it, yet today they are accepted as "gospel." Problem is, it's not the gospel delivered by Christ.

And while we may think nothing will come of it, our LORD is not slack or delaying from his perspective. It's the old pay me now, or pay me later which is always more the costly alternative. We are given ample chance to change our minds about this. We can push aside these counterfeits and pay attention to the real thing as delivered to us in the original documents...or not.

If we choose not to heed our warning mentioned in both Jeremiah and Revelation, then when that "day of his *fierce anger*" arrives marked by a global earthquake due to an asteroid maelstrom indicating the Earth may be knocked off its axis, what will God tell us on this prophetic day *in our future* when we cry out to him to save us? "*As the thief is ashamed when he is found, so is the *House of Israel* ashamed; they, their kings, their princes, their priests and their prophets...for they have turned their back unto me, and not their face [*we refer to this today as lip service; our lips say Jesus Christ, but our actions say Santa Claus; we call our religion Christianity, yet we follow pagan traditions*]: but in their time of trouble they will say, Arise and save us. But where are the gods you have made yourselves? [*Christmas tree lots?*] Let them rise and save you if they can in your time of trouble."[20] I wouldn't hold my breath waiting for some action hero Santa in his sleigh to save the day when Christ unleashes the apocalypse. Obviously, many do.

An evangelical Christian wrote me trying to justify his learning the way of the heathen by explaining, "...Christmas as a child...is a special time of the year. It's not where we lined up and bowed to a tree...When the church hijacked these pagan holidays it was for good reason, to influence the world with biblical worldview and culture. Santa's flying reindeer instead of Thor's chariot. Halloween celebrations instead of Samhain...We have every right to take these things and spin them with the goodness of the Lord as part of the Great Commission...We take something bad and make it good." What can I say? The blind have no fear of the darkness.

You see while our faces, our words, are all about being so righteously Christian, in deed and in action we turn our back on God. Do we listen and take seriously his admonition to "Learn not the way of the pagan?" Do we really fear our LORD? Or do we blindly rush off choosing to do as we please instead, hijacking pagan holidays at our peril?

As a true Christian, why would we not follow what our LORD has set us before us "to influence the world with biblical worldview?" Good question. Which path do we choose? Narrow is the way and straight is the gate that leads to life, but broad is the way and wide is the gate that leads to falling asteroids, a great earthquake and such. What will you choose to do in December then? Will you run with the herd or not?

While you're contemplating the Christmas thing, let's take a look at Easter or Ishtar as it was in the ancient Babylonian religion. Ishtar is the Babylonian goddess of fertility and war. Seems like a rather strange pairing, fertility and war, until you realize wars need human cannon fodder. "Keep those kids coming, we'll need them to die in our wars" must have been the queen of heaven Ishtar's rationale. No doubt the Babylonians would have had bumper stickers on their chariot SUVs that read, "Make love *and* war!" The more modern version would be "No abortions, no peace!"

For all those "Christians" who celebrate Ishtar, Easter is not mentioned in the Biblical record except by example where it is instructing us not follow after its lies and deceptions that take us off the path we were given to walk on. Right about now, some of you may be disagreeing because in the Book of Acts concerning

Peter's arrest by Herod, it plainly says that Herod was "...intending after Easter to bring him forth to the people" proves the early church celebrated Easter. If anything, it proves something else.

A simple look at the original documents provided to us by the apostles shows that the word used is of Aramaic origin and is the word *pascha*, which refers to the paschal or passover lamb Israelites sacrificed on the fourteenth day of Nisan which is the first month in the sacred year marking the death of the first born of Egypt just before Pharaoh agreed to let Israel leave Egypt. The apostles celebrated the Passover, not Easter. More about this later. The word Easter is one of the few outright translation errors in the King James Version [KJV] of the Bible.

Ishtar, the queen of heaven, the goddess of fertility and war, is known by various other names, such as Astarte, Ashtoreth, Easter, etc., depending upon whether it is the Assyrian, Babylonian, or Christian incarnation of this pagan deity. Seems like the House of Israel has a proclivity for this goddess much like it does for evergreen trees. Our ancestors got in a lot of trouble because of, once again, hijacking false gods. It's become a broken record.

Let's go back to the account in the Book of Kings. Solomon has been admonished by God not to take wives outside of Israel because they would turn his heart away from God. You can read it for yourself, but we are told that "*...when Solomon was old, his wives turned away his heart after other gods: and his heart was not perfect with the LORD his God, as was the heart of his father David."[21]

Who was on Solomon's Top Ten hijacked pagan god list? Coming in at number one, "*Solomon went after Ashtoreth the goddess of the Zidonians...." Ashtoreth, of course, is the same goddess of fertility and war, Ishtar or Easter. And what was our LORD's reaction to this? "And the LORD was angry with Solomon," because why? "...because his heart was turned from the LORD God of Israel...."[22] It's the same with us today, lip service aside.

As a result of Solomon's apostasy, Israel was broken into two houses, the House of Judah and the House of Israel. The Christian nations today are the descendants of the House of Israel. The true Jews are the descendants of the House of Judah. What are Christians doing, then, in the name of the LORD every spring? They celebrate Easter, Ishtar, Ashtoreth rather than paying attention to the days our LORD has given us to keep us on the path so our hearts are not turned from the LORD.

Naturally, most will likely argue that they do not celebrate Easter or Ishtar, the Babylonian goddess of fertility, but rather celebrate the resurrection of Christ a la the warped reasoning provided to us above about Christmas and other days of pagan origin. Of course, they go to sunrise services waiting for the *Sun to rise* in the east, that big egg rising into the heaven in spring, the same as the Babylonians. Or perhaps they attend the more mundane church services just after they give their kids a basket of Easter treats including chocolate Easter bunnies [*talk about fertility symbols especially as chocolate is considered an aphrodisiac*] and then probably take the kids to an Easter egg hunt afterwards. The White House lawn is especially popular as a venue. This of course doesn't include the time the kids spend either at school or at home with mom coloring Babylonian fertility eggs for Christ. So of course, Easter has everything to do with Christ and nothing to do with the Babylonian goddess of fertility, Ishtar.

What is perhaps the most telling aspect of the falsity of Easter Sunday allegedly celebrating Christ's rising from the dead is that he didn't arise Sunday morning. Oops. Christianity got the wrong day. But they're close. He arose from the dead late Saturday afternoon on the weekly sabbath *before sunset*. Sunset in Jerusalem for that time of the year is about six pm standard time. We'd probably be fairly accurate in saying Christ was resurrected from the dead sometime between four and five pm. If anything then, it should be Saturday pre-sunset services. For you skeptics, let's take a look at events for the timing here. In this case, we'll work our way back to front using the original documents given to us by the apostles who were actually there.

In John's gospel, we read, "The first day of the week comes Mary Magdalene early, when it was yet dark, unto the sepulcher, and sees the stone taken away from the sepulcher."[23] The first day of the week is Sunday. Mary showed up on Sunday morning early, as it was still dark. And what did she find? Christ had already risen and left, as the stone to the sepulcher was open. She ran to tell the others. Soon thereafter she, Peter and John ran to the sepulcher. Christ was not there. They found the linen burial wear in one place and the cloth napkin that was wrapped around Christ's head in a place by itself.

This leaves us with two possibilities. One, he arose sometime on Sunday very early morning when still dark, before sunrise, and before Mary arrived, or it was at some other time even earlier. It was not later, or closer to sunrise. At this point, take a minute or two and read John's account in chapter twenty through the first eighteen verses. Then think of what Easter is today by comparison. It's not too different in nature than just the shepherds respectfully showing up at the manger at Christ's birth compared to what "Christmas" has become today.

Okay, we know that *before sunrise* Sunday, the first day of the week, when it was still dark, or before dawn's first light, Christ had already risen. Definitely he didn't rise with the Sun. Can we determine when Christ arose? Yes, we can. During his ministry, a certain person of the scribes and Pharisees told Christ they wanted to see a sign from him, you know, to prove who he was. Christ gave him an answer. He said, "An evil and adulterous generation seeks after a sign; and there shall be no sign given to it, but the sign of the prophet Jonas: *For as Jonas was three days and three nights* in the great fish's belly: so shall the Son of man be *three days and three nights* in the heart of the earth."[24]

Two points here, Jonas, or Jonah, was sent to an evil and adulterous people, in Nineveh, to get them to repent of their evil ways and seek forgiveness. They are one of, if not the only people in the Biblical record, who actually listened and changed. Thus, there was an underlying message here for the hypocritical scribes and Pharisees as well as the rest of us. Plus, we discover that Jonah's three days and three nights [Hebrew, *yowm* meaning 24-hour days], twice mentioned for emphasis, means that Christ would be a *full seventy-two hours* in the grave rather than *one day and two nights* as is the common teaching today in order to fit it into an Ishtar Sunday sunrise service.

We know then, Christ arose before sunrise on Sunday and had been in the grave for a full *three days and three nights* when he arose as Matthew stated, "And they shall kill him, and the third day he shall be raised again." Interestingly, the Greek word for day here is *hemera*. While the civil use of the word is a day of 24 hours, the natural day refers to the time between sunrise and sunset, *not between sunset and sunrise*. Using the natural day then, it means Christ arose between sunrise and sunset. Whether we use the natural day and/or the civil day, it says that Christ arose on the third 24-hour period between sunrise and sunset, which is precisely what happened.

The key question is, then, *when was Christ put into the grave?* The common assumption is that it was a Friday sabbath before sunset. For our answer, let's turn to the original account in John. "And after this [*Christ's death*], Joseph of Arimathaea, being a disciple of Jesus, but secretly for fear of the Jews [*in this case, King Herod and those descended from Edom rather than Judah*] besought Pilate that he might take away the body of Jesus: and Pilate gave him leave. He came therefore, and took the body of Jesus...Now in the place where he was crucified, there was a garden; and in the garden a new sepulcher, wherein was never man yet laid. There laid they Jesus because of the Jews' *preparation day*; for the sepulcher was near at hand."[25]

We see Christ being taken and placed in a nearby sepulcher rather hastily because of the preparation day. There are two things to note here. The preparation day is the day before a sabbath day of rest in which no servile work was allowed. The normal chores of gathering wood for a fire to cook a meal, food preparation, etc., were not allowed. Thus, double duty was done on a preparation day for the coming day of rest. There was no extra time to prepare a body for burial to some more distant place on a preparation day. Additionally, Joseph of Arimathaea would need time to get home and cleanse himself in preparation for the high holy day which began at sunset. Consequently, a hasty solution was found.

The second point is that the days for Israel began at sunset, or "even to even" as it says in the Biblical record. The "Saturday Sabbath," the weekly sabbath, according to our current day calendars, begins at Friday sunset. Christ was placed into the grave *before sunset* on a preparation day, again which would have been before six pm in Jerusalem at that time of the year. This is where many church organizations get off the track. They try to squeeze three days and three nights into Friday just before sunset to Sunday morning before sunrise or portions of three days because of the weekly sabbath. It doesn't work for one. Christ was to rise on the third day, not two nights and a day later. And second, obviously this wasn't a reference to the weekly sabbath which is the most common mistake made by those using the Friday sunset timing.

As we'll see when we look at the days set aside for Israel to keep in remembrance, Christ was the Passover lamb sacrifice. The day *after* Passover is a *high* holy day. It is not the weekly holy day or sabbath. As we can read in John's account, this is exactly the case. "The Jews therefore, because it was the preparation day, that the bodies should not remain upon the cross on the sabbath day, (for *that* sabbath was a *high day*)...."[26]

Now we have our three key points to determine Christ's time of resurrection. We know that the sabbath day here was a *high holy day* not the weekly [*Friday evening*] sabbath. We know he was placed in the grave *before sunset* marking the beginning of a high holy day. And we know he was in the belly of the earth a full *three days and three nights*.

What does this tell us then? We know Christ was put in the grave before a sunset. We know by Sunday before sunrise, he was risen. Consequently, the first evening or sunset before sunrise Sunday is Saturday evening or just before the end of the weekly sabbath. Going back three full days and nights takes us to Friday before sunset, Thursday before sunset and Wednesday before sunset. Hence, Christ was crucified, died and was placed in the sepulcher just prior to Wednesday's sunset, probably between four and five pm, just prior to the beginning of the high holy day of unleavened bread, the day after Passover.

Christ was *risen on the third day* just before sunset on the weekly sabbath day after being placed, *three full days and nights* before sunset on a Wednesday Passover day, a preparation day, prior the start of the *high holy day*, none of which was marked by coloring Easter fertility eggs for Christ. It's amazing what we can discover when we go to the original documents delivered to us by the apostles who walked, talked and ate with Christ. You can see, this is a fairly simple matter to figure out when we go to the original source.

How deluded are we in our thinking about Easter? Here's a simple test. If you really believe that Easter has nothing to do with the fertility goddess, make absolutely sure your kids or grandkids don't get any chocolate bunnies or eggs or other Ishtar related treats next Easter. Then when they cry or react angrily, ask yourself, what is it that we are teaching our kids? For the children will react to the essence of what Easter is really all about. "But those things which proceed out of the mouth come forth from the heart...."[27] So often I've heard adults say, "Well, we only celebrate Christmas [or Easter] because of the kids." Are children in this case our teachers, rather than our LORD? Our children are the reason why we shouldn't be observing these counterfeit days. It perpetuates the deceit. If we are ever to break the cycle and get back on track, we need to teach our children the truth. Our children deserve more than lip service from us.

Ishtar, Ashtoreth, Easter by any other moniker is also known in the Biblical record as the queen of heaven. Our ancestors got in trouble with her as well. While this specific example is in direct reference to Judah, who were taken captive by the Babylonians, the principle remains the same. "*The children gather wood, and the fathers kindle the fire, and the women knead their dough to make cakes to the queen of heaven, and to pour out drink offerings to other gods, that they may provoke me to anger."[28] As our evangelical writer above said, "We have every right to take these things and spin them with the goodness of the Lord as part of the Great Commission." Uh, okay, but if you do this, then what?

"*Do they provoke me to anger, says the LORD? Do they not provoke themselves to the confusion of their own faces?"[29] Huh? Our LORD says we are confused? How can this be? He must be mistaken, for our evangelical writer told us, "When the church hijacked these pagan holidays it was for good reason, to influence the world with biblical worldview and culture." Who are you going to believe then? Before you decide, consider this.

"*Therefore, thus says the LORD God; Behold my anger and my fury will be poured out upon this place, upon man, and upon beast… and it shall burn and not be quenched."[30] In the case of Judah, Jerusalem was laid ruin, the temple and palaces destroyed and set fire to, and, "for good reason," they ended up as slaves for seventy years in Babylon. Of course, it's harder to learn lessons from our ancestors when we've lost sight of who they are.

From our perusal of the original documents, then, it appears that God does not take to kindly to our hijacking pagan festivals in his name, whether it is Christmas or Easter. Why do we hijack these pagan festivals, mistakenly thinking we are doing so for "good reason," as did our forefathers? They got into trouble big time. Are we modern sophisticated geniuses who think the results will be different for us? Einstein, famously, gave us the answer. "Stupidity is doing the same things over and over and expecting different results." But he did add that there is a difference between stupidity and genius. "Genius has its limits." It appears that the children of Israel have no limits. No wonder our LORD says we are "altogether stupid and foolish; the tree is a doctrine of vanities."

Christianity, the House of Israel today is deceived as were our ancestors. It is this history we should examine and learn from rather than doing the same things over and over again. "All scripture is given by inspiration of God and is profitable for doctrine, for reproof, for correction, for instruction in righteousness," as Paul pointed out to Timothy.[31] Or we can choose to ignore sound advice.

But, heck, on the plus side, when the sixth seal starts off with a bang from the heavens, unveiling the sixth empire of the Book of Revelation, Babylon the Great, Christians already will be celebrating Easter, the Babylonian queen of heaven, the goddess of fertility and war. It is just one less thing Christians will need to learn from our Babylonian masters…again. These dualities just keep on showing up.

We began this discussion of Christmas and Easter talking about the principle of duality in the Biblical record. The physical/spiritual duality is found in the handiwork of God. This same duality is found in the days of which we should be mindful. Theologically, it is totally lacking with both Christmas and Easter not to mention the other counterfeit pagan religious days hijacked by Christianity today.

It should be plain to all that there is no spiritual Biblical second birth of Christ portrayed by Christmas with some glowing cosmic evergreen tree showering us with birthday presents. There is no spiritual death of Christ a second time to another resurrection. Although no doubt some enterprising Christians will probably set about trying to refute the word of God on this matter to prove themselves more righteous and knowledgeable than our LORD. It will result only in more confusion. As the Biblical record says, God is not the author of confusion.[32] As Christians, who does that leave us with as the instigator of confusion?

Rather than mess around with twisting hijacked pagan festivals into some sort of justified so-called "Christian" celebration, why don't we respect the days God did set aside for us to observe, that honor him as our King and Savior? It seems like such a straightforward, simple thing to do. They are quite incredible not only in their physical meaning, but are much more so in their spiritual fulfillment by Christ.

As an added bonus at no extra charge, they have meaning for what's taking place in the world right now as opposed to the counterfeits, which keep us mindlessly ignorant as "lip service Christians," spinning over and over in the same circles year after year after year. And no hijacking "pagan festivals for Christ" is required. Plus the counterfeits can't hold a candle to them. It's not even close as we'll soon find out in the following chapters.

We can do better. Theologically, we don't have to settle for a banged up '84 fossil fueled Clunkmobile. We can have a new, clean energy Aston Martin coupe. However, if we remain blind, we won't know the difference by looking. For those of you preferring the new Aston Martin, by way of theological metaphor only, please turn the page to the next chapter in our exciting adventure. It's still possible to rescue the hijacked elephant.

Chapter Two
Archetypes: The Duality of Days

Before we get into the discussion of what days of observance were set aside by God for us, let me reiterate one vital point of understanding for Christians. Christ said plainly, "I am not sent except unto the lost sheep of the House of Israel."[33] He meant what he said and said what he meant. The indigenous Christian nations of the world today are the sons of Israel. And all *twelve* sons are mentioned in Genesis chapter forty-nine. It is the prophetic chapter dealing with identities of the sons of Israel regarding that which "shall befall you in the last days."

The twelve sons of Israel today, with the exception of Simeon and Levi, who are scattered among their brother's countries, have national identities. The Jews, those descended from Judah, one of Israel's twelve sons, are just one of the sons of Israel with a national identity today.[34] They are the nation state of Israel.

There is a popular Christian misperception that the "Old Testament" is for the Jews and the New Testament is for the "Gentiles." However, the Bible or Biblical record is written to the same people. Biblically, the Jews and the indigenous Christian nations are those people who are the descendants of Isaac to whom the birthright belongs.[35] If we simply remove the page that separates the last book of the Old Testament in the Biblical record from the first page of Matthew in the New, we will have a much clearer understanding of the history of Israel's *twelve* sons.

It is true that the conditions and relationship of the House of Israel and the House of Judah have changed relative to each other since the breaking of the bands of brotherhood between them at Christ's first coming.³⁶ Until Christ's first coming and his death and resurrection, the House of Israel was a divorcee.³⁷ Since Christ's death, the House of Judah, in terms of a covenant relationship, is a widow.³⁸ And it shall remain officially so, nationally, until Christ's return,³⁹ portrayed by one of the days set aside for us to look forward to. But the contents of both the Old Testament and the New Testament are for the edification and benefit of the same people.

The day portrayed by Christ's return to establish the kingdom of God on Earth, the day that some Christians more than eagerly await, was a day of special observance for Israel, *all Israel*, initially back in the Book of Leviticus in the Old Testament. Yet how many Christians are aware of this today?

The day portraying Christ's second coming was given to Israel for observance throughout their generations not long after all Israel left the bondage in Egypt and *all* passed though the sea. And they, *all our brothers of Israel, all twelve of them*, drank of that spiritual Rock, *and that Rock was Christ* as the apostle Paul, the apostle to the *gentiles* told the Christians at Corinth in the first century.⁴⁰

Christ was that spiritual Rock that guided all Israel out of bondage to Egypt. And it is Christ who has guided *all* Israel out of the bondage to the law covenant or sin. We are no longer in bondage to the law, but justified by faith unto grace. The first covenant has passed away.

Thus, we have a connection, a missing link as it were, to our forefathers. As Paul explains, "Wherefore the law [*given to all Israel by Moses*] was our schoolmaster to bring *us* to Christ, that we might be justified by faith. But after that faith is come, we are no longer under a schoolmaster. For you are all the children of God by faith in Christ Jesus."[41] Paul's *us* here is a reference to all Israel.

First, ask yourself, who was under the law or the first or old testament? Was it the gentiles of the world? No, it was *all* Israel. "Neither by the blood of goats and calves, but by his own blood, Christ entered in once into the holy place having obtained eternal redemption for us. For if the blood of bulls and goats and the ashes of a heifer sprinkling the unclean, sanctifies to the purifying of the flesh: how much more shall the blood of Christ, who through the eternal Spirit offered himself without spot to God, purge your conscience from dead works to serve the living God? And for this cause he [*Christ*] is the mediator of a new testament that by means of death, for the *redemption of the transgressions that were under the first [old] testament.*"[42]

Who were the only people on Earth that were transgressors under the first testament or law delivered to Moses? Was it the gentiles of the world or all Israel? Therefore, who was Christ sent to redeem? It was those under the first testament. And they aren't the gentiles of the world.

Who does Paul here say "entered once into the holy place?" Christ. And where is that holy place to which Paul is making reference? Is it somewhere on the face of the Earth among some group of gentiles? No, that holy place was the portion of *Israel's* temple reserved for the priests only. Christ, our high priest spiritually fulfilled that which the priests of *Israel* used to do physically in the physical temple on behalf of the sons of Israel. Here's that duality again.

Our Israelite ancestors, who had the spirit of man dwelling in them, had a physical temple where God dwelt, specifically the Holy of Holies as it was called, and where the Ark of the Covenant was located. Yet once we receive the Spirit of God, our bodies are to be the temple of God wherein his Spirit resides.[43] Again, we see the physical archetype and its spiritual counterpart. And as we will read later on, the day that signaled this event, the receiving of the Holy Spirit, is also one of the days set aside by God to guide us along life's path.[44]

Rather than the death of a bull or goat sacrificed by the priests of Levi for the sins of Israel, Christ removed our transgressions and obtained an eternal inheritance for Israel, *all Israel*, or as Paul has told us, for the redemption of the transgressions who were under the first covenant or testament. Only one people can claim to have been under the first covenant. And those people are Israel, including the lost sheep of the House of Israel to whom Christ said he was sent.

In the coming chapters, we'll readily come to see the duality of the physical observance of the holy days under the first or Old Testament and their spiritual fulfillment by Christ under the terms of the second or new covenant. And both the theologically paltry pagan counterfeits of Christmas or Easter will be rather noticeable by their complete and utter absence.

Before we get into the details of these days, and the dualities that are the waypoints for the House of Israel, we're going to step back a bit to get a feel for the big picture first. Theologically, within the Biblical record, we have seven eras or defined periods of time set out for us since the "let there be light," "Big Bang" creation of our universe, the first heavens and Earth.

Archetypes: The Duality of Days

The first is the creation period. It is the time since the Big Bang just prior to the creation of man. This is the time period that includes the entire universe and all creature life on Earth who had the spirit of a creature within them. This includes the creatures of the sea, those that fly through the air and all land creatures including hominids. The second or Adamic period begins with the creation of adam, with the spirit of man, through Noah and the flood just prior to Abraham. The third or Abrahamic period goes from Abraham to just prior to Moses. The fourth or Moses period begins with Moses and continues up to the resurrection of Christ. Theologically, the next is the Christian period, which goes from the time of the fulfillment of Pentecost to just prior to the return of Christ. Next, we have the Millennial time period heralded by Christ's return and the peaceful time of the Millennium up to the last, or seventh theological period when a new heaven and new Earth are created.

As you can see from this, there is plenty of human history ahead of us, but not without some radical alterations in between. The periods of interest for us here concerning the days God set aside for Israel include the time of Abraham, then Moses, then Christ at his first coming. If we were taking one of those IQ tests where they ask us, which one of the three doesn't belong, which one would you choose here?

The answer would be B, Moses. The reason for this is that Abraham is the father of the faithful. And with Christ, our redemption and salvation is through faith in Christ. Moses and the law gets left out because the law covenant was a temporary fix to get us from A to C, Abraham to Christ or as we read in the book of Galatians, "Wherefore the law was our schoolmaster to bring us to Christ that we might be justified by faith…And if you are Christ's, then you are Abraham's seed, and heirs according to the promise."[45]

So let's take a look at Abraham here first to garner a better understanding of why the law covenant was a bridge between Abraham and Christ. We first come across Abraham in chapter eleven of Genesis in the generations descended from Noah. At this point, Abraham is known as Abram. Abram took a wife whose name was Sarai. She is the second woman mentioned by name in the Biblical record. The first was Eve.

God said to Abram, "*Get out of your country, and from your relatives, and from your father's house and into a land that I will show you. And I will make of you a great nation [*which is all Israel*], and I will bless you and make your name great; and you shall be a blessing: And I will bless them that bless you, and curse them that curse you: and in you shall all families of the earth be blessed."[46]

This is a great way to start out married life. So Abram did as he was directed and left. He ended up in a land called Bethel and built an altar to God in the mountain in the east of Bethel. *Beyth-El* in Hebrew means house of God.

Later, in the time of the nations of Israel, it became the place of worship, "the king's chapel," at Mount Bethel for Ephraim, who became the kingly line of the House of Israel, which was the "stone" that smote the image on its feet in 1918 as seen by Nebuchadnezzar in his dream more than 2500 years earlier. Thus, the land of Mount Bethel, located about 17 kilometers north of Jerusalem, returned into the hands of the descendants of Ephraim once again for the first time in thousands of years in 1918. Bethel should not be confused with Bethlehem, the birthplace of King David of Judah and the birthplace of Christ, which is about eight kilometers south of Jerusalem.

Archetypes: The Duality of Days

After a detour into Egypt for a period of time with his wife Sarai, Abram returned to the area of Bethel. God once again blessed Abram there in Bethel. "*For all the land which you see, to you will I give it, and to your seed forever. And I will make your seed as the dust of the earth: so that if a man can number the dust of the earth, then shall your seed be numbered also."47

After these and other events you can read about in Genesis, Abram was concerned that he had no children of his own to pass along the blessing he had received from God because his wife Sarai had borne him no children. Sarai said to Abram, "*Behold now, the LORD has restrained me from bearing [*or giving birth*]: I pray you that you go in unto my handmaid; it may be that by her I may obtain children by her."48

Hagar, Sarai's Egyptian handmaid, gave birth to a son from Abram, who was eighty-six years old at the time. His son's name was Ishmael, meaning, "God will hear" in Hebrew. Ishmael is the father of the Arab nations of the world today, hence Islam's claim back to Abraham as their father.

When Abram was ninety-nine years old, God revealed the extent of the promises that Abram was blessed with by God. "*Behold, *my covenant* is with you and you shall be a father of many nations. Neither shall your name any more be called Abram, but your name shall be Abraham [*father of a great multitude*]; for a father of many nations have I made you. And I will make you exceedingly fruitful, and I will make nations of you, and kings shall come out of you. *And I will establish my covenant between me and you and your seed after you in their generations for an everlasting covenant, to be a God to you, and to your seed after you*. And I will give to you, and to your seed after you, the land wherein you are a stranger, all the land of Canaan [*Bethel was* *in the land of Canaan*], for an everlasting possession; and I will be their God."⁴⁹

God also established the covenant of circumcision with Abraham at this time too. Abraham, then ninety-nine, and Ishmael, thirteen, along with all the males that were of Abraham's household were circumcised that same day. Now if all this wasn't more than enough for one day, ninety-nine years old or not, God told Abraham his wife would no longer be called Sarai, but rather Sarah [*princess*]. And God continued to tell Abraham, "*I will bless her, and will give you a son also of her, and she shall be a mother of nations; kings of people shall be of her."⁵⁰ These were the children of the circumcision.

So what was Abraham's reaction to this incredible news just after being circumcised? Abraham fell on his face and laughed. While we have the benefit of hindsight, Abraham said in his heart with less than stellar faith, greatly paraphrasing here, "Yeah, right. I'm ninety-nine and Sarah's ninety, we don't even have sex anymore, and she's going to give birth? Hahaha." Obviously, he wasn't the father of the faithful yet.

"*And God said, Sarah your wife shall bear you [*give birth to*] a son indeed; and you shall call his name Isaac [*Hebrew meaning, he laughs; God has a sense of humor too*]: and I will establish my covenant with him for an everlasting covenant, and with his seed after him. As for Ishmael, I have heard you: Behold I blessed him, and will make him fruitful, and will multiply him exceedingly; twelve princes shall he produce, and I will make him a great nation. But my covenant will I establish with Isaac, which Sarah shall bear to you at this set time next year."⁵¹

This is pertinent to our present day situation, which is why Paul

Archetypes: The Duality of Days

tells us "that in Isaac shall your seed be called." Why? Only Israel can trace their birthright back to Isaac. Ishmael cannot and neither can Israel's brother, Edom, though both can lay claim to Abram or Abraham.

Now when Sarah overheard the LORD tell Abraham she would give birth to a son, she laughed to herself saying, "*After I am waxed old shall I have pleasure my lord being old also? And the LORD said to Abraham, Wherefore did Sarah laugh, saying, Shall I of a surety, bear a child, which am old? Is there anything too hard for the LORD? Then Sarah denied, saying, I laughed not; for she was afraid. And he said, No; but you did laugh."[52]

All this brings us to the event that made Abraham the father of the faithful, but this time it was no laughing matter. Remember, the theological principle of duality is central to both Abraham and Christ. And the law covenant, as opposed to the Abrahamic covenant, is a temporary bridge between the two. Let's take a look at some of the dualities that are found between Abraham, Isaac and Christ. Then when we get to the law, we will further see the duality in the days God set aside for all Israel to physically observe and why they are a bridge from Abraham to Christ.

Let's read the account in Genesis. God said to Abraham, "*Take now your son, your only son Isaac, whom you love and go to the land of Moriah and offer him there for a burnt offering upon one of the mountains which I will tell you of."[53]

We can only imagine the thoughts that must have gone through Abraham's mind here. One of them might have been, "maybe I shouldn't have fell down laughing." "*...Abraham took the wood for the burnt offering, and laid it upon Isaac his son; and he took the fire in his hand, and a knife, and they went both of them together...And he [*Isaac*] said, Behold the fire and the wood, where is the lamb for a burnt offering? And Abraham said, My son, God will provide himself a lamb for the burnt offering: so they went both of them together. And they came to the place, which God had told him of; and Abraham built an altar there, and laid the wood in order, and bound Isaac his son, and laid him on the altar upon the wood. And Abraham stretched forth his hand, and took the knife to slay his son."[54]

Now we aren't told what were Abraham's thoughts nor the reaction of Isaac his son was when he was bound and placed on the altar. But whatever your thoughts are about this, hold on to them for the moment.

The angel of the LORD called out and told Abraham not to lay his hand upon his son. So we know Abraham was committed to do the will of God. Abraham was told, "*...for now I know that you fear God, seeing that you have not withheld your son, your only son from me."[55] The word fear here is an adjective in Hebrew meaning to reverence God. As we can see, this was not "lip service" on the part of Abraham.

Of course, we know that God did provide a lamb to be sacrificed on that wood altar. "*And Abraham called the name of that place Jehovah-jireh [*meaning the LORD will provide*]: as it is to this day, in the mount of the LORD it shall be seen."[56]

Because of Abraham's faith and reverence of God, an angel appeared to Abraham a second time and said, "*By myself have I sworn, says the LORD, for because you have done this thing, and have not withheld your son, your only son, that in blessing I will bless you and multiplying I will multiply your *seed* as the stars of the heaven, and as the sand which is upon the sea shore; and

Archetypes: The Duality of Days

your *seed* shall possess the gate of his enemies; And in your *seed* shall all the nations of the earth be blessed because you have obeyed my voice."[57]

Okay, let's take a look at this. While this may appear to be a cruel thing to ask of Abraham, it marks the beginning of the duality between Abraham, Isaac and Christ. Abraham was willing to sacrifice his only son. God, our Father, *did* sacrifice his only begotten son, as a sin offering for the transgressions of Abraham's descendants [*you and me*] that by faith in Christ, and not by obedience to the law, we are redeemed. So while God stayed Abraham's hand, our Father offered his son or as Abraham prophetically said, "My son, God will provide himself, a lamb..." This and events that followed with Moses marked what became the Passover as we'll see.

Secondly, Isaac carried the wood on his back that was to be the altar upon which he was to be offered as a sacrifice. Christ carried the wooden cross on his back that became the altar of his sacrifice for us.

Both Isaac and Christ did their father's will. And while Isaac was bound and placed on the altar, Abraham's faith saved Isaac. Yet it is Christ's faith, in death and in resurrection that has saved us, Abraham's children, the lost sheep of the House of Israel.

And what is particularly interesting, the mountain in Moriah where Abraham was shown of God to place Isaac on the altar as a sacrifice became the site of the temple mount in Jerusalem where the sacrifices in Solomon's temple were made. "*Then Solomon began to build the house of the LORD at Jerusalem in mount Moriah, where the LORD appeared unto David his father, in the place that David had prepared in the threshingfloor of Ornan the Jebusite."[58]

And you can take the dualities a step further in that Isaac and Christ both had what could be termed "miraculous" circumstances for birth.

This sort of duality is replete throughout the Biblical record. It ties the past into the present and into our future in our relation with God and his promises to our forefather Abraham. Neither Christmas, nor Easter has any such duality or relationship. They are hijacked pagan festivals that serve only to take us from our birthright and knowledge and understanding of who we are and what our responsibilities are towards God today.

Perhaps, then, we can understand God's anger towards us. He did give his only begotten son as a sacrifice for us, and we turn our backs on God, blindly justifying our stupidity and ignorance thinking God is angry with everyone else except us. It is going to be a very rude awakening when Santa doesn't show up to save all those Christian derrieres.

At this point, you may be wondering why then did the law covenant get added? Why didn't our ancestors just follow Abraham's footsteps in faith? We could ask the same question about Christianity. Why didn't we stay on the path set forth in the first century by Christ and delivered to us by his apostles?

We find our answer in the Book of Galatians written by the apostle Paul. You see Paul was upbraiding the Galatians that once they accepted Christ in faith, they veered back into keeping the law. But as Paul's answer is pertinent to us as much today as it was then, let's read it directly from the original.

"O foolish Galatians, who has bewitched you, that you should not obey the truth, before whose eyes Jesus Christ has been evidently set forth, crucified among you? This only would I learn of you, Did you receive the Spirit by the works of the law or by the hearing of faith? Are you so foolish? Having begun in the Spirit, are you now made perfect by the flesh? Have you suffered so many things in vain? If yet in vain.

"Even as Abraham believed God, and it was accounted to him for righteousness. Know you therefore that they, which are of faith, the same are the children of Abraham. And the scripture, foreseeing that God would justify the nations [*Greek, ethnos*] through faith, preached before the gospel unto Abraham, saying, In you shall all nations be blessed. So then they which be of faith are blessed with faithful Abraham.

"For as many as are of the works of the law are under the curse: for it is written, Cursed is everyone that continues not in all things, which are written in the book of the law to do them. But that no man is justified by the law in the sight of God, it is evident: for the just shall live by faith. And the law is not of faith: but the man that does them shall live in them.

"Christ has redeemed us from the curse of the law, being made a curse for us: for it is written, Cursed is everyone that hangs on a tree: That the blessing of Abraham might come on the nations [*of Israel*] through Jesus Christ [*who was sent only to the lost sheep of the House of Israel*]; that we might receive the promise of the Spirit through faith.

"Brothers I speak after the manner of men; Though if it be a man's covenant, yet if it is confirmed, no man disannuls or adds thereto. Now to Abraham and his seed were the promises made. He didn't say, And to seeds, as of many, but as of one; And to your seed which is Christ. And this I say, the covenant, that was confirmed before of God in Christ, the law, which was four hundred and thirty years after, cannot disannul, that it should make the promise of none effect. For if the inheritance be of the law, it is no more of promise: but God gave it to Abraham by promise.

"*Wherefore then serves the law? It was added because of transgressions*, till the seed should come to whom the promise was made; and it was ordained by angels in the hand of a mediator."[59]

In other words, our ancestors in the House of Israel, as well as Judah, couldn't stay away from paganism and idols. You probably recall the story of the Israelites making the Golden Calf while Moses was on Mt. Sinai getting the Ten Commandments. They had gotten so far away from the understanding of the promises and way of life led by Abraham after several hundred years in Egypt, that God laid down the law, so to speak. And God spelled out exactly what they needed to do. There was no ambiguity. There was no room for second-guessing. It was put in place, and it was all or nothing. Or as Paul put it, "cursed is everyone that continues not in all things, which are written in the book of law to do them" if you choose to put yourself under the law.

It is so hypocritical for any Christian to self-righteously cherry pick points written in the law in the Old Testament. If you are going to use the law to condemn someone's behavior saying it must be followed, then you are bound to follow all the law, every single word of it. Problem is, no one can do this. It is physically impossible. There is no temple. There are no Levite priests in service there obviously. And would you go back to sacrificing bulls and goats? How about stoning people for working on the Sabbath [*Friday sunset to Saturday sunset*]? That would cut down on mall retail sales for sure. Of course, you could sell off your teenager into servitude for some quick cash. The point of all this is that it is ludicrous for Christians to go back to the law in any shape or form. Our lives are to lead us in faith to Christ as it did our forefather Abraham.

Yet it was in the law, the schoolmaster, the bridge that the days ordained by God for all Israel to observe were written down and pointed us to Christ and the faith we have through the Spirit of God.

Let's take a cursory look at these days, these high holy days as they were called to distinguish them from the weekly holy day or Sabbath. The days for the Israelites to observe, or be held in remembrance throughout all their generations are found written in the law.

Our forefathers were instructed by God, "*These are the statutes and judgments [*which included the high holy days*], which you shall observe to do in the land, which the LORD God of your fathers [*Abraham, Isaac and Israel*] has given you to possess it, all the days that you are upon the earth. You shall utterly destroy all the places, wherein the people, which you shall possess, served their [*pagan*] gods, upon the high mountains, upon the hills and under every green tree. And you shall overthrow their altars, and break their pillars and burn their groves with fire; and you shall hew down the graven images of their gods, and destroy the names of them out of that place."[60]

Well God's position on pagan practices seems pretty clear. Although it does differ somewhat in principle from that which our modern day evangelical Christian boldly stated in chapter one. "When the church hijacked these pagan holidays it was for good reason, to influence the world with biblical worldview and culture. Santa's flying reindeer instead of Thor's chariot. Halloween celebrations instead of Samhain...We have every right to take these things and spin them with the goodness of the Lord as part of the Great Commission...We take something bad and make it good." Indeed, our modern day Christian has perfectly described the hijacked elephant.

The very obvious point is that God not only does not want us to hijack pagan holidays, but to utterly destroy all the places in which they were observed and the names of them out of those places. Apply this to Christmas and Easter and the landscape of the world, both geographically and economically, would be altered dramatically. But that's another day.

Let's take a look at these high holy days or days of convocation, the feast days exactly as they appear in the original document set out to our ancestors by Moses. This will provide us with a very clear picture of what these days were. In the following chapters, we will address each one of these days and their relevance for us with Christ's fulfilling them spiritually on our behalf. The physical/spiritual duality of these days will become very clear. They are found in Leviticus chapter twenty-three.

"*And the LORD spoke unto Moses, saying, Speak unto the children of Israel, and say unto them, concerning the feasts of the LORD, which you shall proclaim holy convocations...These are the feasts of the LORD, holy convocations, which you shall proclaim in their seasons.

"In the fourteenth day of the first month at even [sunset] is the LORD's Passover. And on the fifteenth day of the same month is the feast of unleavened bread unto the LORD: seven days must

Archetypes: The Duality of Days

you eat unleavened bread. In the first day you shall have a holy convocation: you shall do no servile work therein. But you shall offer an offering made by fire unto the LORD seven days: in the seventh day is a holy convocation: you shall do no servile work therein.

"And the LORD spoke unto Moses, saying, Speak unto the children of Israel, and say unto them, When you are come into the land which I give unto you, you shall reap the harvest thereof, then you shall bring a sheaf of the firstfruits of your harvest unto the priest: And he shall wave the sheaf before the LORD, to be accepted for you: on the morrow after the [*weekly*] Sabbath the priest shall wave it. And you shall offer that day when you wave the sheaf, a he lamb without blemish of the first year for a burnt offering unto the LORD.

"And the meat offering thereof shall be two tenth deals [or parts] of fine flour mingled with oil, an offering made by fire unto the LORD for a sweet savor: and the drink offering thereof shall be of wine, the fourth part of a hin [*which is about five quarts, thus a quarter of this amount*]. And you shall eat neither bread, nor parched corn, nor green ears, until the selfsame day you have brought an offering unto your God: it shall be a statute forever throughout your generations in all your dwellings." These are the high holy days of unleavened bread.

"And you shall count unto you from the morrow after the Sabbath, from the day that you brought the sheaf of the wave offering; seven Sabbaths shall be complete: even unto the morrow after the seventh Sabbath shall you number fifty days; and you shall offer a new meat offering unto the LORD.

"And you shall bring out of your habitations two wave loaves of two tenth deals: they shall be of fine flour; they shall be baked with leaven; they are the firstfruits of the LORD. And you shall offer with the bread seven lambs without blemish of the first year, and one young bullock, and two rams: they shall be for a burnt offering unto the LORD, with their meat offering, and their drink offerings, even an offering made by fire, of the sweet savour unto the LORD.

"Then shall you sacrifice one kid of the goats for a sin offering, and two lambs of the first year for a sacrifice of peace offerings. And the priest shall wave them with the bread of the firstfruits for a wave offering before the LORD, and with two lambs: they shall be holy to the LORD for the priest. And you shall proclaim on the selfsame day, that it may be a holy convocation unto you: you shall do no servile work therein: it shall be a statue for ever in all your dwellings throughout your generations. And when you reap the harvest of your land, you shall not make clean riddance of the corners of your field when you reap, neither shall you gather any of the gleaning of your harvest: you shall leave them unto the poor, and to the stranger: I am the LORD your God." This is known as Pentecost, which is why we are to count fifty days after the seventh Sabbath.

"And the LORD spoke unto Moses, saying, Speak unto the children of Israel, saying in the seventh month, in the first day of the month, shall you have a Sabbath, a memorial, a holy convocation. You shall do no servile work: but you shall offer and offering made by fire unto the LORD." This is known as the Day of Trumpets.

"And the LORD spoke unto Moses, saying, also on the tenth day of this seventh month there shall be a day of atonement: it shall be a holy convocation unto you; and you shall afflict your souls,

Archetypes: The Duality of Days

and offer an offering made by fire unto the LORD. And you shall do no work in that same day: for it is a day of atonement, to make atonement for you before the LORD your God.

"For whatsoever soul it be that shall not be afflicted in that same day, he shall be cut off from among his people. And whatsoever soul it be that does any work in that same day, the same soul will I destroy from among his people. You shall do no manner of work: it shall be a statue forever throughout your generations in all your dwellings. And it shall be unto you a Sabbath of rest, and you shall afflict your souls: in the ninth day of the month from even to even, shall you celebrate your Sabbath." This is known as the day of Atonement.

"And the LORD spoke unto Moses, saying, Speak unto the children of Israel, saying, The fifteenth day of this seventh month shall be the feast of tabernacles [*temporary dwellings*] for seven days unto the LORD. On the first day shall be a holy convocation: you shall do no servile work therein. Seven days you shall offer an offering made by fire unto the LORD: on the eighth day shall be a holy convocation unto you; and you shall offer an offering made by fire unto the LORD: it is a solemn assembly; and you shall do no servile work therein.

"Also in the fifteenth day of the seventh month, when you have gathered in the fruit of the land, you shall keep a feast unto the lord seven days: on the first day shall be a Sabbath and on the eighth day shall be a Sabbath. And you shall take to you on the first day the boughs of goodly trees, branches of palm trees, and the boughs of thick trees, and willows of the brook; and you shall rejoice before the LORD your God seven days. And you shall keep it a feast unto the LORD seven days in the year. It shall be a statue for ever in your generation: you shall celebrate it in the seventh month.

"You shall dwell in booths seven days; all that are Israelites born shall dwell in booths: that your generations may know that I made the children of Israel to dwell in booths, when I brought them out of the land of Egypt: I am the LORD your God.

"And Moses declared unto the children of Israel the feasts of the LORD."[61]

"These are the feasts of the LORD which you shall proclaim to be holy convocations, to offer an offering made by fire unto the LORD, a burnt offering, and a meat offering, a sacrifice, and drink offerings, everything upon his day: besides the [*weekly*] sabbaths of the lord and besides your gifts and beside all your vows, and beside all your freewill offerings, which you give unto the LORD."[62]

Here we have the days set out by God through Moses for all the people of Israel to observe throughout their generations. No Christmas. No Easter. However, if I were to guess, about now you're thinking, "These are the days we need to be mindful of? How in the world can these days possibly have any meaning for me as a Christian? What's with the sheaf waving and convocations? They are more foreign than Christmas and Easter!"

From a cursory perspective, I couldn't argue with you about that. However, these days are extremely relevant to us today once we understand what they represent and we shift away from riveting our attention on the physical details of observance. This is another case of the truth being stranger than fiction. Yet, we won't need a secret decoder ring to find out the hidden meaning because the meaning is out in plain sight for us to see. It's just that Christmas and Easter block our view.

Archetypes: The Duality of Days

All we have to do is read the original documents given to us, then follow the waypoints. And that's precisely what the following chapters will do with each of the seven holy days of convocation. You are going to discover some incredible facts about Christianity you never knew existed. By the time you finish reading, you'll probably be astounded with what you discover, namely the lost saga of mankind's most amazing story.

Remember, the New Testament plainly shows Christ was sent to the lost sheep of the House of Israel and ultimately to the House of Judah as well. These high holy days are the days that unfold in their fullness in Christianity through Christ. We are in the midst of living these days as Christ is fulfilling them on a spiritual level. For within these days are contained three key elements. The first is the *actual event* that took place concerning our ancestors in the House of Israel, all Israel for that matter. The actual events took place from the time of the passover in Egypt, to passing through the sea, the wandering in the wilderness for forty years, and finally crossing into the land promised them by God as part of the covenant he made with Abraham and Isaac.

Note that Moses, "the lawgiver," did not pass into the promised land with Israel. Yet from the time of the events preceding the Passover, when the firstborn sons of Egypt were slain by the angel of God, Moses, had been the key figure in Israel's history. But the law is our schoolmaster to bring us to Christ. And Moses brought the children of Israel to the border of the land "which I [*the LORD*] swore unto their fathers to give them." This is a reference back to Abraham when he returned from Egypt and went again to Bethel.

We read in the Book of Joshua, "*Now after the death of Moses the servant of the LORD, it came to pass that the LORD spoke unto Joshua, the son of Nun, Moses' minister saying, Moses my servant is dead; now therefore arise, go over this Jordan, you and all this people, unto the land which I do give them, to the children of Israel."[63] The people of Israel including our ancestors of the House of Israel were given into the hands of Joshua to lead them across the Jordan River in the land given by covenant promise to Abraham, the father of the faithful. The lawgiver Moses, a Levite, was not to take them there. The message is that the law can't get to where God has promised us. It has to be by faith.

Joshua, the son of Nun, was of the tribe or nation of Ephraim. As you may recall, Ephraim was blessed by Israel as his firstborn in place of Reuben. And Joseph, father of Ephraim and Manasseh, was the reason why Israel was in Egypt to begin with. Ephraim, from whom Joshua was descended, was chosen to be the kingly line of the House of Israel as you may also remember. Christ was sent only to the lost sheep of the House of Israel. The name Joshua means, "Jehovah is salvation." The name Jesus means, "Jehovah is salvation." There is incredible elegance and beauty in the duality contained in the word of God for his people. Moses, and the law brought Israel to "Jehovah is salvation" both physically, coming out of bondage in Egypt and spiritually, by Christ, king of Israel, leading the House of Israel out of bondage to the law and sin so they can receive the fullness of the promises given to Abraham and Isaac.

This is the point made by the apostle Paul. "Knowing that a man is not justified by the works of the law, but by faith of Jesus Christ, even we have believed in Jesus Christ, that we might be justified by the faith of Christ...."[64] We are justified by faith of Jesus Christ because Christ was the sin offering on our behalf. Another duality. The physical sacrifices of bulls and goats and then the sacrifice of Christ for us spiritually.

"For where a testament is, there must also of necessity be the death of the testator. For a testament is of force after men are dead: otherwise it is of no strength at all while the testator lives. Whereupon neither the first testament was dedicated without blood. For when Moses had spoken every precept to all the people according to the law, he took the blood of calves and goats, with water, and scarlet wool, and hyssop, and sprinkled both, the book and all the people, saying, This is the blood of the testament which God has enjoined unto you.

"Moreover he sprinkled with blood both the tabernacle, and all the vessels of the ministry. And almost all things are by the law purged with blood; and without shedding of blood is no remission.

"It was therefore necessary that the patterns of things in the heavens should be purified with these; but the heavenly things themselves with better sacrifices than these. For Christ is not entered into the holy places made with hands, which are the figures of the true; but into heaven itself, now to appear in the presence of God for us: nor yet that he should offer himself often, as the high priest enter into the holy place every year with blood of others; for then must he often have suffered since the foundation of the world: but now once in the end of the world [*Greek, aion, meaning end of the age*] has he appeared to put away sin by the sacrifices of himself.

"And as it is appointed unto men once to die, but after this is the judgment: so Christ was *once offered* to bear the sins of many; and unto them that look for him shall he appear the second time without sin unto salvation."[65]

The second key element is the *remembrance*. That's what we read above in outlining the days of observance for Israel as delivered by Moses. The days spelled out by Moses in the law covenant to Israel were feast days. They were not meant to be onerous and burdensome, but rather days to celebrate in joy especially when we know what they portend for us in our future.

The third key element therefore is the *spiritual fulfillment* of these days by Christ as it is in the "pattern of things in the heavens."[66]

Upon examining each day mentioned by Moses, we will examine the event's occurrence in Israel's history. Then we will look at the day from the perspective of Christ's fulfillment on a spiritual level. By doing so, we will see each day's physical/spiritual duality, but more importantly we will see how meaningful these days are for Christians, the lost sheep of the House of Israel.

And we will truly come to see what Paul meant when he told the Christians in Corinth, "Moreover brethren, I would not have you ignorant, how that *all our brothers* were under the cloud and *all* passed through the sea; and *all* were baptized unto Moses in the cloud and in the sea; and *all* ate the same spiritual meat; and *all* drank the same spiritual drink: for they drank of that *spiritual Rock* that followed them: and *that Rock was Christ*."[67]

It needs to be pointed out that this is not some metaphorical expression of Christ's presence with all Israel, both the House of Israel and the House of Judah as they would become. Christ was there with them in the Old Testament as he is with us also in the New Testament.

Remember, the Bible, the Biblical record is one complete book written to the same people. It is one story replete with dualities.

Archetypes: The Duality of Days

While the condition of the people, the characters in our story, has changed in relation to God and with each other, the Biblical record is for all Israel, both the House of Israel and the House of Judah. This is why we find in both the Old Testament and the New Testament the same quote, "Behold the days come, says the LORD, that I will make a new covenant with the House of Israel and the House of Judah…."[68] The apostle of Christ, Paul, a Benjamite quoted the prophet of our LORD, Jeremiah, son of a priest in the land of Benjamin. Duality again.

It's time we Christians realize our true history and put away the hijacked pagan traditions that take us away from our LORD Jesus Christ. Our LORD made a covenant with our forefathers Abraham and Isaac. They were passed on to our forefather Israel in what is the Genesis Birthright.[69] We are increasingly separated daily from this knowledge because we are ignorant of our heritage. Our LORD is angry with us because of all he has done for us, including laying down his life on behalf of each and everyone of us. We foolishly turn our back on him thinking we are wise to hijack pagan holidays in his name.

For those of us willing to stand up and seek the truth of our ancestral history, let's begin by learning about the duality of the days our LORD, Jesus Christ established for us as found in the original document of the Biblical record.

Chapter Three
Passover, Days of Unleavened Bread and Christ

"Do not think that I came to destroy the Law or the Prophets. I did not come to destroy, but to fulfill."

Apart from the Passover, you've probably never even heard about the Days of Unleavened Bread much less that Christ fulfilled them. As I noted in chapter six of the *The Blind Man's Elephant*, Christ's first coming radically changed the relationships between the House of Judah and the House of Israel. The fact of the matter is that by fulfilling these days, Christ purposefully severed the covenant relationship with the House of Judah, which the apostle Paul points out in his letter to the Romans; and Stephen clearly pointed out to the high priest, which resulted in his martyred death. The reconciliation of the House of Judah occurs on another of the high holy days yet in our future.

Specifically, the Passover is not a high holy day of convocation. Convocation simply means a calling together, an assembly. Thus, on days of convocation everyone of Israel came together for a specific purpose, depending on each high holy day. The high holy sabbath days were joyous feast days, with the possible exception of the Day of Atonement, which meant they were a celebration, a special time of remembrance.

The closest thing we had to what these days were like for the House of Israel would be Thanksgiving Day. As a kid growing up more than fifty years ago, Thanksgiving was as big a deal as Christmas. We looked forward to it the whole month of November. It was a very special occasion. Even though we were a blue-collar family, I remember my dad getting dressed up in a white starched dress shirt and carefully selecting which tie he would wear. Mom planned the logistics of the Thanksgiving meal with the same dedication a field general would give to his battle plans. And while the day was a sumptuous feast with everyone leaving the table stuffed as much as the turkey had been, it was a solemn day as well. Pausing to sincerely give thanks to God for our blessings, individually, as a family and as a nation was the focal point of the day.

Thanksgiving today appears to have become not much more than an inconvenient speed bump in the four to five month long Christmas season adorned with football games and TV commercials that marks the jumping off point for the largest retail sales day ahead of Christmas. But the aptly named Abraham Lincoln in the midst of the most serious war the US has been involved in, the Civil War, took time in 1863 to reflect upon that crisis time as Americans were dying on American soil in huge numbers. The republic itself was in mortal danger.

Showing incredible leadership in that most unstable of times unparalleled in US history, he made a proclamation establishing Thanksgiving Day. Just to be clear, he did not establish "Turkey Day." One was established to set aside a national day of giving thanks to God. The other is growing into a day that appears dedicated to food consumption and watching football games perhaps with a token nod to giving thanks. To set the tone of remembrance for what we will read in this, and the following chapters, and being mindful of current circumstances in the world, I thought it appropriate to include President Lincoln's proclamation in its entirety.

"The year that is drawing towards its close has been filled with the blessings of fruitful fields and healthful skies. To these bounties, which are so constantly enjoyed that we are prone to forget the source from which they come, others have been added, which are of so extraordinary a nature, that they cannot fail to penetrate and soften even the heart which is habitually insensible to the ever watchful providence of Almighty God. In the midst of a civil war of unequalled magnitude and severity, which has sometimes seemed to foreign States to invite and to provoke their aggression, peace has been preserved with all nations, order has been maintained, the laws have been respected and obeyed, and harmony has prevailed everywhere except in the theatre of military conflict; while that theatre has been greatly contracted by the advancing armies and navies of the Union. Needful diversions of wealth and of strength from the fields of peaceful industry to the national defence, have not arrested the plough, the shuttle, or the ship; the axe had enlarged the borders of our settlements, and the mines, as well of iron and coal as of the precious metals, have yielded even more abundantly than heretofore. Population has steadily increased, notwithstanding the waste that has been made in the camp, the siege and the battle-field; and the country, rejoicing in the consciousness of augmented strength and vigor, is permitted to expect continuance of years, with large increase of freedom.

"No human counsel hath devised nor hath any mortal hand worked out these great things. They are the gracious gifts of the Most High God, who, while dealing with us in anger for our sins, hath nevertheless remembered mercy.

"It has seemed to me fit and proper that they should be solemnly, reverently and gratefully acknowledged as with one heart and voice by the whole American people. I do therefore invite my fellow citizens in every part of the United States, and also those who are at sea and those who are sojourning in foreign lands, to set apart and observe the last Thursday of November next, as a day of Thanksgiving and Praise to our beneficent Father who dwelleth in the Heavens. And I recommend to them that while offering up the ascriptions justly due to Him for such singular deliverances and blessings, they do also, with humble penitence for our national perverseness and disobedience, commend to his tender care all those who have become widows, orphans, mourners or sufferers in the lamentable civil strife in which we are unavoidably engaged, and fervently implore the interposition of the Almighty Hand to heal the wounds of the nation and to restore it as soon as may be consistent with the Divine purposes to the full enjoyment of peace, harmony, tranquillity and Union."

The days set aside by our LORD for our remembrance throughout all our generations have special meaning for us today. But, as with Abraham Lincoln's proclamation written not that long ago, we have lost sight of the true meaning and significance those days hold for us. Let's look at the remembrance of the Passover first and then the Days of Unleavened Bread.

The Passover and Days of Unleavened Bread Remembrance: "*And the LORD spoke unto Moses, saying, Speak unto the children of Israel, and say unto them, concerning the feasts of the LORD, which you shall proclaim holy convocations…These are the feasts of the LORD, holy convocations, which you shall proclaim in their seasons.

"In the fourteenth day of the first month at even [*sunset*] is the LORD's Passover. And on the fifteenth day of the same month is the feast of unleavened bread unto the LORD: seven days must you eat unleavened bread. In the first day you shall have a holy convocation: you shall do no servile work therein. But you shall offer an offering made by fire unto the LORD seven days: in the seventh day is a holy convocation: you shall do no servile work therein.

"Speak you unto all the congregation of Israel, saying, In the tenth day of this month they shall take to them every man a lamb, according to the house of their fathers, a lamb for an house: And if the household be too little for the lamb, let him and his neighbor next unto his house take it according to the number of the souls; every man according to his eating shall make your count for the lamb.

"Your lamb shall be without blemish, a male of the first year: you shall take it out from the sheep, or from the goats: And you shall keep it up until the fourteenth day of the same month: and the whole assembly of the congregation of Israel shall kill it in the evening. And they shall take of the blood, and strike it on the two side posts and on the upper door post of the houses, wherein they shall eat it.

"And they shall eat the flesh in that night, roast with fire, and unleavened bread; and with bitter herbs they shall eat it. Eat not of it raw, nor sodden at all with water, but roast with fire; his head with his legs, and with the purtenance [*internal organs*] thereof.

"And you shall let nothing of it remain until the morning; and that which remains of it until the morning you shall burn with fire. And thus shall you eat it; with your loins girded, your shoes on your feet, and your staff in your hand; and you shall eat it in haste: it is the LORD's passover.

"For I will pass through the land of Egypt this night, and will smite all the firstborn in the land of Egypt, both man and beast; and against all the gods of Egypt I will execute judgment: I am the LORD. And the blood shall be to you for a token upon the houses where you are: and when I see the blood, I will pass over you, and the plague shall not be upon you to destroy you, when I smite the land of Egypt.

"And this day shall be unto you for a memorial; and you shall keep it a feast to the LORD throughout your generations; you shall keep it a feast by an ordinance for ever."

"*And the LORD said unto Moses and Aaron, T*his is the ordinance of the passover*: There shall no stranger eat thereof: But every man's servant that is bought for money, when thou hast circumcised him, then shall he eat thereof. A foreigner and a hired servant shall not eat thereof. In one house shall it be eaten; you shall not carry forth ought of the flesh abroad out of the house; neither shall you break a bone thereof."

"*Seven days shall you eat unleavened bread*; even the first day you shall put away leaven out of your houses: for whosoever eats leavened bread from the first day until the seventh day, that soul shall be cut off from Israel.

"And in the first day there shall be an holy convocation, and in the seventh day there shall be an holy convocation to you; no manner of work shall be done in them, save that which every man must eat, that only may be done of you.

"And you shall observe the feast of unleavened bread; for in this selfsame day have I brought your armies out of the land of Egypt: therefore shall you observe this day in your generations by an ordinance for ever.

"In the first month, on the fourteenth day of the month at even, you shall eat unleavened bread, until the one and twentieth day of the month at even. Seven days shall there be no leaven found in your houses: for whosoever eats that which is leavened, even that soul shall be cut off from the congregation of Israel, whether he be a stranger, or born in the land. You shall eat nothing leavened; in all your habitations shall you eat unleavened bread."[70]

"*And Moses said unto the people, Remember this day, in which you came out from Egypt, out of the house of bondage; for by strength of hand the LORD brought you out from this place: there shall no leavened bread be eaten.

"And it shall be when the LORD shall bring thee into the land of the Canaanites, and the Hittites, and the Amorites, and the Hivites, and the Jebusites, which he swore unto thy fathers to give you, a land flowing with milk and honey, that you shall keep this service in this month.

"Seven days you shall eat unleavened bread, and in the seventh day shall be a feast to the LORD. Unleavened bread shall be eaten seven days; and there shall no leavened bread be seen with you, neither shall there be leaven seen with you in all your quarters. And you shall show your son in that day, saying, This is done because of that which the LORD did unto me when I came forth out of Egypt.

"And it shall be for a sign unto you upon your hand, and for a memorial between your eyes, that the LORD's law may be in your mouth: for with a strong hand has the LORD brought you out of Egypt. You shall therefore keep this ordinance in his season from year to year." [71]

Before we take a look at the actual event in history that these days were observed in remembrance of, there a few things that should pop out at you in terms of dualities. The Passover lamb was to be without blemish. Christ is that Lamb sacrificed for sin. He was without blemish or sin. No bones were to be broken when eating the Passover lamb. It was said of Christ that not one bone of his was broken. When the crucifixion took place, the other two men there had their legs broken that they would die more quickly, but Christ was already dead at that point.

Let's read what took place to bring about the high holy days and their remembrance. For all that is taking place today, and in the future stem from the events that began thousands of years ago in Egypt.

The Event in Israel's History: The events that resulted in the Passover in Egypt all began with our forefather, Joseph, ending up in Egypt. As we read, "And the patriarchs [*Israel's sons*], moved with envy, sold Joseph [*their brother*] into Egypt: but God was with him, And delivered him out of all his afflictions, and gave him favor and wisdom in the sight of Pharaoh king of Egypt; and he made him governor over Egypt and all his house.

"Now there came a dearth [*famine*] over all the land of Egypt and Chanaan, and great affliction: and our fathers found no sustenance. But when Jacob [*Israel*] heard that there was corn in Egypt, he sent out our fathers first. And at the second time Joseph was made known to his brethren; and Joseph's kindred was made known unto Pharaoh. Then sent Joseph, and called his father Jacob to him, and all his kindred, threescore and fifteen souls. So Jacob went down into Egypt, and died, he, and our fathers, And were carried over into Sychem, and laid in the sepulcher that Abraham bought for a sum of money of the sons of Emmor, the father of Sychem.

"But when the time of the promise [*covenant*] drew nigh, which God had sworn to Abraham, the people grew and multiplied in Egypt, Till another king arose, which knew not Joseph. The same dealt subtlety with our kindred, and evil entreated our fathers, so that they cast out their young children, to the end they might not live. In which time Moses was born, and was exceeding fair, and nourished up in his father's house three months: And when he was cast out, Pharaoh's daughter took him up, and nourished him for her own son.

"And Moses was learned in all the wisdom of the Egyptians, and was mighty in words and in deeds. And when he was full forty years old, it came into his heart to visit his brethren the children of Israel. And seeing one of them suffer wrong, he defended him, and avenged him that was oppressed, and smote the Egyptian:

"And the next day he showed himself unto them as they strove, and would have set them at one again, saying, Sirs, you are brethren; why do you wrong one to another? But he that did his neighbor wrong thrust him away, saying, Who made you a ruler and a judge over us? Will you kill me, as you did the Egyptian yesterday? Then fled Moses at this saying, and was a stranger in the land of Madian, where he begat [*fathered*] two sons.

"And when forty years were expired, there appeared to him in the wilderness of mount Sinai an angel of the Lord in a flame of fire in a bush. When Moses saw it, he wondered at the sight: and as he drew near to behold it, the voice of the LORD came unto him, Saying, I am the God of your fathers, the God of Abraham, and the God of Isaac, and the God of Jacob.

"Then Moses trembled, and didn't dare to look. Then said the LORD to him, Put off your shoes from your feet: for the place where you stand is holy ground. I have seen, I have seen the affliction of my people, which is in Egypt, and I have heard their groaning, and am come down to deliver them. And now come, I will send you into Egypt. This Moses, whom they refused, saying, Who made you a ruler and a judge? the same did God send to be a ruler and a deliverer by the hand of the angel which appeared to him in the bush. He brought them out, after that he had showed wonders and signs in the land of Egypt, and in the Red sea, and in the wilderness forty years."

"This is that Moses, which said unto the children of Israel, *A prophet shall the LORD your God raise up unto you of your brethren, like unto me; him shall you hear.*"[72] This is a reference to Christ by Moses.

This historical account of Israel's sojourn in Egypt quoted above, including this last point, was made to the high priest. What is particularly interesting about this account of Moses and the children of Israel is that it isn't found at all in the Old Testament or the Jewish Bible. All this is written in the New Testament. It is part of the martyr Stephen's account to the high priest in the Book of Acts essentially telling him the old way has passed. The physical office of the high priest had been passed over. Essentially, Stephen was pointing out to the high priest that he was made redundant just as Moses said would happen.

Consequently, a momentous and fundamental change took place for Israel with Christ's first coming. The bridge between Abraham and Christ, the law covenant, had served its useful purpose. Christ, did not come to destroy the law or the prophets, that which is written in the first two divisions of the Old Testament, but to *fulfill* that which was written as he plainly stated in Matthew chapter five. The seven holy days given to Israel by Moses were now to be fulfilled on a higher stage, that is, Christ will spiritually fulfill them on our behalf as our high priest as we'll see in the coming chapters. This is why they have more meaning for us today than ever before.

When Stephen was martyred by stoning, the witnesses laid down their clothes at the feet of a young man named Saul. It is this same Saul that became the apostle Paul who later wrote to the Christians in Galatia that the law, delivered to the children of Israel by Moses, was our schoolmaster to bring us to Christ.

The office of high priest was no longer a physical entity. Christ now spiritually fulfilled that office. The temple that the high priest sat in was replaced, too, as the apostle to the gentiles, Paul pointed out. "But Christ being come a high priest of good things to come, by a greater and more perfect tabernacle, not made with hands, that is to say not of this building."[73] As the apostle John said, "For the law was given by Moses, but grace and truth came by Jesus Christ."[74] No more does the House of Israel need a physical temple and a man to fill the office of high priest.

Before we get into Christ fulfilling the Passover, let's take a closer look at the events that transpired in Egypt. Egyptians set taskmasters over all of Israel to make their life so miserable, they would want to leave Egypt. As it says in Genesis, "*And the Egyptians made the children of Israel to serve with rigor: and they made their lives bitter with hard bondage."[75]

Eventually, the Pharaoh called for all male babies born of Israel to be cast into the river for the explicit purpose of drowning. This lead to the familiar story of Moses' birth when, at three months of age, he was placed in a basket in the river. A daughter of Pharaoh found him, gave him his name, and raised him as her own son.

This Pharaoh eventually died. And over time, "*...the children of Israel sighed by reason of the bondage, and they cried, and their cry came up unto God by reason of the bondage. And God heard their groaning and God remembered his covenant with Abraham, Isaac and Jacob [Israel]."[76]

Moses, who was in exile, was chosen by God to go back to Egypt to bring the children of Israel out of their bondage. God told Moses, "*I will stretch out my hand, and smite Egypt with all my wonders which I will do in the midst thereof: and after that he [*Pharaoh*] will let you go."[77] As we may remember, it wasn't without some convincing that the Pharaoh finally allowed Israel to leave.

So Moses took his wife and children and set off to return to Egypt now that all those who sought to kill him were dead. Upon arrival and convincing the elders and children of Israel of their mission to lead the children of Israel out of Egypt, Moses and his older brother Aaron, who became the first high priest of Israel, went to see the Pharaoh.

In the initial meeting with Pharaoh, we had the world's first recorded "throw down." It was Moses and Aaron versus the Egyptian magicians. Aaron threw down his staff and it became a serpent. The Pharaoh called in his guys and they threw down their staffs, which became serpents as well. Only Aaron's serpent ate the Egyptian's serpent staffs. Pharaoh was ticked off and refused to let Israel leave Egypt.

The next morning, Moses and Aaron went to see the Pharaoh again. But, he hadn't changed his mind. With the same staff that ate the other serpents, God had Aaron strike the river. It was turned into blood. The fish died. And it got stinky real fast. Then, by God's direction Aaron stretched forth his staff and all the waters of Egypt, the streams, pools, ponds, and even the water stored in vessels, all turned to blood. Still the Pharaoh was resolute. This continued for seven days.

God commanded Moses to go back to see the Pharaoh. This time it was frogs. There were frogs in the well water, frogs in the beds, frogs in the ovens, frogs climbing all over the Egyptians. Heaps and heaps of frogs everywhere. However, if Pharaoh agreed to let Israel leave, then the frogs would die off, except in the river. So Pharaoh conceded. And as the frogs died as Moses had said, everywhere except in the river, Pharaoh changed his mind or "hardened his heart" as we are told.

So God told Aaron to stretch forth his staff and strike the dust of the land so that lice was upon man and beast alike. The Egyptian magicians couldn't do anything to stop it. They even told Pharaoh that this was the "finger of God" doing this. Strange the Egyptians didn't say it was the hand of God, just the finger. Point taken. Nevertheless, Pharaoh dug his heels in and refused to let the Israelites go.

The LORD told Moses to get up early and go stand before Pharaoh when he was going down to the water. "*Tell him, my LORD says let my people go, that they may serve me." If Pharaoh refuses, then tell him I will send swarms of flies upon every Egyptian, their houses, even the ground they walk on. But, only in the land of Goshen will there not be flies in Egypt so that Pharaoh knows that "I am the LORD in the midst of the earth."[78]

Pharaoh stayed the course once again. And the plague of flies filled Egypt except Goshen. This time Pharaoh decided to change course. He told Moses to go sacrifice to your LORD in Egypt. Moses countered with three days journey from Egypt. Pharaoh countered with, "Okay go to the wilderness but not too far away." Moses warned Pharaoh not to change his mind again and "stay the course" as he had done before.

Moses left, and entreated God to stop the plague of flies. As soon as the last of the flies was gone, Pharaoh reneged on his word. As the insects and frogs weren't getting through to Pharaoh, God told Moses to tell Pharaoh that unless his people were let free, then a "very grievous murrain," a highly contagious deadly disease shall strike down the Egyptian's cattle, horses, asses, camels, oxen, and sheep. This would be a very expensive disaster for any agrarian economy. But of all the animals of Israel, none shall die. Still the Pharaoh stayed the course and all the cattle of Egypt died. None died of the Israelites.

Next the LORD said to Moses and Aaron, take handfuls of ashes and before the Pharaoh's presence, sprinkle it towards the heavens.[79] Then tell Pharaoh that the dust in all the land of Egypt shall be a "*boil breaking forth blains [*inflammatory, swelling infection of the skin with a hard pus-filled core*] upon man and beast throughout all Egypt. The magicians of Egypt couldn't even stand before Moses and Aaron this time because of the boils. If you give this just a little thought, imagine these boils over all parts of your body. Normal bodily functions including walking or sitting would be extremely painful. We are told, "The LORD hardened the heart of Pharaoh."

"*And the LORD said unto Moses, Rise up early in the morning, and stand before Pharaoh, and say unto him, Thus says the

LORD God of the Hebrews, Let my people go, that they may serve me. For I will at this time send all my plagues upon your heart, and upon your servants, and upon your people; that you may know that there is none like me in all the earth. For now I will stretch out my hand, that I may smite you and your people with pestilence; and you shall be cut off from the earth. *And in very deed for this cause have I raised you up, for to show in you my power; and that my name may be declared throughout all the earth.* As yet exalt you yourself against my people, that you will not let them go?"[80]

If you recall from *The Blind Man's Elephant*, this is essentially the same point God made to Nebuchadnezzar, king of Babylon. And it is the point made to the rest of us with the exact timing of the five empires in succession over 2520 years that came to pass. God rules in the empires of men despite what we may think. As the apostle Peter said, God is not slack as men would count slackness. His perspective of time is different than ours. And this same point will once again become apparent with the sixth empire as explained in the Book of Revelation.

But Pharaoh remained stubborn. "*Behold, tomorrow about this time I will cause it to rain a very grievous hail, such as has not been in Egypt since the foundation thereof even until now. Send therefore now, and gather your cattle, and all that you have in the field; for upon every man and beast which shall be found in the field, and shall not be brought home, the hail shall come down upon them, and they shall die. He that feared the word of the LORD among the servants of Pharaoh made his servants and his cattle flee into the houses: And he that regarded not the word of the LORD left his servants and his cattle in the field."[81] There's always some who insist on learning the hard way.

This continued with the hail, then with locusts and then with a thick darkness so that the Egyptians had to move about by touch. This lasted for three days. However, there was light in the houses of the Israelites. Finally Pharaoh told Moses and Aaron they could go but only if they left their flocks and herds. Obviously Egypt was pretty depleted of just about everything on land at this point. But Moses said, "No, they will go with us too." Pharaoh said never mind, you can't go. For the "LORD hardened his heart." But the Pharaoh called Moses in and told him to get away from him and Egypt pretty much saying, "If I see your face again, you're a dead man."

But there was one more plague that was to fall upon Egypt by the hand of God. And it is the precursor of the day that Christ began fulfilling the promises of the Spirit he made to Abraham, Isaac and Israel.

"*Then Moses called for all the elders of Israel, and said unto them, Draw out and take you a lamb according to your families, and kill the passover. And you shall take a bunch of hyssop, and dip it in the blood that is in the basin, and strike the lintel and the two side posts with the blood that is in the basin; and none of you shall go out at the door of his house until the morning. For the LORD will pass through to smite the Egyptians; and when he sees the blood upon the lintel, and on the two side posts, *the LORD will pass over the door, and will not suffer the destroyer to come in unto your houses to smite you*. And you shall observe this thing for an ordinance to you and to your sons for ever."[82]

This is a specific example of a physical event having its spiritual duality fulfilled by Christ. It is this ordinance that Christ fulfilled on that Passover night about 2000 years ago. There is a reason why Christ said he was sent only to the lost sheep of the House of Israel.

"*And it shall come to pass, when you are come to the land which the LORD will give you, according as he has promised, that you shall keep this service.

"And it shall come to pass, when your children shall say unto you, What do you mean by this service? That you shall say, It is the sacrifice of the LORD 's passover, who passed over the houses of the children of Israel in Egypt, when he struck the Egyptians, and delivered our houses. And the people bowed the head and worshipped.

"And the children of Israel went away, and did as the LORD had commanded Moses and Aaron, so did they.

"And it came to pass, that at midnight the LORD struck all the firstborn in the land of Egypt, from the firstborn of Pharaoh that sat on his throne unto the firstborn of the captive that was in the dungeon; and all the firstborn of cattle.

"And Pharaoh rose up in the night, he, and all his servants, and all the Egyptians; and there was a great cry in Egypt; for there was not a house where there was not one dead.

"And he called for Moses and Aaron by night, and said, Rise up, and get you forth from among my people, both you and the children of Israel; and go, serve the LORD, as you have said."[83]

But what is the custom of Christians today concerning Christ's Passover sacrifice? What would we say to our children? How do we answer them when they ask, "What do you mean by this service?" We should say, "It is the sacrifice of the LORD's passover, who passed over the houses of the children of Israel in Egypt, when he struck the Egyptians, and delivered our houses. And now he has spiritually fulfilled this day for us." Instead, given our following after Ishtar, we'd have to say our children, "We color Easter fertility eggs for Christ because...."

Christ fulfills the Passover: We should note that the Passover is mentioned in 27 verses in the New Testament including the one mistranslation of Easter, which really is *pascha* in the original manuscripts meaning Passover. Thus, if anything, the text shows us that the Passover was being observed by Israel in the first century. As we read above, the Passover ordinance was not just for the Jews, or the sons of Judah, as is the common misperception, but for all twelve patriarchs of Israel and their children.

Thus, when it was time for Christ to offer himself up as a sin offering, it was on behalf of all the children of Israel. If it were just for the children of Judah, the Jews, Christians would be up the creek without the proverbial paddle.

Paul explained it to Christians this way. "For the law [*given to all Israel*] having a shadow of good things to come, and not the very image of the things, can never with those sacrifices which they offered year by year continually make the comers thereunto perfect. For then would they not have ceased to be offered? Because that the worshippers once purged should have had no more conscience of sins.

"But in those sacrifices there is a remembrance again made of sins every year. For it is not possible that the blood of bulls and of goats should take away sins. Wherefore when he comes into the world, he says, Sacrifice and offering you would not, but a body have you prepared me: In burnt offerings and sacrifices for sin you have had no pleasure.

"Then said I, Lo, I *am* come (in the volume of the book it is written of me) [*Psalm 40*] to do your will, O God. Above when he said, Sacrifice and offering and burnt offerings and offering for sin you would not, neither had pleasure therein; which are offered by the law;

"Then said he, Lo, I come to do your will, O God. He takes away the first [*covenant*], that he may establish the second.

"By whose will we are sanctified through the offering of the body of Jesus Christ *once* for all."[84]

The point Paul is making here is that Christ was the sacrificial Lamb that was offered once for all transgressions for those who were under the first covenant. His death fulfilled the terms of the first covenant by which sacrifices and observances had to be made every year in remembrance. Now, the second covenant is established first with the children of the House of Israel to whom Christ said he was sent…"Lo, I come to do your will, O God."

Let's take a look, however, at the very last physical observance of Passover under the law covenant when Christ ate the Passover meal with his apostles.

"And the first day of unleavened bread, when they killed the passover, his disciples said unto him, Where will you that we go and prepare that you may eat the passover? And he sent forth two of his disciples, and said unto them, Go you into the city, and there shall meet you a man bearing a pitcher of water: follow him.

"And wheresoever he shall go in, say you to the good man of the house, The Master said, Where is the guest chamber, where I shall eat the passover with my disciples? And he will show you a large upper room furnished and prepared: there make ready for us. And his disciples went forth, and came into the city, and found as he had said unto them: and they made ready the passover. And in the evening he came with the twelve."[85]

By way of clarification, it should be pointed out that the Passover, along with the two holy days of convocation, specifically the Days of Unleavened Bread had come to be popularly named as one. But as we read above, the Passover was not a holy day of convocation or a part of the Days of Unleavened Bread by law, but rather the day following Passover was the first official day of unleavened bread. However those of Israel at the time came to generically include Passover among the observed "days of unleavened bread."

Another point that should be clarified is that Christ came to observe the Passover in the evening, which was the sunset time, along with the twelve apostles. This is another duality. The Passover in Egypt protected all twelve sons of Israel and their families. And it was at this Passover meal with Christ that these same twelve were told, "And I appoint unto you a kingdom, as my Father has appointed unto me; That you may eat and drink at my table in my kingdom, and sit on thrones judging the *twelve tribes of Israel*."[86]

Why would Christ say anything like this to his apostles if he came to save the "gentiles of the world?" Why wouldn't he tell his apostles they were sent to the gentiles of the world and would sit on thrones judging them? Maybe it's because he said, "I am not sent except to the lost sheep of the House of Israel." And at the end of this meal, why didn't Christ tell the apostles he would join them hunting for Easter eggs after his resurrection as a remembrance for all the gentiles in their generations?

Let's go back to the actual Passover meal Christ ate with his apostles and see what took place there.

"And he said unto them, With desire I have desired to eat this passover with you before I suffer: For I say unto you, I will not any more eat thereof, *until it be fulfilled in the kingdom of God*." Christ was referring to his fulfilling the Passover, the first duality he fulfilled. Christ did eat again with the apostles after his resurrection.

"And he took the cup, and gave thanks, and said, Take this, and divide it among yourselves: For I say unto you, I will not drink of the fruit of the vine, until the kingdom of God shall come." Christ did not drink any wine with the apostles after his resurrection.

"And he took bread, and gave thanks, and brake it, and gave unto them, saying, This is my body which is given for you: this do in remembrance of me. Likewise also the cup after supper, saying, This cup is the new testament in my blood, which is shed for you."[87] Christ's death by his shedding of blood as the sacrificial lamb and resurrection marked the end of the first covenant, and the beginning of the new covenant, no longer of the flesh, but now fulfilled of the spirit.

This Passover meal was a special observance the night before Christ became the sacrificial Passover lamb for the sins of Israel. Again the Passover ordinance was made with one people only. But this particular Passover meal was a special meal for Christ and the twelve who were to sit on thrones judging the twelve tribes of Israel. Christianity, however, looks upon this as the

Lord's supper from which the practice of communion is derived. Lord's being a possessive noun and thus meaning Christ's supper with his apostles. A possessive noun is a noun that normally doesn't end in the letter "s," and is normally made possessive by adding the apostrophe "s" ['s].

Now this is important to know because in the King James Version of this supper's account is written as "Lord's," which is incorrect. In the original Greek, it is an adjective, *kyriakos*, and not the possessive noun, *kyrios*. This is a big difference. When Paul is writing to the Corinthians about the *Lords* supper, it is not a reference to Christ's supper, but correctly it is describing the type of supper. In this descriptive case, it is a supper of Lords or a supper belonging to Lords. Specifically, it was in reference to the fact that at this last Passover supper under the terms of the old covenant made with Israel, the twelve apostles were told they would sit on thrones judging the twelve nations of Israel as kings or lords. This is where the problem lies for many Christian churches today. Let's read Paul's account.

"When you come together therefore into one place, this is not to eat the Lords supper. For in eating every one takes before his own supper: and one is hungry, and another is drunken. What? have you not houses to eat and to drink in? *or* do you despise the church of God, and shame them that have not? What shall I say to you? shall I praise you in this? I praise you not." Thus, the current custom of "taking communion" is not something the apostle Paul sanctioned. In fact, he condemned it.

"For I have received of the Lord that which also I delivered unto you, That the Lord Jesus the same night in which he was betrayed took bread: And when he had given thanks, he broke it, and said, Take, eat: this is my body, which is broken for you: this do in remembrance of me.

"After the same manner also he took the cup, when he had supped [*eaten supper*], saying, This cup is the new testament in my blood: this do *you*, as oft as *you* drink it, in remembrance of me.

"*For as often as you eat this bread, and drink this cup, you do show the Lord's death till he come.*"

"Wherefore whosoever shall eat this bread, and drink this cup of the Lord, *unworthily*, shall be guilty of the body and blood of the Lord."

"For he that eats and drinks *unworthily*, eats and drinks damnation to himself, not discerning the Lord's body."[88]

Just to be clear, the word Lord's body here in Greek is *kyrios*, a masculine noun and is a reference to the body of Christ. Thus the apostrophe 's' makes it a possessive noun completely different than the adjective used for the *Lords* supper. In the Old Testament, when referring to the LORD's Passover, the word LORD is a proper noun, which is Yehovah. Every Passover up to the Lords supper used the proper noun. But as Paul correctly pointed out, it is the Lords, *kyriakos*, supper.

The first point we need to make clear is that this was a supper of Lords. Just like the upper house of British government is the House of Lords. It is a descriptive term, an adjective describing its members who are lords. All the people at that Passover supper were lords or kings.

Secondly, in the church at Corinth, this had become essentially a festive social type meal. Paul is telling them to eat and drink in their own homes if they're hungry and or if they want to get drunk.

Third, Paul is pointing out to them that Christ gave these commands only to these twelve lords, his apostles, not to everyone in the world. "For as often as <u>you</u> eat this bread, and drink this cup, <u>you</u> do show the Lord's death till he come." It was a supper of lords. It was to these twelve lords that were told to do so as often as they ate and drank to show the *Lord's death till he come*. It had a timing element to it. And when did Christ come back from the dead? He was risen before sunset on the weekly sabbath, and saw the apostles later on the first day of the week, Sunday.

So this commemoration was for these twelve apostles only, to keep them in remembrance until Christ would arise from the dead as he said. And did Christ command them to "take this cup and divide it among the gentiles of the world?" No, it was to be divided amongst themselves, the lords.

In reality then, the twelve apostles, the twelve lords, observed this practice for about four days. It is not an eternal remembrance for all generations. It was a specific command to these twelve lords for a specific period of time only.

And what does Paul say about whosoever eats and drinks unworthily? They shall be found guilty of the body and blood of Christ and drink damnation unto themselves. This has nothing to do with going to confession, saying some "Our Fathers and Hail Mary's" so we can be "worthy" for a weekly communion service. This misses the entire point made by Paul and other apostles.

This was a one-time supper of Lords to whom Christ gave a

specific command for a specific period of time...until he arose from the dead. Who of us will stand up and proclaim ourselves to be a lord with Christ, worthy to sit on the thrones of Israel judging them? Any takers? It's time for the tradition of "communion" to be reconsidered, otherwise as Paul said, "you drink damnation to yourself not discerning the Lord's body."

Christ also said he would not drink the fruit of the vine until he sat down with the twelve in the kingdom of heaven. And while Christ ate with the disciples after his resurrection, he did not drink wine. "...he said to them do you have any meat here? And they gave him a piece of broiled fish, and of a honeycomb. And he took it and did eat before them. And he said unto them, These are the words I spoke unto you, while I was yet with you, that *all things must be fulfilled, which were written in the law of Moses, and in the prophets and in the psalms, concerning me*."[89] The law, prophets and the psalms are the three main sections of the Tanakh or Old Testament as canonized by Ezra and duly recognized here by Christ.

We've gone into a bit of detail here with the Passover even though it is not a high holy day. Nevertheless, it is the fulcrum that marked the turning point in the current history of the House of Israel with Christ's fulfillment of the Passover in the first century. It marked the changing of the guard for Israel, specifically the House of Israel.

Which is the more likely scenario, then, concerning Christianity and Christ, of whom all things must be *"fulfilled, which were written in the law of Moses, and in the prophets and in the psalms, concerning me."* That Christ, the Redeemer, the spiritual Rock that Israel drank of when coming out of bondage in Egypt, would be sent to redeem the lost sheep of the House of Israel because of their sins, as the Passover lamb, and whose apostles were told by Christ at that Passover meal that they would be kings sitting on thrones judging the twelve nations of Israel? Or is it that Christ was arbitrarily accepted by a bunch of gentiles of the world? The answer is very plain to see. The indigenous Christian nations of the world today are descendants of the nations of Israel.

Christ came once to bring us out of bondage to the law. We are no longer slaves to the law. As Christ said, the law is not done away, but is to be fulfilled. Christ is fulfilling the law on our behalf. It began with that Passover nearly 2000 years ago. We now are under grace through faith as he has met the terms and conditions for the law on our behalf by his death. And the only people who had a law covenant with God as written by Moses was Israel. No gentiles were involved.

The Passover has been fulfilled for us. Abraham was willing to sacrifice his firstborn son, Isaac. God our Father did this on our behalf with his Son, our king and savior Jesus Christ, who is our sacrificial lamb concerning the law. The original Passover and Days of Unleavened Bread took place on the night when our LORD brought our ancestors out of Egypt, out of bondage on their journey to the land promised by Him that we would prosper in our own land honoring God in our lives daily. This has happened. The firstborn males of all Egypt were killed and the sons of Israel were passed over that night. This became a remembrance under Moses and the law to be observed by all Israel throughout their generations. That is, until the "schoolmaster," the law, brought us to Christ. This is where our forefathers were in the first century and where we are today.

As the first Passover marked the beginning of the physical journey that ended with Israel crossing the Jordan into the land promised to Abraham and his seed, the fulfillment by Christ of the Passover is the first event on our spiritual journey towards the new heaven and Earth when, no longer in the flesh, we shall be immortal. The rest of the high holy days lead us to that day when, spiritually speaking, we will cross the river Jordan. And it is those days that we will be looking at next on our journey.

As you will see clearly with our discussion of the holy days, each one is a waypoint for us in God's plan. So many people say today life has no meaning. We ask where are we going, what's the purpose of life? This is one of the deceits that both Christmas and Easter foist upon us. They take us away from the path set out before us that can give us meaning. Instead, they keep us spinning in circles, the same circles, year after year after year, going nowhere. We are spinning round, chasing our spiritual tails, dizzy with meaningless fables in place of the truth.

The high holy days, conversely, are a linear journey with a physical and spiritual duality. These days are not Jewish days meant just for the House of Judah. They are days for Israel, all Israel, who passed under the cloud and through the sea and drank of that spiritual rock, which was Christ. And Christ said he was sent only to the lost sheep of the House of Israel at his first coming. We need to put aside the counterfeits designed to keep us away from our true destiny and boldly embrace that which our king and savior gave his life in the flesh on our behalf that we might have life everlasting.

But keep in mind the Passover is done. It is complete. Christ fulfilled it. We can no longer "observe" it in the flesh. That day is gone. There are new days yet to be fulfilled that we need to be looking towards and what they mean in our lives today. But we need no longer "observe" days as we were required under the terms of the old covenant as Paul told the Galatians. Christ is fulfilling them on our behalf.

As the spirit in man is a shadow of the spirit of God, we are now to live our lives as the original documents delivered to us by Christ's apostles direct us, in fullness of the spirit rather than the shadow of the physical observance of days. This is the duality of the days God set aside for us. The Biblical record is alive. It has meaning for us today and for our future as well.

While the Passover was not considered a high holy day, the Days of Unleavened Bread were. As the Passover and Days of Unleavened Bread are bound together, let's take a look at the physical event of those days when Israel left Egypt and took unleavened bread with them for their journey. It should be pointed out that at this time, the Israelites received their calendar too. "*…the LORD spoke to Moses in the land of Egypt, saying This month shall be unto you the beginning of months: it shall be the first month of the year to you."[90] Passover and the Days of Unleavened Bread occur in the first month of the Israelite lunar calendar, which is spring time or the time of the vernal equinox.

The Event in Israel's History: "*And the Egyptians were urgent upon the people, that they might send them out of the land *in haste*; for they said, We will all be all dead. And the people [*Israel*] took their dough before it was leavened, their kneading troughs being bound up in their clothes upon their shoulders. And the children of Israel did according to the word of Moses; and they borrowed of the Egyptians jewels of silver, and jewels of gold, and raiment: And the LORD gave the people favor in the sight of the Egyptians, so that they lent unto them such things as they required. And they spoiled the Egyptians."[91]

The reference here to the spoil given to Israel by the Egyptians could be considered "The accumulated earnings of many years being paid them at this moment, the Israelites were suddenly enriched, according to the promise made to Abraham (Gen 15:14), and they left the country like a victorious army laden with spoil (Psa 105:37; Eze 39:10)."[92]

The reference here to the spoil being borrowed or lent is a verb meaning in context to ask for. Given the circumstances that Egypt had been decimated by all the plagues, their labor base greatly depleted by Israel's departure and the fact that psychologically the Egyptians figured they'd all be dead if circumstances didn't change fast, so the sooner the Israelites left, the better. Hence the desire to give them whatever they ask for, but just get them out of Egypt as soon as possible.

"*And the children of Israel journeyed from Rameses to Succoth, about six hundred thousand on foot that were men, beside children. And a mixed multitude went up also with them; and flocks, and herds, even very much cattle.

"And they *baked unleavened cakes* of the dough which they brought forth out of Egypt, for it was not leavened; because they were thrust out of Egypt, and could not linger, neither had they prepared for themselves any food.

"Now the sojourning of the children of Israel, who dwelt in Egypt, was four hundred and thirty years. And it came to pass at the end of the four hundred and thirty years, even the selfsame day it came to pass, that all the hosts [Hebrew, tsaba, army] of the LORD went out from the land of Egypt.

"It is a night to be much observed unto the LORD for bringing them out from the land of Egypt: this is that night of the LORD to be observed of all the children of Israel in their generations. All the congregation of Israel shall keep it."[93]

This is the night immediately following the Passover, which would begin at sunset according the Hebrew counting of days. Thus, if a Tuesday at sunset, according to our solar calendar, was the Passover, then the first high day of unleavened bread would be observed beginning at Wednesday sunset. And it would be a high holy day marking the day that Israel came out of Egypt when they ate unleavened bread because of their hasty departure. Also, on the seventh day after this day, it too would be the second high holy day of unleavened bread.

How are the Days of Unleavened Bread and Christ connected? And what does it mean for Christianity today? Perhaps we should begin by asking what's the significance of unleavened bread opposed to leavened bread. Leavened bread of course, is the bread we normally use to make sandwiches or toast for breakfast in the morning. Yeast added to the dough and then kneaded causing the flour and water mix to rise, puffing it up, so when it is baked we have a loaf of bread or specifically leavened bread. Take the same mixture, but add no leavening agent and it will not rise. It will be flat. This thin, brittle bread is unleavened bread. When Israel left Egypt in a hurry, they didn't have time to add a leavening agent, knead the dough, and allow time for it to rise. In a hurry, they were able only to take with them the flour and water mixture, thus the unleavened bread.

But this duality of unleavened bread has a symbolic purpose directly related to each and every Christian's life. Unleavened bread represents a life without sin, out of bondage to the law and therefore out of bondage to sin. The Israelites came out of bondage in Egypt. They were set free once the firstborn males of Egypt had been killed. Christ was the Passover lamb sacrificed to take away our sins. When we accept this on our behalf as a Christian, we are to repent, which is to change from our old, puffed up, vain life, take off the old and put on the new life without leaven or sin. To mix metaphors, we don't put new wine in old wineskins.

If you want to see what it was like for our ancestors of the House of Israel to successfully get all leaven out of their lives, try one time to get leaven physically out of your life. Then, live without any leaven, not just bread, for a week. It will be an eye opening experience. You'll be surprised to find leavening agents in things you never thought of beer drinkers. And you won't be able to get all the leaven out of your life. The spiritual lesson is that we humans, with the spirit of man, can't get sin out of our lives, Christ had to do it for us. But try one time just to see what an immense effort it takes to get only physical leavening out of our life. The same holds more than true for the spiritual as well.

It's more than just not using anything with leavening in it, any leaven, but it's getting rid of all the old leaven out of your life, and house, and car, and garage, and desk, and toaster, and sofa, and refrigerator, and oven, etc, etc. If you want to get an idea of what a real spring cleaning is, try this just once. You will have profound new respect for getting leaven out of your life, both physically and spiritually. It takes a lot of work, focus and dedication. If you really give this a shot, I'd be willing to guess, sometime after your weeks of preparation and the week without leaven are through, you'll discover some leaven you missed...like crumbs in an old suitcase tucked away in the basement.

Paul made this same point about living an unleavened Christian life to the Corinthians. "It is reported commonly that there is fornication among you, and such fornication as is not so much as named among the gentiles, that one should have his father's wife. And you are puffed up [leavened], and have not rather mourned, that he that has done this deed might be taken away from you... In the name of our Lord Jesus Christ, when you are gathered together, and my spirit, with the power of our Lord Jesus Christ, to deliver such a one unto Satan for the destruction of the flesh, that the spirit may be saved in the day of the Lord Jesus." Here's that physical-spiritual duality again showing us that the spirit takes precedent over the physical.

The point made by Paul is the same principle that God makes to the House of Israel about the Christmas tree and celebration when he will shake the foundations of the Earth with the opening of the sixth seal. It will serve as a destruction of the flesh that the spirit may be saved.

Paul is reminding them that our new lives are to be lived spiritually-minded every day, "Your glorying [*in sin*] is not good. Don't you know that a little leaven leavens the whole lump? Purge out therefore the old leaven [*the hijacked pagan festivals*], that you may be a new lump, as you are unleavened. For even Christ our Passover is sacrificed for us: therefore let us keep the feast, not with old leaven, neither with the leaven of malice and wickedness; but with the unleavened bread of sincerity and truth."[94]

It is thought that Paul wrote this letter to the Corinthians about 55 CE. If anything then, the church in the first century would be living the feast of unleavened bread spiritually, and was not celebrating Easter. Later in this same letter Paul reminds these same Corinthians about how "all our fathers were under the cloud and passed through the sea. And were all baptized unto Moses in the cloud and in the sea." This is the exact time historically that the lost sheep of the House of Israel ate of that original unleavened bread. Now being baptized unto Christ, and the receiving of the Holy Spirit, we are to put away the leavening, the sin out of our lives.

As Paul mentions here, the feast of the Days of Unleavened Bread are not to be kept once a year with the eating of the physical unleavened bread, nor with the leaven of malice and wickedness, but with unleavened sincerity and truth. This is why Christianity is a daily way of life. Christianity isn't something we do on Sunday or Christmas or Easter.

The duality of the Days of Unleavened Bread is that as Christians we are to put our old ways out of our lives. It is a call for change. We no longer need to look back to the law. We are to live in faith. This is the key point here. Christ redeemed us. He bought us back. But, we have a responsibility to put forth a personal effort, as faith without works is dead. While we look to Christ and trust in him for our salvation, we cannot just sit on our "spiritual derrieres" waiting for Christ to live our lives for us. We need to be pro-active daily in our faith in Christ, rather than observing hijacked festivals certain days a year.

Our forefathers were to observe eating unleavened bread for seven days with the first day and the last day being high holy days. The duality of the week represents an entire cycle of mankind and creation. As we saw in *The Blind Man's Elephant*, the six days of creation were not six, 24-hour Earth days. They were days of undetermined length in relation to our ability to observe time. Christ covered the sins of Israel including those who lived and died before his first coming. "And so all Israel shall be saved: as it is written, There shall come out of Sion the Deliverer, and shall turn away ungodliness from Jacob: For this is my covenant unto them, when I shall take away their sins."[95]

By fulfilling of the Days of Unleavened Bread, we have a liberty that Christ gave us. We are set free from the bondage of Egypt, from sin that came from the Law of Moses. It is this liberty from the law that places a higher responsibility on a Christian. We are policed through God's Spirit within us rather than the spirit of man, or flesh. We are to live our lives in the Spirit, getting rid of the leavening of the flesh. Paul tell us then, "Stand fast, therefore, in the liberty wherewith Christ has made us free, and be not entangled again with the yoke of bondage."[96]

In other words, don't go back there again. Some of the Christians in Galatia were claiming that physical circumcision was a requirement that must be kept. But Paul reminded them that "if you are circumcised, [*meaning it is a requirement of one's faith*] Christ shall profit you nothing...For in Jesus Christ neither circumcision avails anything, nor uncircumcision, but faith which works by love."[97]

The point Paul makes to them is that for awhile you were living in faith through the Spirit as Christ intended it, why are you now turning back to the ways of the flesh and sin when you were set free from bondage in the liberty given to us by Christ? Christ has fulfilled the Days of Unleavened Bread.

Paul asks them, "...who does hinder you that you should not obey the truth? This persuasion comes not from him that calls you. A little leaven leavens the whole lump...."[98] If they start down this road, first with circumcision, next it will be something else, and then something else. Before you know it, you'll believe anything that comes down the road including the notion that we must hijack pagan holidays for observance to lead heathens to Christ. Paul was correct; a little leaven leavens the entire lump called Christianity today.

Paul continues, "For brethren, you have been called unto liberty; only don't use liberty for an occasion of the flesh, but by love serve one another. For all the law is fulfilled in one word, in this, 'You shall love your neighbor as yourself.' But if you bite and devour one another, take heed that you are not consumed of one another. I say then, Walk in the Spirit, and you shall not fulfill the lust of the flesh…But if you are led of the Spirit, you are not under the law…If we live in the Spirit, let us also walk in the Spirit."[99]

The duality of Passover and the original Days of Unleavened Bread live on for the lost sheep of the House of Israel today. Most Christians are still lost as to this truth and purpose of Christ. There is a reason why Christ is the Lamb sacrificed for the sins of Israel. The only people who can sin are those who are under the law covenant. The law covenant was given only to Moses and the children of Israel upon leaving Egypt. While anyone can do good or evil, only those under the law covenant can transgress the law, which can then be legally accounted as sin.

Ironically, Christian pastors harp on about sin all the time, yet it is an *old covenant condition* that legally applied *only* to Old Testament Israel. Then these same pastors claim they are not of Israel, but are gentiles. If gentiles, then they can't transgress the law covenant, which is the definition of sin.[100]

The Passover sacrifice of Christ has covered our sins as Christians, the lost sheep of the House of Israel. And now that we are no longer in bondage under the law, we are to keep the leaven of sin out of our lives as our forefathers brought unleavened bread out of the bondage to Egypt.

Christ has fulfilled both the Passover and the high holy Days of Unleavened Bread. We, as Christians, have been given a liberty greater even than our forefather Abraham experienced in his life. Yet we stupidly and foolishly hijack pagan holidays blindly thinking we honor Christ. We do no such thing. Instead, we make him fiercely angry. We dishonor him and his life. We dishonor his death, and to our confusion, the truth of the purpose of his resurrection. Gleefully ignorant, we are following fables in place of the truth.

The Passover and the two high holy Days of Unleavened Bread are two, of the seven, holy days of convocation fulfilled so far by Christ. These actual events took place in Egypt led by Moses. The next actual event took place in the land promised to Abraham under Joshua, "Yehovah is salvation," who was told, "My servant Moses [the lawgiver] is dead...go over this Jordan."

Christ fulfilled these days by his death under the law of Moses. The resurrection of Jesus, "Yehovah is salvation," "crossing the Jordan," put the law by which we were counted as dead behind us, opening the way for the new covenant of the Spirit, which marks the beginning of Christianity, established upon better promises than the law covenant. They are the promises given to Abraham. Our next chapter examines another duality, the third holy day of convocation given to our forefathers to keep in remembrance throughout all our generations.

Chapter Four
Pentecost, the First Fruits and Christianity

We have seen very clear evidence that the days observed by our forefathers of the House of Israel, under the law given by Moses to all Israel, have a duality to them. Christ was the Passover lamb taking us from under the bondage of the law and sin portrayed by Israel coming out of Egypt. The Bible, the Biblical record is one complete book written to the same people. And as we know, Christ plainly said, "I am not sent except unto the lost sheep of the House of Israel."[101]

Pentecost, as it is known in the New Testament, is a fulfilling of the Old Testament high holy day of convocation when the sheaf, or bundle of grain representing the first fruits of the summer harvest, was waved before the LORD. This annual high holy day of Pentecost had huge implications. It symbolically portrayed the day that would mark the beginning of Christianity. But first, let's read exactly what Israel was to do in observance of this day.

The Holy Day Remembrance: "*And the LORD spoke unto Moses, saying, speak unto the children of Israel, and say unto them, When you be come into the land which I give unto you, and shall reap the harvest thereof, then you shall bring a sheaf of the first fruits of your harvest unto the priest:

"And he shall wave the sheaf before the LORD, to be accepted for you: on the morrow after the Sabbath the priest shall wave it.

"And you shall offer that day when you wave the sheaf a he [*male*] lamb without blemish of the first year for a burnt offering unto the LORD.

"And the meat offering thereof shall be two tenth deals [*or parts*] of fine flour mingled with oil, an offering made by fire unto the LORD for a sweet savor: and the drink offering thereof shall be of wine, the fourth part of a hin [*which is about five quarts, thus a quarter of this amount*]. And you shall eat neither bread, nor parched corn, nor green ears, until the selfsame day you have brought an offering unto your God: it shall be a statute forever throughout your generations in all your dwellings.

"And you shall count unto you from the morrow after the Sabbath, from the day that you brought the sheaf of the wave offering; seven Sabbaths shall be complete: Even unto the morrow after the seventh Sabbath shall you number fifty days; and you shall offer a new meat offering unto the LORD.

"You shall bring out of your habitations two wave loaves of two tenth deals: they shall be of fine flour; they shall be baked with leaven; they are the first fruits unto the LORD; And you shall offer with the bread seven lambs without blemish of the first year, and one young bullock, and two rams: they shall be for a burnt offering unto the LORD, with their meat offering, and their drink offerings, an offering made by fire, of sweet savour unto the LORD.

"Then you shall sacrifice one kid of the goats for a sin offering, and two lambs of the first year for a sacrifice of peace offerings.

"And the priest shall wave them with the bread of the first fruits, a wave offering before the LORD, with the two lambs: they shall be holy to the LORD for the priest.

"And you shall proclaim on the selfsame day, that it may be an holy convocation unto you: you shall do no servile work therein: it shall be a statute for ever in all your dwellings throughout your generations.

"And when you reap the harvest of your land, you shall not make clean riddance of the corners of your field when you reap, neither shall you gather any gleaning of your harvest: you shall leave them unto the poor, and to the stranger: I am the LORD your God."[102]

All of this represents the summer harvest or the first harvest of the year. It is a smaller harvest compared to the fall harvest, which is another high holy day. There are a few duality points that you may have already picked up in reading how our forefathers were to observe this day.

First, "You shall offer that day when you wave the sheaf a he lamb without blemish of the first year...." This was not an accidental or arbitrary feast celebration given to Israel in the time of Moses. It was specifically created to provide an example to Israel of what was to come. For all these holy days are waypoints, beacons that light the way forward into God's plan, the story in the Biblical record. The duality here is that Christ was that Lamb sacrificed for us, without blemish, that we might have liberty in Christ, free from the bondage to the law, living life in the Spirit.

As the apostle Peter wrote, "Forasmuch as you know that you were not redeemed [103] with corruptible things, as silver and gold, from your vain conversation received by tradition from your fathers [*of Israel*]; but with the precious blood of Christ, as of a lamb without blemish and without spot: Who verily was foreordained before the foundation of the world, but was manifest in these last times for you...."[104] This is related to what Paul wrote to the Romans, "For whom he did foreknow, he also did predestinate to be conformed to the image of his Son, that he might be the *firstborn* among many brethren."[105]

The second duality point here is the timing of this particular holy day. "*And you shall count unto you from the morrow after the [*weekly*] Sabbath, from the day that you brought the sheaf of the wave offering; seven Sabbaths shall be complete: even unto the morrow after the seventh Sabbath shall you number fifty days; and you shall offer a new meat offering unto the LORD."[106] There is to be fifty days counted from the day after the weekly sabbath after the second high holy Day of Unleavened Bread. If the second high holy Day of Unleavened Bread was a Thursday, then the counting of fifty days began on the next weekly sabbath on what is our Friday evening at sunset. Seven weekly sabbaths were completed, and then on the day after the seventh weekly sabbath, this was to be the day the waving of the sheaf was done. Pentecost simply means to count fifty.

Specifically included in the observance of the first fruits of the harvest was this admonition, "*And when you reap the harvest of your land, you shall not make clean riddance of the corners of your field when you reap, neither shall you gather any gleaning of your harvest: you shall leave them unto the poor, and to the stranger: I am the LORD your God."[107] The principle here is that while Israel was favored before God and would be blessed, it was a responsibility of Israel to be mindful of the poor and the stranger. Thus, the poor could go into the fields to gather food, as could a passing stranger. Those who are spiritually poor or strangers from Israel, too, should not be forgotten. It is a principle for the nations of Israel today.

We have an example of the spiritual duality to this principle given to us in the story of the Canaanite woman, a stranger, not of Israel, who sought out Christ to heal her daughter. "And, behold, a woman of Canaan came out of the same coasts, and cried unto him, saying, Have mercy on me, O Lord, Son of David; my daughter is grievously vexed with a devil. But he answered her not a word. And his disciples came and besought him saying, Send her away; for she cries after us. But he answered and said, I am not sent except unto the lost sheep of the house of Israel. Then came she and worshipped him, saying, Lord, help me. But he answered and said, It is not meet [*good*] to take the children's bread, and to cast it to dogs. And she said, Truth, Lord: yet the dogs eat of the crumbs, which fall from their masters' table. Then Jesus answered and said unto her, O woman, great is your faith: be it unto you even as you will. And her daughter was made whole from that very hour."[108]

The Historical Event: The actual historical event of waving the sheaf offering, the counting of fifty days, occurred every year that Israel was in the land given to them by promise. They were to take the first fruits of the harvest and offer them up to God. It was also a way of reminding Israel to keep their focus on God first and by doing so, their harvests, and lives, would be full and blessed. It is this way with Pentecost today, but in matters of the Spirit rather than the physical.

The Fulfillment by Christ: Let's go back then to that Pentecost day, nearly 2000 years ago when the apostles and disciples were gathered together. It marked the very first Pentecost of the new era, a day that remains until this day, the most significant day in Christianity, as it was the day Christianity began. No longer was the Old Testament sheaf offering in effect. Christ told the disciples:

"But the Comforter, which is the Holy Spirit, whom the Father will send in my name, he shall teach you all things, and bring all things to your remembrance, whatsoever I have said unto you."[109]

The spiritual fulfillment of Pentecost was about to take place. Let's read of the account in the Book of Acts.

"And when the day of Pentecost was fully come, they were all with one accord in one place. And suddenly there came a sound from heaven as of a rushing mighty wind, and it filled the entire house where they were sitting. And there appeared unto them cloven tongues like as of fire, and it sat upon each of them. And they were all filled with the Holy Spirit, and began to speak with other tongues, as the Spirit gave them utterance."[110]

The "day of Pentecost was *fully* come." This reference is to the fact that previous Pentecosts were observances of the Old Testament ordinances, remembrances as given to Israel by Moses to be observed in their land. This is signifying that the *fulfillment* of the day of Pentecost by Christ was now a fact.

I don't wish to get into a discussion here about "speaking in tongues." But suffice to say, this is explained in the context of the account. However, it was an outward sign of the event that had just transpired. And it was occurring in front of educated people in Jerusalem, devout men and men of every nation of Israel. This certainly would be considered a credible audience, and therefore serve as a reliable witness of the event. As such, word of this event would spread rather quickly drawing the crowds that gathered there.

"And there were dwelling at Jerusalem Jews, devout men, out of every nation under heaven. Now when this was noised abroad, the multitude came together, and were confounded, because that every man heard them speak in his own language. And they were all amazed and marveled, saying one to another, Behold, are not all these which speak Galileans? And how is it we hear every man in our own tongue, wherein we were born?"[111]

All this caused quite a stir for nothing before had ever been seen or heard like this in Jerusalem. Naturally some were asking what this meant, and others thought they were all suffering from the effects of too much wine. However Peter, who was there with the other apostles, stood up to speak.

"You men of Judaea, and all that dwell at Jerusalem, be this known unto you, and listen to my words: For these are not drunken, as you suppose, seeing it is the third hour of the day [about 9 am]. But this is that which was spoken by the prophet Joel…."[112]

Joel, a prophet, wrote his book about 790 BCE, which is the Assyrian period of the first seven of the books of the minor prophets in the Old Testament. It was the Assyrians who, as you may recall from *The Blind Man's Elephant*, took the *House of Israel* into captivity, upon the divorce from their covenant relationship with God, because of their ungodliness in following false gods they had hijacked.

The Assyrians took the House of Israel captive first in the lands of Zebulon and Naphtali in Galilee. This, too, was the very area in which Christ began his ministry to redeem the lost sheep of the House of Israel. As Paul wrote, "And it shall come to pass, that in the place where it was said to them, You are not my people; there shall they be called the children of the living God."[113] Paul was quoting a prophecy of Hosea.[114] It is not a reference here to "gentiles of the world," but rather to the divorced covenant condition of the House of Israel at the time of the Assyrian captivity.

As David Brown explains in his commentary, "*I will call them my people, which were not my people; and her beloved, which was not beloved*--quoted, though not quite to the letter, from Hosea 2:23 , a passage relating immediately, *not to the heathen*, but to the kingdom of the ten tribes [*House of Israel*]; but since they had *sunk to the level of* the heathen, who were "not God's people," and in that sense "not beloved," the apostle legitimately applies it to the heathen, as "aliens from the commonwealth of Israel and strangers to the covenants of promise" (so 1Ptr 2:10)."[115]

And on that day of Pentecost nearly 2000 years ago, the fulfilling of Hosea's prophecy came to be. It was the day the children of the House of Israel first received the Holy Spirit as promised. They became the redeemed children of the living God.[116]

As we read above, "Behold, are not all these which speak Galileans?" Matthew Henry points out in his Biblical Commentary, "They observe that the speakers are all Galileans, that know no other than their mother tongue; they are despicable men, from whom nothing learned nor polite is to be expected. God chose the weak and foolish things of the world to confound the wise and mighty. Christ was thought to be a Galilean, and his disciples really were so, unlearned and ignorant men."[117]

Men of Israel from all over the Roman Empire, as well as devout men, which would be highly educated for the day, were present and were amazed that Galileans, who speak no other languages, were speaking and every one there *understood* what they were saying yet in their own language. This would have to be considered the first miracle of the Christian era. News of this would spread everywhere. If this event had happened today, it would be twittered and, no doubt, available on YouTube.

Peter continues quoting Joel, saying "And it shall come to pass in the last days, says God, I will pour out of my Spirit upon all [*Greek, pas, meaning each individually*] flesh: and your sons and your daughters shall prophesy, and your young men shall see visions, and your old men shall dream dreams: And on my servants and on my handmaidens I will pour out in those days of my Spirit; and they shall prophesy: And I will show wonders in heaven above, and signs in the earth beneath; blood, and fire, and vapor of smoke: The sun shall be turned into darkness, and the moon into blood, *before* that great and notable day of the Lord come: And it shall come to pass that whosoever shall call on the name of the Lord shall be saved."[118]

As you recall from our earlier chapters, this "The sun shall be turned into darkness, and the moon into blood, before that great and notable day of the Lord" event mentioned above occurs in context with the House of Israel keeping "Christmas" as we witnessed in Jeremiah ten. And as you further may recall, God asks Israel, 'In *your time* of trouble will your gods save you?' Christianity is not calling on the name of our Lord, but rather calling upon the name of the hijacked Santa and the Easter bunny, Ishtar the Babylonian goddess.

Peter tells the assembly on this day of Pentecost, "You men of Israel, hear these words; Jesus of Nazareth, a man approved of God among you by miracles and wonders and signs, which God did by him in the midst of you, as you yourselves also know: Him, being delivered by the determinate counsel and foreknowledge of God, you have taken, and by wicked hands have crucified and slain: Whom God has raised up, having loosed the pains of death: because it was not possible that death should have a hold on him." Peter goes on to talk of David, king of Israel who made reference to Christ "For David speaks concerning him, I foresaw the Lord always before my face, for he is on my right hand, that I should not be moved:"[119]

We now come to a very important point. On this very first day of Christianity, concerning the very first miraculous event, Peter, the Rock upon whom Christ said he would build his church, concluded his remarks in Acts on that Pentecost day nearly 2000 years ago by saying to the gentiles of the world...well, nothing. Peter makes absolutely no reference to them whatsoever.

What Peter did say on this most momentous of days in the history of Christianity was, "Therefore let *all the House of Israel* know assuredly, that God has made that same Jesus, whom you have crucified, both Lord and Christ [*messiah*]...Repent, and be baptized every one of you [*House of Israel*] in the name of Jesus Christ for the remission of sins and you shall receive the gift of the Holy Spirit."[120]

Read that again. This is one of the most significant statements in the New Testament. It unquestionably shows that both Christ and Peter knew to whom Christ was sent. And if you wish to talk about a "great commission" for Christianity, it is for *all the House of Israel* to repent, be baptized in the name of Jesus Christ for the remission of sins.

Peter addressed his remarks to "*all the House of Israel*... whom you have crucified." All the nations of the House of Israel were scattered all over the Roman Empire. And with those men present from all the nations, word of this would spread abroad to them in addition to the apostle Paul's journeys. It was the House of Israel that was divorced from God because of her iniquities and transgression before God that made it necessary for Christ to fulfill the terms of the Old Testament with his death. It was not something done by the "gentiles of the world."

The popular John 3:16 does not refer to the gentiles of the world either. "For God so loved the world that he gave his only begotten son that whosoever shall believe on him shall have life everlasting." The word for world here is the Greek *kosmos*. It is not a reference to people as some mistakenly think. It is a reference to the orderly arrangement. The orderly arrangement was the covenant relationship the House of Israel had with God. The divorce of the House of Israel made it necessary for Christ to give his life to restore the House of Israel, indeed, all Israel into the place God has chosen for them. The fulfillment of this arrangement ultimately was to be by promise and not the law. It was from the very beginning meant to be spiritual rather than physical. This is the meaning of John 3:16. And this is why Peter said that the House of Israel was responsible for crucifying Christ.

Christ gave his life that a new covenant with the children of the House of Israel individually would be made first, and at his second coming nationally with the Houses of Israel and Judah. This fulfillment of Pentecost, and the receiving of the Holy Spirit for those of the House of Israel, marked the first day of the fulfilling of the new covenant. We receive God's Spirit, which is housed in us rather than a temple made of stone, as Peter said, by changing our way of life, which is repentance, and being baptized.

Paul told the Corinthians as we read earlier that all our brothers of Israel were baptized with Moses in the sea, and all drank from the spiritual rock, and that Rock was Christ. This took place after the passover in Egypt, and after leaving Egypt with unleavened bread. The duality of the day of Pentecost is very apparent.

This duality is marked physically by the keeping of the law in the flesh with the observances of the high holy days versus their fulfillment by Christ in the Spirit. Paul explained it to the Christians in Rome, "There is therefore now no condemnation to them which are in Christ Jesus, who walk not after the flesh, but after the Spirit. For the law of the Spirit of life in Christ Jesus has made me *free from the law of sin and death*."[121] Remember, Moses delivered the law covenant only to the children of Israel, not the gentiles of the world.

"For what the law could not do, in that it was weak through the flesh, God sending his own Son ["*I am not sent except to the lost sheep of the House of Israel*"] in the likeness of sinful flesh, and for sin, condemned sin in the flesh: That the righteousness of the law might be fulfilled in us, who walk not after the flesh, but after the Spirit. For they that are after the flesh do mind the things of the flesh; but they that are after the Spirit the things of the Spirit. For to be carnally minded is death; but to be spiritually minded is life and peace.

"Because the carnal mind is enmity against God: for it is not subject to the law of God, neither indeed can be, so then they that are in the flesh cannot please God. But you are not in the flesh, but in the Spirit, if so be that the Spirit of God dwells in you. Now if any man has not the Spirit of Christ, he is none of his.

"And if Christ is in you, the body is dead because of sin; but the Spirit is life because of righteousness. But if the Spirit of him that raised up Jesus from the dead dwell in you, he that raised up Christ from the dead shall also quicken [*make alive*] your mortal bodies by his Spirit that dwells in you. Therefore, brethren, we are debtors, not to the flesh, to live after the flesh. For if you live after the flesh, you shall die: but if you through the Spirit do mortify the deeds of the body, you shall live. For as many as are led by the Spirit of God, they are the sons of God."[122]

As we discussed in chapter one of *The Blind Man's Elephant*, there have been three creations of life. The first creation was that of creatures of the sea, the air and land as we read in Genesis. All these creatures have a spirit in them that returns to the dust of the earth along with their bodies at death. With Adam came the spirit of man. This set mankind's potential above those of creatures. While the human body dies and returns to the dust of the earth, the spirit of man returns to God. Those with the spirit in man shall be judged on that Great Judgment Day to be read out of the Book of Life. Those who are the first fruits, those who have lived from the time of Christ's first coming up to his second coming, who repent, are baptized and receive the Holy Spirit, it is this Spirit that makes alive our mortal bodies on this mortal stage. However, we are no longer counted as being alive to the flesh, as a son of man, but alive in the Spirit, as a son of God, if God's Spirit dwells in us.

The apostle John explains, "Behold, what manner of love the Father has bestowed upon us, that we should be called the sons of God: therefore the world knows us not, because it knew him not. Beloved, now are we the sons of God, and it does not yet appear what we shall be: but we know that, when he shall appear, we shall be like him; for we shall see him as he is.

"And every man that has this hope in him purifies himself, even as he is pure. Whosoever commits sin transgresses also the law: for sin is the transgression of the law. And you know that he [*Christ*] was manifested to take away our sins; and in him is no sin. Whosoever abides in him sins not: whosoever sins has not seen him, neither known him. Little children, let no man deceive you: he that does righteousness is righteous, even as he is righteous.

"He that commits sin is of the devil; for the devil sins from the beginning. For this purpose the Son of God was manifested, that he might destroy the works of the devil.

"Whosoever is born of God does not commit sin; for his seed remains in him: and he cannot sin, because he is born of God. In this the children of God are manifest, and the children of the devil: whosoever does not righteousness is not of God, neither he that loves not his brother. For this is the message that you heard from the beginning, that we should love one another."[123]

A comment about "...he cannot sin, because he is born of God." Remember, sin is defined as transgression of the law delivered by Moses to Israel. If we are no longer under the law, we can't violate or transgress the law. It's simple logic. However, as Paul warned us, we are not to use our liberty in Christ as license to do as we please. We can't hide from God and we can't fool him. And those who sincerely repent, are baptized and seek first the kingdom of God having God's Spirit are led of the Spirit in the righteousness of God, not man. By their fruits you shall know them.

Now with the fulfillment of Pentecost by Christ, the feast of the first fruits of the smaller summer harvest, we have God's Holy

Spirit that gives life to our fleshly bodies. The Spirit of God was not available to anyone, including the children of the House of Israel, prior to this day nearly 2000 years ago. The summer harvest, spiritually marks the first resurrection, a gathering of those of the House of Israel who repent, are baptized and receive the Holy Spirit between Christ's first coming and his second coming.

The apostle John also wrote the book of Revelation. "And I saw thrones, and they sat upon them, and judgment was given unto them: and I saw the souls of them that were beheaded for the witness of Jesus, and for the word of God, and which had not worshipped the beast, neither his image, neither had received his mark upon their foreheads, or in their hands [*sixth empire in Revelation*]; and they lived and reigned with Christ a thousand years. But the rest of the dead lived not again until the thousand years were finished. This is the first resurrection.

"Blessed and holy is he that has part in the first resurrection [*the first fruits of Christ*]: on such the second death has no power, but they shall be priests of God and of Christ, and shall reign with him a thousand years."[124]

The great judgment day, "And I saw the dead, small and great, stand before God; and the books were opened: and another book was opened, which is the book of life: and the dead were judged out of those things which were written in the books, according to their works,"[125] is the fall harvest marked by another high holy day, which we'll discuss in another chapter later in the book.

The waving of the sheaf by the priests under the law was an annual festival held on the day specified by Moses to the children of Israel. They arrived at this day by counting fifty from the weekly sabbath day after the second high holy Day of Unleavened Bread.

The waving of the sheaf signified to our forefathers the day of the harvest of the first fruits of the summer harvest beginning in May in the northern hemisphere. The children of Israel had been brought out of bondage in Egypt and were now free in their own land as promised to Abraham and his seed. "Now to Abraham and his seed were the promises made. He said not, And to seeds, as of many; but as of one, And to your seed, which is Christ."[126]

The law was a bridge to bring us from Abraham to Christ. "Wherefore the law was our schoolmaster to bring us unto Christ, that we might be justified by faith. But after that faith is come, we are no longer under a schoolmaster."[127] As such, Christ is fulfilling the high holy days of the law that were given to all Israel. His fulfilling of the Passover and the Days of Unleavened Bread through his death and resurrection dissolved the Old Testament or the law covenant. Christ paid our debt under the terms of the law covenant on our behalf.

On that Pentecost day nearly 2000 years ago, God's Spirit was made available to those who repent [*change*], are baptized and receive the Spirit of God, that they would be the first fruits of the kingdom of God. "But now is Christ risen from the dead, and become the first fruits of them that slept. For since by man came death, by man came also the resurrection of the dead. For as in Adam all die, even so in Christ shall all be made alive. But every man in his own order: *Christ the first fruits*; afterward they that are Christ's at his coming."[128] "For whom he did foreknow, he also did predestinate to be conformed to the image of his Son, that he might be the *firstborn* among many brethren."[129]

Adam marked the advent of the spirit of man compared to all previous life on Earth that had the spirit of a creature. Another step up happened on Pentecost nearly 2000 years ago. "But when the Comforter is come, whom I will send unto you from the Father, even the Spirit of truth, which proceeds from the Father, he shall testify of me:"[130] With Christ, the sending of the Comforter, or God's Holy Spirit, on that Pentecost day, the Spirit of God now gives life in the Spirit rather than in bondage to the lusts of the flesh. As Paul told us, "Flesh and blood cannot inherit the kingdom of God. For if you live after the flesh, you shall die: but if you through the Spirit do mortify the deeds of the body, you shall live."[131]

The duality of Pentecost should be very clear. When our ancestors came out of Egypt and were settled in their own land as promised to Abraham, they were to offer up the first fruits of their summer harvest to God. We read the details of what was to be done. Typically, the summer harvest begins sometime in May and ends about the beginning of September. The annual observance of Pentecost took place usually in what is our mid-May or so depending on the timing of the second high holy Day of Unleavened Bread with the lunar calendar. This marks the historical annual cycle of the summer harvest and was the physical observance of Pentecost. The next annual high holy day takes place in early [first part of second week] to late September [last week of the month] on our current day calendars due to differences between the lunar/solar calendar cycles.

Spiritually, Christ was the first fruit, and the rest of those who repent, are baptized and receive God's Spirit will be gathered to Christ at his second coming. This is the first resurrection, or perhaps more clearly, this is the resurrection of the first fruits. We are in the summer harvest now, which is the time between Christ's first coming and his second coming. The next holy day to be fulfilled by Christ, yet in our future, will mark the end of the spiritual summer harvest, culminating in Christ's return and the gathering of his first fruits, which is the first resurrection.

Spiritually then, the summer harvest has been ongoing for nearly the past 2000 years. It is not surprising that all those who live in these "last days," the time between Christ's first coming and his second coming, believe Christ will return in their generation. The apostles in the first century believed this to be so as have every generation of Christians since. Our generation is no exception.

In fact, you can go back, at least, to the past one hundred and fifty years and find evidence of groups of Christians thinking Christ's return was imminent. Records show that since 1970, each and every year has someone predicting Christ's return. This past millennium is a notable example with some even picking out a specific month and day. The year 2012 is the next big date already set for the "end of the world" or apocalypse based on the Mesoamerican Long Count calendar used by the Mayans. The date they've chosen is either December 21st or as some say, the 23rd. Their calculations were based on "natural time," to which our current day Roman/Gregorian based calendar is contrary. Their natural time calendars were based on the 13 moon, or month, year. This is the same calendar in the Old Testament used by Israel.[132]

Despite this, Christ said that no man knows when he will return except that it will be *unexpected*. We are told in the parable of the virgins, "Watch therefore, for you know neither the day nor the hour wherein the Son of man comes."[133] No doubt some will claim that this doesn't preclude knowing the year. The point of the parable is twofold: one, we need to live our lives daily seeking the perfection of the Spirit rather than being weighed down by the lusts of the flesh. Two, none of us knows when our time in our fleshly bodies is up. Someone may be looking to

December 21ˢᵗ 2012 for Christ's return, but if that person dies of a heart attack tomorrow, for all intents and purposes, Christ's return for that person happened much earlier on a day and hour totally unexpected.

But perhaps this phenomena is not without reason for as Paul pointed out to the Romans, "And not only they, but ourselves also, which have *the first fruits of the Spirit*, even we ourselves groan within ourselves, waiting for the adoption, to wit, the redemption of our body."[134] In other words, Christians do look forward to the return of Christ. Unfortunately some forget the purpose of living in the Spirit one day at a time and instead tend to focus on a day and hour in the future none of us will know until it happens.

In the meantime, in the Spirit we are living in the fulfillment era of the summer harvest. The summer harvest will end at Christ's return. "Of his own will begat he us with the word of truth, that we certainly should be the first fruits of his creatures [or those things created]."[135] The day of Pentecost has been fulfilled by Christ and is being fulfilled in everyone that repents, is baptized and receives God's Spirit up to the return of Christ.

In the nearly 2000 years past, Christ has fulfilled the Passover, and the three high holy days of convocation, which are the Days of Unleavened Bread and Pentecost. As we've seen these days were to be physically observed by our forefathers in the House of Israel as well as the House of Judah. These days, and prophesies in the Old Testament pointed the House of Israel towards their fulfillment by Christ. And on that day of Pentecost nearly 2000 years ago, which officially marked the beginning of Christianity with the Spirit of God dwelling in us rather than in a physical temple made of stone under the terms of the Old Covenant, the apostle Peter got up to speak. We read that his remarks unequivocally were addressed, not to the gentiles of the world, but to the House of Israel. Christ plainly said, "I am not sent except to the lost sheep of the House of Israel."

But as we have lost our identity over the past two millennia, we have also lost sight of the path we should be walking before God and our LORD Jesus Christ. Yet according to our evangelical writer in chapter one, "When the church hijacked these pagan holidays it was for good reason, to influence the world with the biblical worldview and culture. Santa's flying reindeer instead of Thor's chariot. Halloween celebrations instead of Samhain..." There is no good reason to hijack pagan holidays. It dishonors Christ. Furthermore, our writer claims it is "to influence the world with the biblical worldview?" How can you possibly "influence the world with the biblical worldview" when you haven't a clue as to what the Biblical view is? If you did, you wouldn't be out there hijacking pagan holidays.

In fact, the very word holiday is a corruption of holy day. In place of the holy days that Christ is fulfilling on our behalf, we are substituting Christmas and Easter among other holidays. In our ignorance, we stupidly think this pleases God. But as we read in Jeremiah, the day is coming when the House of Israel will think differently. In the meantime, it is better that we learn the easy way. And this is one of the reasons for writing this book. We can pay now, or we can pay later. Later is always much more expensive.

What have we seen to this point? A very clear picture should have emerged by now of the relevancy and duality of the holy days given to Israel and their fulfillment by Christ. The irrelevancy of Christmas and Easter should be very clear as well. It should be very clear that the Biblical record, the Bible is one book written

Pentecost, the First Fruits and Christianity

to the same people. And it should be very clear that the time between Christ's first coming and his return is the time of the "summer harvest" of his first fruits for those who have God's Spirit dwelling in them. And it should be very clear that Christ was sent to the House of Israel whose descendants are the Christian nations of the world today.

This ends the portion of the book that deals with the first three of our waypoints fulfilled, the Passover, the Days of Unleavened Bread and Pentecost. As these three Old Testament high holy days of our story have been fulfilled, that leaves four more high holy days yet to be fulfilled by Christ. And if we've read the description of all seven of the high holy days in the Old Testament, we should have a pretty good idea of what is to come.

If Christianity today was mindful of it's ancestry, and then paid attention to what's written for us, we'd know where we stand in the plan of God. Not only that, but we'd know that there is a plan. Life would have meaning. As it is, life seems to be without meaning. We just wander around aimlessly without a clue of who we are and what we should be doing. We spend our time like rats in a cage running on the same wheel over and over again. Christmas and Easter commemorate looking back into the corrupted pagan past. There is nothing to point us to the future. Christ was born. He was crucified. They point to a weak savior. One is a baby, the other is dead on a cross. No wonder so many people think God doesn't exist or that God is not active in our daily lives. These hijacked pagan holidays give us no clue as to our identity or where we are headed. Yet the high holy days make very clear who we are, where we've been, where we are and where we're headed.

This is the beauty of the duality contained in each day. It makes it easier for us to see the past and the future. There is a pattern, a design that is easy to recognize once we know what to look for. God has communicated to us about life. It's just that we'd rather follow after some foolish heathen traditions. It is to our own confusion as we are told. And today Christianity is certainly confused. What else can we call more than 30,000 versions of one original truth?

Ask the average Christian a question about what you've read here so far and they won't have a clue. In fact, they will be confused very likely asking you, "What in the world are you talking about?" Worse yet, as with our evangelical writer, they will justify their reasons for holding on to lies and fables. That was the subject of *The Blind Man's Elephant*. Christians have been following the wrong path. That elephant is not the one delivered to us in the original document canonized by the apostles who walked and talked and learned directly from Christ.

It's time that we discover our identity once again. It's time we return to the truth delivered to us by the first century elephant rather than chasing after an elephant described by blind men. So in the following chapters, we will examine the other days given by Moses for our ancestors to observe when they came into the land promised them, and of the promises made to Abraham and his seed, Christ. They outline for us major events in our future. And when we examine them, one by one, we will see very clearly the plan God has set before us yet to unfold. We will be able to connect the events described in the Biblical record, notably the Book of Revelation, with events in our lives today and in our future.

They are the next four waypoints, which were set out for us nearly four thousand years ago. The next four outline the days reaching more than a thousand years into our future. And as we have seen with the first three high holy days being fulfilled and how they are so thoroughly described in the Biblical record, we too will discover, probably for the first time, just how intertwined our lives are today with events described in the Biblical record. The Biblical record is no collection of fairy tales best suited for Sunday school classrooms. But rather it is a book that is not for the faint of heart. For it deals with some very harsh realities and events that probably are not too far distant in man's future. We just don't know when.

We should keep in mind a very important point, however, made by the apostle Paul concerning the observances of days as Paul wrote about to the Colossians and the Laodiceans. "For I would that you knew what great conflict I have for you, and for them at Laodicea, and for as many as have not seen my face in the flesh; That their hearts might be comforted, being knit together in love, and unto all riches of the full assurance of understanding, to the acknowledgement of the mystery of God, and of the Father, and of Christ; in whom are hid all the treasures of wisdom and knowledge. And this I say, lest any man should beguile you with enticing words.

"For though I am absent in the flesh, yet am I with you in the spirit, in joy beholding your order, and the steadfastness of your faith in Christ. As you have therefore received Christ Jesus the Lord, so walk in him: Rooted and built up in him, and established in the faith, as you have been taught, abounding therein with thanksgiving. Beware lest any man spoil you through philosophy and vain deceit, after the tradition of men [*such as Christmas and Easter*], after the rudiments of the world, and not after Christ.

"For in him dwells all the fullness of the Godhead bodily. And you are complete in him, which is the head of all principality and power: In whom also you are circumcised with the circumcision made without hands, in putting off the body of the sins of the flesh by the circumcision of Christ: And you, being dead in your sins and the uncircumcision of your flesh, he has made us alive together with him, having forgiven you all trespasses;

"Blotting out the handwriting of ordinances that was against us [the law], which was contrary to us, and took it out of the way, nailing it to his cross; having spoiled principalities and powers, he made a show of them openly, triumphing over them in it.

"Let no man therefore judge you in meat, or in drink, or in respect of an holyday, or of the new moon, or of the Sabbath: which are a shadow of things to come; but the body is of Christ.... Wherefore if you be dead with Christ from the rudiments of the world, why, as though living in the world, are you subject to ordinances?..."[136]

In other words, we don't need to physically observe any days now, period. We don't need to be concerned with dates. Christ has covered all this on our behalf. We are no longer under the law, but living daily in the Spirit with the liberty Christ has given to us. Thus, there is no need that we observe any one day, including those past and those yet in our future, physically by going "to church." The body of Christ, those who have his Spirit dwelling in them, are the *ekklesia*, the church, of God. Our attention is to be on living our lives fully in the Spirit each and every day, seeking first the kingdom of God.

It is the next high holy day fulfilled by Christ on our behalf that marks the advent of what is the civil new year, the ushering in of the kingdom or government, if you will, of God. It is, as most Christian denominations think of it, the second coming of Christ. They have no idea it will be the fulfilling of another Old Testament high holy day.

As you may recall, the sacred new year started in the spring. It was marked by the Passover on the tenth day of the new year in the month of Nisan [*or Abib*],[137] which occurs in our late March or early April. Nisan, the name of the first month of the sacred new year means *their flight*. This, of course, is a reference to Israel fleeing Egypt and for Christians marks a fleeing from bondage and sin into life in the Spirit. Christ is the high priest that covered our sins. The time of the entire summer harvest is the *sacred* year. "Blessed and holy is he that has part in the first resurrection [*the first fruits of Christ*]: on such the second death has no power, but they shall be priests of God and of Christ, and shall reign with him a thousand years."

However, a big change takes place with the next high holy day. It is the day that will once and for all answer the philosophical question, "Does God exist?" It is the advent of the *civil* new year, the first day of Tishri, the seventh month, when Christ will return, but this time as king, in power and might subduing all the nations of the world, bringing the kingdom of God to Earth. It will be a much different arrival than what the apostle John wrote of in the New Testament, "Fear not, daughter of Sion [*an obvious reference to Israel, not the gentiles of the world*]: behold, your King [*Christ*] comes, sitting on an ass's colt."[138]

John was paraphrasing Zechariah's prophesy in the Old Testament. "*Rejoice greatly, O daughter of Zion; shout, O daughter of Jerusalem: behold, your King comes unto you: he is just, and having salvation; lowly, and riding upon an ass, and upon a colt the foal of an ass."[139]

The preceding should make it very clear that Christ was sent to the lost sheep of the House of Israel and not the gentiles of the world. One would hardly consider the gentiles to be the daughters of Zion and Jerusalem.

"*And I will cut off the chariot from Ephraim [*House of Israel*], and the horse from Jerusalem [*House of Judah*], and the battle bow shall be cut off: and he shall speak peace unto the nations: and his dominion shall be from sea to sea, and from the river to the ends of the earth."[140]

The last part of this quote is talking about peace for the House of Israel and for Judah. It is to happen in our future. And it is portrayed by one of the days yet to be fulfilled by Christ our King. Let's take a look, then, at the next four high holy days given to our ancestors of the House of Israel. They, too, are a part of God's plan.

Chapter Five
Christ's Return, Trumpets and the Civil New Year

The Day of Trumpets, which heralds the beginning of the new civil year, in its duality marks the second coming of Jesus Christ. It is the day that Christians, unknowingly, have been looking forward to for millennia. And it was a high holy day that was observed millennia before that by the children of Israel. It's all part of the same story; just the circumstances of its characters have changed.

It is the first of the high holy days we are discussing that have yet to be fulfilled by Christ. There are many relevant events that will occur just before and on this day in our future. And while we don't know when this day will occur exactly, it is a future date that has left in its wake thousands of false prophets who predicted a date when the "world would end." Despite the one hundred percent failure rate of those who've preceded them, and that scientists have proven man cannot know the future;[141] we still have no shortage of those who will tell us when Christ will return. It's been this way from the very start.

"And as he sat upon the Mount of Olives, the disciples came unto him privately, saying, Tell us, when shall these things be? and what shall be the sign of your coming, and of the end of the world? And Jesus answered and said unto them, Take heed that no man deceive you."[142] The first thing Christ did was to warn his apostles concerning those predicting his return and the end of the world. In fact, the surest way to tell if a self-proclaimed predictor is wrong is if that person gives you a date. If you're reading this hoping to get a date, then I would suggest one of the on-line dating services.

Modern Christianity that celebrates the hijacked Ishtar festival is devoid of any understanding of the purpose of the intervening time between Christ's first and second coming. But as we've just read, it is the summer harvest of the first fruits of Christ. Those Christian first fruits are of the House of Israel. Peter was very clear to whom he was addressing his remarks on that Pentecost day nearly 2000 years ago. "Therefore let *all the House of Israel* know assuredly, that God has made that same Jesus, whom you have crucified, both Lord and Christ [messiah]...Repent, and be baptized every one of you [*House of Israel*] in the name of Jesus Christ for the remission of sins and you shall receive the gift of the Holy Spirit."[143] It is no coincidence either that Christ said "I am not sent except to the lost sheep of the House of Israel." And it is equally clear; Christ was not sent to the "gentiles of the world."

Modern day Christianity has lost sight of this elephant. It's been hijacked. In its place we have fables and traditions of men. Even though Christians are looking forward to Christ's return, hardly any understand his return will fulfill the Day of Trumpets given to our forefathers nearly four thousand years ago. Let's read the ordinance for the memorial Day of Trumpets.

The Holy Day Remembrance: "*And the LORD spoke unto Moses, saying, Speak unto the children of Israel, saying, In the seventh month, in the first day of the month, shall you have a sabbath, a memorial of blowing of trumpets, an holy convocation. You shall do no servile work therein: but you shall offer an offering made by fire unto the LORD."[144]

"*And in the seventh month, on the first day of the month, you shall have an holy convocation; you shall do no servile work: it is a day of blowing the trumpets unto you. And you shall offer a burnt offering for a sweet savor unto the LORD; one young bullock, one ram, and seven lambs of the first year without blemish: And their meat offering shall be of flour mingled with oil, three tenth deals for a bullock, and two tenth deals for a ram, And one tenth deal for one lamb, throughout the seven lambs: And one kid of the goats for a sin offering, to make an atonement for you: Beside the burnt offering of the month, and his meat offering, and the daily burnt offering, and his meat offering, and their drink offerings, according unto their manner, for a sweet savor, a sacrifice made by fire unto the LORD."[145]

The Historical Event: Like the day of Pentecost in Old Testament Israel, the Day of Trumpets was an annual memorial for the children of Israel while in the land given by promise to Abraham. It was to take place at an appointed time each year as set forth in the law. But it was not the only occasion in which trumpets were used. Trumpets were sounded at the beginning of every new moon, or month, too. "*Also in the day of your gladness, and in your solemn days, and in the beginnings of your months, you shall blow with the trumpets over your burnt offerings, and over the sacrifices of your peace offerings; that they may be to you for a memorial before your God: I am the LORD your God."[146]

However, the first day of the seventh month marked a special annual occasion that was a high holy day. This day had special meaning for Israel as Robert Jamieson explains. "That which is here made peculiar to this festival is that it was *a memorial of blowing of trumpets*. They blew the trumpet every new moon, but in the new moon of the seventh month it was to be done with more than ordinary solemnity; for they began to blow at sun-rise and continued till sun-set. This is here said to be a memorial, perhaps of the sound of the trumpet upon mount Sinai when the law was given, which must never be forgotten. Some think that it was a memorial of the creation of the world, which is supposed to have been in autumn; for which reason this was, till now, the first month. The mighty word by which God made the world is called *the voice of his thunder* [Psalm 104:7]; fitly therefore was it commemorated by blowing of trumpets, or a memorial of shouting, as the Chaldee renders it; for, *when the foundations of the earth were fastened, all the sons of God shouted for joy,* [Job 38:6,7]."[147]

As we'll discover when examining this day's duality, it foresaw the day when Christ would return to Earth at his second coming. Surprisingly, of those who do predict the date for Christ's return, I don't recall any of them picking the first day of Tishri, the seventh month. And now would not be a good time to start predicting either. Because just when we think we've got it covered, we will be surprised for his coming will be as "a thief in the night." "Therefore be you also *ready*: for in such an hour as *you think not*, the Son of man comes."[148]

We would do well to heed the words of James in order to be ready. "But whoso looks into the perfect law of liberty, and continues therein, he being not a forgetful hearer, but a doer of the work, this man shall be blessed in his deed."[149] In other words, we need to live our lives doing what Christians need to be doing. Myopically setting dates is not one of them. Besides, as we've just read, Christ won't return when we think he will, but when we think he *won't*. If you'd like to read what Christ has to say in detail, then read Matthew chapter twenty-four.

The actual blowing of the trumpets in Israel could not be done by just anyone. The trumpets were to be blown by the sons of

Aaron, sons of the high priest. "Neither the Levites nor any in the common ranks of the people could be employed in this office of signal giving. In order to attract greater attention and more faithful observance, it was reserved to the priests alone, as the Lord's ministers; and as anciently in Persia and other Eastern countries the alarm trumpets were sounded from the tent of the sovereign, so were they blown from the tabernacle, the visible residence of Israel's King."[150]

As we've seen with other holy days, this ordinance was to be observed throughout Israel's generations. "*And the sons of Aaron, the priests, shall blow with the trumpets; and they shall be to you for an ordinance for ever throughout your generations."[151]

The blowing of the trumpets also served another purpose for Israel. "*And if you go to war *in your land* against the enemy that oppresses you, then you shall blow an alarm with the trumpets; and you shall be remembered before the LORD your God, and you shall be saved from your enemies."[152]

We have an example of the blowing of trumpets to sound an alarm with Moses. "*And Moses sent them to the war, a thousand of every tribe, them and Phinehas the son of Eleazar the priest, to the war, with the holy instruments, and the trumpets to blow in his hand."[153]

We even have an example of the House of Judah, the Jews, sounding the trumpets of war when going to war against their brothers of the House of Israel. "*And, behold, God himself is with us [*House of Judah*] for our captain, and his priests with sounding trumpets to cry alarm against you. O children of [*the House of*] Israel, fight you not against the LORD God of your fathers; for you shall not prosper."

Turns out Abijah, King of Judah was right. "*And when Judah looked back, behold, the battle was before and behind: and they cried unto the LORD, and the priests sounded with the trumpets. Then the men of Judah gave a shout: and as the men of Judah shouted, it came to pass, that God smote Jeroboam and all Israel before Abijah and Judah. And the children of Israel fled before Judah: and God delivered them into their hand."[154]

This principle should be well heeded today by the House of Israel. For as we have forsaken our heritage to hijack false gods, we would be wise to remember that in times past the hand of God has delivered the children of the House of Israel to its enemies. It is prophesied to happen again for this very reason when the sixth seal is opened prior to the sounding of the seven trumpets leading to Christ's return.

In the book of Revelation, the church in the last days before Christ's return are warned, "Because you say, I am rich, and increased with goods, and have need of nothing; and know not that you are wretched, and miserable, and poor, and blind, and naked: I counsel you to buy of me gold tried in the fire, that you may be rich; and white raiment, that you may be clothed, and that the shame of your nakedness do not appear; and anoint your eyes with eye salve, that you may see. As *many as I love, I rebuke and chasten*: be zealous therefore, and repent."[155]

Probably the best-known example in the Biblical record of trumpets sounding for war is the example of Jericho. In fact, the fall of Jericho led by Joshua after leading Israel across the river Jordan contains a remarkable dualism related to the fall of Babylon the Great, the sixth empire or beast of Revelation, as we'll discuss later. "*Now Jericho was straightly shut up because of the children of Israel: none went out, and none came in. And the LORD said unto Joshua, See, I have given into your hand Jericho, and the king thereof, and the mighty men of valor. And you shall compass the city, all your men of war, and go round about the city once. Thus shall you do six days.

"And seven priests shall bear before the ark seven trumpets of rams' horns: and the seventh day you shall compass the city seven times, and the priests shall blow with the trumpets. And it shall come to pass, that when they make a long blast with the ram's horn, and when you hear the sound of the trumpet, all the people shall shout with a great shout; and the wall of the city shall fall down flat, and the people shall ascend up every man straight before him.

"And Joshua the son of Nun called the priests, and said unto them, Take up the ark of the covenant, and let seven priests bear seven trumpets of rams' horns before the ark of the LORD … And it came to pass, when Joshua had spoken unto the people, that the seven priests bearing the seven trumpets of rams' horns passed on before the LORD, and blew with the trumpets: and the ark of the covenant of the LORD followed them. And it came to pass, when Joshua had spoken unto the people, that the seven priests bearing the seven trumpets of rams' horns passed on before the LORD, and blew with the trumpets: and the ark of the covenant of the LORD followed them.

"And Joshua had commanded the people, saying, You shall not shout, nor make any noise with your voice, neither shall any word proceed out of your mouth, until the day I bid you shout; then shall you shout… And it came to pass on the seventh day, that they rose early about the dawning of the day, and compassed the city after the same manner seven times: only on that day they compassed the city seven times.

"And it came to pass at the seventh time, when the priests blew with the trumpets, Joshua said unto the people, Shout; for the LORD has given you the city. So the people shouted when [*the priests*] blew with the trumpets: and it came to pass, when the people heard the sound of the trumpet, and the people shouted with a great shout, that the wall fell down flat, so that the people went up into the city, every man straight before him, and they took the city. And they utterly destroyed all that was in the city, both man and woman, young and old, and ox, and sheep, and ass, with the edge of the sword."[156]

The feast of blowing the Trumpets portrays the return of Christ, the fall of the sixth empire, Babylon the Great, which is Edom, the sealing of 144,000 of the sons of Israel, and the first resurrection. In fact, the Day of Trumpets fulfillment by Christ essentially covers everything from chapter seven through chapter twenty in the book of Revelation. It might be useful at this point to read through these chapters so as to have a familiarity with them as we discuss the events of the Day of Trumpets fulfillment by Christ. Keep in mind, however, that chapters twelve, thirteen, fourteen, and seventeen are inset chapters. This simply means they are not in chronological order. They are meant to amplify particular subjects. Chapter twelve for example explains and expands on the role of the church in this sequence of events.

To help matters a bit, as this can be a trifle confusing the first time reading through it, let's summarize some events. The *sixth seal* is opened by Christ prior to his return on the Day of Trumpets.[157] It sets in motion a period of forty-two months in which the Earth will be subject to the power of the beast and the false prophet, *a sixth empire* that follows the five mentioned in Daniel's prophecy. "And there was given unto him a mouth speaking great things and blasphemies; and power was given unto him to continue forty two months."[158]

As we read in great detail in chapter six, The Genesis Birthright in *The Blind Man's Elephant*, the sixth empire of man is that of Edom. Edom sold the birthright to his younger brother Israel. He has vowed to kill his brother Israel [*Jacob*][159] and regain the physical birthright, which he will do because Christ will deliver us into their hands as we have, and continue to deal irresponsibly with our inheritance, our birthright. When Edom gains dominion over Israel, he will control the physical birthright openly. This is the time of trouble for Christianity or the time of Jacob's trouble, which we first discussed in the context of Jeremiah chapter ten. These are the circumstances prior to Christ's return marked by the civil Day of Trumpets.

The children of the House of Israel, Christianity today, are totally oblivious to our national identity. While we look forward to the return of Christ, we have no idea that the opening of the sixth seal is a chastising from God upon us. When the seal is opened, "The sun shall be turned into darkness, and the moon into blood, *before* that great and notable day of the Lord come..." and the events of that day will fall upon us before Babylon the Great falls.[160] We read of the same event in Revelation, "And I beheld when he [*Christ*] had opened the sixth seal, and, lo, there was a great earthquake; and the sun became black as sackcloth of hair, and the moon became as blood...."[161]

And why must the children of Israel, Christianity, suffer through this time? You may recall earlier from chapter one in context of the Christmas celebration, we read in Jeremiah, "*But the LORD is the true God, he is the living God, and an everlasting king: at his wrath the earth shall tremble, and the nations [*Israel*] shall not be able to abide his indignation. Thus shall you say unto them, The gods that have not made the heavens and the earth, they shall perish from the earth, and from under these heavens. He has made the earth by his power, he has established the world by his wisdom, and has stretched out the heavens by his discretion...

"Every man is brutish [*stupid*] in his knowledge: every founder is confounded by the graven image: for his molten image is falsehood, and there is no breath in them. They are vanity, the work of errors: in the time of their visitation they shall perish. The portion of Jacob [*House of Israel*] is not like them: for he is the former of all things; and Israel is the rod of *his inheritance*: The LORD of hosts is his name... For the pastors are become stupid, and have not sought the LORD: therefore they shall not prosper, and all their flocks shall be scattered."[162]

This is a strong warning from our LORD for the church, Christianity, the House of Israel, to be zealous and change our ways. The events of the sixth seal are directly tied to our hijacking pagan holidays and gods. It is a warning that largely goes unnoticed because we are told by our LORD, "every man is stupid in his knowledge."

We don't know who we are, what we should be doing, or where we are headed. False holidays blind us to our heritage. Christ is returning as a king, in a war marked by the blowing of trumpets at his return to destroy evil, the sixth empire, and to establish the kingdom of God on Earth. Because of our hijacking these pagan days and forsaking our birthright inheritance, Christians, the children of Israel will pay a heavy price before that day. It is difficult to imagine that anyone who wishes to be saved from this would be found keeping the hijacked pagan celebrations of Christmas and Ishtar given what we've just read.

Yet one of the primary purposes of Christ's second coming, marked by the Day of Trumpets, begins with the redemption the 144,000 of the nation of Jacob, or Israel. "*Hear the word of the LORD, O you nations, and declare it in the isles afar off, and say, He that scattered Israel will gather him, and keep him, as a shepherd does his flock. [*This is a promise national in scope to Israel*] For the LORD has redeemed Jacob, and ransomed him, from the hand of him that was stronger than he."[163]

The last part of the sentence in Jeremiah, "ransomed him, from the hand of him that was stronger than he," is a specific reference to Edom [*Herod et al*] at Christ's first coming and referenced in Genesis concerning the birth of Esau/Edom and Jacob/Israel. "*And the LORD said unto her [*Rebekah*], Two nations are in your womb, and two manner of people shall be separated from your bowels; and one people shall be stronger [*Edom*] than the other people [*Israel*]; and the elder [*Edom*] shall serve the younger."[164]

Christ paid the ransom for the divorced House of Israel and the House of Judah. Edom had gained control over the House of Judah by the first century CE. Christ's death and resurrection changed the path that leads to the inheritance, which was chronicled in chapter six of *The Bind Man's Elephant*. It is now of the Spirit and of faith rather than of the flesh and the Law. "For even the Son of man came not to be ministered unto, but to minister, and to *give his life a ransom for many.*"[165]

Christ was sent only to the lost sheep of the House of Israel at his first coming. As Paul pointed out in Romans eleven, the natural branches, the House of Judah, were broken off at that time. The Day of Trumpets, however, opens the door to Christ's fulfilling a future day of redemption, national in scope, that awaits Jacob, both the nations of Israel and Judah, as we'll read in the next chapter.

The overall outline for these events leading up to Christ's return is as follows: There are seven seals followed by the seven trumpets followed by seven plagues. The seventh seal opens. There is silence in heaven for half an hour. After this, seven trumpets sound in order. The fifth trumpet sounds, which is the first woe. Woe here as used in the Greek is an interjection signifying an exclamation of grief. We could say today that "woe" is akin to hearing really bad news, much, much worse than 9/11 and exclaiming, "Oh, s**t!" The sixth trumpet sounds and the second and third woes occur. Then the seventh trumpet sounds, which in turn initiate the seven last plagues somewhat reminiscent of the plagues when Israel was redeemed from Egypt.

In total then, we have seven seals, the last of which gives way to seven trumpets, the last of which gives way to seven last plagues. The first of the seven seals was opened immediately after Christ's first coming, and the last of the seven plagues occurs just prior to his return. This is the period referred to in the Biblical record as the "last days."

Thus, we have sequential events in a series of three sevens. Throughout the Biblical record, there are all sorts of number dualities such as Israel spending 40 years in the wilderness while Christ spent 40 days in the wilderness fasting. While interesting and noteworthy, we need to be careful not to build our theology chiefly around numbers. Nevertheless, in the Biblical record, the number seven signifies completion. The number three signifies perfection.

Leading up to the sounding of the trumpets on the Day of

Trumpets, there are seven seals. Let's read them. They begin in chapter six of Revelation.

"And I saw when the Lamb [Christ] opened one of the seals, and I heard, as it were the noise of thunder, one of the four beasts saying, Come and see. And I saw, and behold a white horse: and he that sat on him had a bow; and a crown was given unto him: and he went forth conquering, and to conquer.

"And when he had opened the second seal, I heard the second beast say, Come and see. And there went out another horse that was red: and power was given to him that sat thereon to take peace from the earth, and that they should kill one another: and there was given unto him a great sword.

"And when he had opened the third seal, I heard the third beast say, Come and see. And I beheld, and lo a black horse; and he that sat on him had a pair of balances in his hand. And I heard a voice in the midst of the four beasts say, A measure of wheat for a penny, and three measures of barley for a penny; and see you hurt not the oil and the wine.

"And when he had opened the fourth seal, I heard the voice of the fourth beast say, Come and see. And I looked, and behold a pale horse: and his name that sat on him was Death, and Hell followed with him. And power was given unto them over the fourth part of the earth, to kill with sword, and with hunger, and with death, and with the beasts of the earth.

"And when he had opened the fifth seal, I saw under the altar the souls of them that were slain for the word of God, and for the testimony which they held: And they cried with a loud voice, saying, How long, O Lord, holy and true, do you not judge and avenge our blood on them that dwell on the earth? And white robes were given unto every one of them; and it was said unto them, that they should rest yet for a little season, until their fellow servants also and their brethren, that should be killed as they were, should be fulfilled."[166]

The first four seals are commonly referred to as the "Four Horsemen of the Apocalypse." Many people who read the account in Revelation believe these five seals will be opened at some future date. However, a careful reading makes clear that the events of the first five opened seals are occurring and have occurred since Christ first coming.

Seal number one, opened by the Lamb, meaning Christ, is a reference to false prophets. False prophets sprang up almost immediately in the early church. Paul wrote to the church in Corinth about 55 CE warning them, "For if he that comes preaches another Jesus, whom we have not preached, or if you receive another spirit, which you have not received, or another gospel, which you have not accepted…. For such are false apostles, deceitful workers, transforming themselves into the apostles of Christ. And no marvel; for Satan himself is transformed into an angel of light."[167] How commonly ironic that Christmas trees decorated with lights have an angel sitting atop them. While popular in Christianity today, hijacked pagan celebrations are deceits that have been transformed into "holidays of light."

It is worthy of note that in the gospel of Matthew, the warning about false prophets is tied into the metaphor of a tree by Christ. "Beware of false prophets, which come to you in sheep's clothing, but inwardly they are ravening wolves. You shall know them by their fruits. Do men gather grapes of thorns, or figs of thistles? Even so every good tree brings forth good fruit; but a corrupt tree brings forth evil fruit. A good tree cannot bring forth evil fruit, neither can a corrupt tree bring forth good fruit. Every tree that brings not forth good fruit is hewn down, and cast into the fire."[168]

The apostle Peter warned, in the 60's CE about false prophets, too. "But there were false prophets also among the people, even as there shall be false teachers among you, who privily [*secretly*] shall bring in damnable heresies, even denying the Lord that bought them, and bring upon themselves swift destruction."[169]

The apostle John warned about false prophets towards the end of the first century. "Beloved, believe not every spirit, but try the spirits whether they are of God: because many false prophets are gone out into the world. Hereby you know the Spirit of God: Every spirit that confesses that Jesus Christ is come in the flesh is of God: And every spirit that confesses not that Jesus Christ is come in the flesh is not of God: and this is that spirit of antichrist, whereof you have heard that it should come; and even now already is it in the world."[170] As we can plainly see, the apostles were warning of false prophets and the spirit of the antichrist well before the end of the first century.

The second seal is war. Remember, Christ said during his earthly ministry, "Think not that I am come to *send* peace, I am come not to *send* peace, but a sword."[171] Who opened the five seals, the second of which sent war? Christ, the Lamb.

In our context, they would be wars fought because of religion. Josephus, one of the first century's most notable historians, who was born about 37 CE and lived to 101 CE, wrote a very thorough work of the time called, *The Wars of the Jews*. And all one has to do is make a cursory look from the beginning of the first century until present day to realize that wars over religion are nearly too numerous to mention. The Pharisees, right off the bat, were out persecuting and killing Christians. Saul, later becoming the apostle Paul, was one of the most passionate in this pursuit. As mentioned, the Romans fought wars with the Jews that led to the destruction of Jerusalem. And so it went through to the Crusades, to the break between the Roman Catholic Church and the German Protestant princes in the Thirty Years War. Today, the House of Israel and Judah are fighting in the Middle East and Muslims are enemies once again. And so it shall be until Christ's foot touches on the Mount of Olives at his return.

The third seal is that of famine. Famines can be the result of wars disrupting normal farming routines, food distribution as well as droughts, insect plagues among others. A cursory look through the history of the past 2000 years or so shows no shortage of famines particularly in Europe. Perhaps most noteworthy was the Irish famine in the 1840s in which upwards of a million people are said to have starved to death.

The fourth seal is pestilence or disease which also brings with it death. Of course, war and famine result very often in pestilence. Healthy sanitation is severely degraded or becomes non-existent. Influenzas and other illnesses have taken a large toll throughout the centuries. And a fourth part of the world will be killed by war, hunger, disease and with the beasts of the earth.

Matthew Henry in his Biblical commentary explains it this way. "After the opening of these seals of approaching judgments, and the distinct account of them, we have this general observation, that God *gave power to them over the fourth part of the earth, to kill with the sword, and with hunger, and with death, and with the beasts of the earth, v. 8.* He gave them power, that is, those instruments of his anger, or those judgments themselves; he who holds the winds in his hand has all public calamities at his command, and they can only go when he sends them and no further than he permits. To the three great judgments of war, famine, and pestilence, is here added *the beasts of the earth*, another of God's sore judgments, mentioned in Ezekiel 14:21 and mentioned here the last, because, when a nation is depopulated by the sword, famine, and pestilence, the small remnant that continue in a waste and howling wilderness encourage the wild beasts to make head against them, and they become easy prey. Others, by *the beasts of the field*, understand brutish, cruel, savage men, who, having divested themselves of all humanity, delight to be the instruments of the destruction of others."[172]

Perhaps we should point out that there are many who claim God is absent from our everyday lives simply because we cannot "see" him. But we would do well to remember that all these afflictions are let loose on us by the hand of God upon opening of these seals. Of course, our instinctive human reaction would be to ask why? What did we do? But perhaps the better question to ask is, what should we be doing?

The fifth seal is the death of those killed for the Word of God. This, too, has been occurring from the time just after Christ's first coming. Stephen, as we read in an earlier chapter, was likely the first martyr for the Word of God. Included in this list are the apostles James, Peter and Paul. And so it has continued throughout the centuries to this day.

The point here is that all five of these seals have been occurring since the first century. When the sixth seal is opened, which will be before the day of Christ's return or the Day of Trumpets, we will know that the events of the "end time" are upon us for certain. Before any prognosticators deliver their dates, the sixth seal will need to be opened.

"And I beheld when he [*Christ*] had opened the sixth seal, and, lo, there was a great earthquake; and the sun became black as sackcloth of hair, and the moon became as blood; And the stars of heaven fell unto the earth, even as a fig tree casts her untimely figs, when she is shaken of a mighty wind. And the heaven departed as a scroll when it is rolled together; and every mountain and island were moved out of their places. And the kings of the earth, and the great men, and the rich men, and the chief captains, and the mighty men, and every bondman, and every free man, hid themselves in the dens and in the rocks of the mountains; And said to the mountains and rocks, Fall on us, and hide us from the face of him that sits on the throne, and from *the wrath of the Lamb*: For *the great day of his wrath* is come; and who shall be able to stand."[173]

"**Alas! for that day is great, so that none is like it: it is even the time of Jacob's trouble;* but he shall be saved out of it."[174] And as you may recall, this terrible time is mentioned in context as the result of Christmas celebrations in Jeremiah chapter ten as addressed to the House of Israel. It should be noted too that it is a time of Jacob's, or Israel's, trouble. It is not referred to as the time of the "gentiles of the world's" trouble. But, it is this time of trouble that current day Christians are hoping to be "raptured" away from. Why?

If Christians, indeed are the "*gentiles* of the world," and this is the time of Israel's trouble, it raises the logical question then, why should Christians be concerned? This only applies to Israel. The "rapture" is only necessary in order for the children of Israel to escape.

In fact, this day of Jacob's troubled was prophesied to Moses before Israel even entered into the promised land after coming out of Egypt. "*And the LORD [*Christ*] appeared in the tabernacle in a pillar of a cloud: and the pillar of the cloud stood over the door of the tabernacle. And the LORD [*Christ*] said unto Moses, Behold, you shall sleep with your fathers; and this people will rise up, and go a whoring after the gods of the strangers of the land, to what place they go to be among them, and will forsake me, and break my covenant, which I have made with them. Then *my anger shall be kindled against them in that day*, and I will forsake them, and I will hide my face from them, and they shall be devoured, and many evils and troubles shall befall them; so that they will say in that day, Are not these evils come upon us, because our God is not among us?

"*And I will surely hide my face *in that day* for all the evils which they shall have wrought, *in that they are turned unto other gods*. Now therefore write you this song for you, and teach it the children of Israel: put it in their mouths, *that this song may be a witness for me* against the children of Israel. For when I shall have brought them into the land which I swore unto their fathers, that flows with milk and honey; and they shall have eaten and filled themselves, and waxen fat; then will they turn unto other gods, and serve them, and provoke me, and break my covenant. And it shall come to pass, when many evils and troubles are befallen them, that this song shall testify against them as a witness; for it shall not be forgotten out of the mouths of their seed: for I know their imagination which they go about, even now, before I have brought them into the land which I swore."[175]

This song is first mentioned in the Torah or the law in the Old Testament. It is not mentioned in the Biblical record again until we see a reference to it in the Book of Revelation. This song is to be a witness against the children of Israel. It is a song of personal and national significance much like a national anthem is for nations today. "National songs take deep hold of the memories and have a powerful influence in stirring the deepest feelings of a people. In accordance with this principle in human nature, a song was ordered to be composed by Moses, doubtless under divine inspiration, which was to be learnt by the Israelites themselves and to be taught to their children in every age, embodying the substance of the preceding addresses, and of a strain well suited to inspire the popular mind with a strong sense of God's favor to their nation."[176]

This time of Jacob's trouble precedes the Day of Trumpets that marks the day of Christ's return. It is the sixth seal. The time of Jacob's trouble lasts for forty-two months. The opening of the seventh seal begins the Day of Trumpets.

If only 144,000 are to be saved, we have to believe then that of the nearly two billion people who are Christians, the immense majority will perish from the House of Israel as well as Judah. Certainly this is the time of Jacob's trouble. No wonder it shall be said, "And they said to the mountains and rocks, Fall on us, and hide us from the face of him that sits on the throne, and from the *wrath of the Lamb*: For the great day of his wrath is come; and who shall be able to stand." And if it were not for God's promise and plan, all Israel, indeed all mankind, would be destroyed.

Paul makes the point to the Romans when he quotes Isaiah, "Esaias also cries concerning Israel, Though the number of the children of Israel be as the sand of the sea, a remnant [*144,000*] shall be saved: For he will finish the work, and cut it short in righteousness: because a short work will the Lord make upon the earth. And as Esaias said before, Except the Lord of Sabaoth had left us a seed, we had been as Sodom, and been made like unto Gomorrha."[177] That is, all Israel would be utterly destroyed.

The Lord of Sabaoth is the Lord of the armies of God. The word should not be confused for the word Sabbath. Yet just prior to the very first Sabbath day, it was recorded, "*Thus the heavens and the earth were finished, and all the host of them."[178] The word host is *tsaba* or *ts^ebaah* in Hebrew. It refers to a mass of persons organized for war or in this case, the armies [*tsabaoth*] of the LORD.

As we've read, the Biblical record is one book and one story. From the very beginning, as part of God's plan outlined in the high holy days for Israel, the high holy Day of Trumpets was destined to be preceded by the time of Jacob's trouble and followed by the blowing of the trumpets when the Lamb of God shall make war against the beast and the ten kings that give their power and strength to him and the Lamb shall overcome him.[179]

It is clear the remnant, the 144,000 that are sealed are of Israel. But they aren't sealed until after the seals are opened including the sixth seal. "And *after* these things I saw four angels standing on the four corners of the earth, holding the four winds of the earth, that the wind should not blow on the earth, nor on the sea, nor on any tree. And I saw another angel ascending from the east, having the seal of the living God: and he cried with a loud voice to the four angels, to whom it was given to hurt the earth and the sea, And I saw another angel ascending from the east, having the seal of the living God: and he cried with a loud voice to the four angels, to whom it was given to hurt the earth and the sea, And I heard the number of them which were sealed: and there were sealed an hundred and forty and four thousand of all the tribes of the children of Israel."[180]

That the 144,000 sealed are from the children of Israel leads us back to two points. One, Christ said he was not sent except unto the children, the lost sheep, of the House of Israel. And second, as this is the time of Jacob's trouble, it includes both the Houses of Israel and Judah.

The duality of the high holy days is very clear here as well. This is a part of the plan of God from the beginning for Jacob. "Not according to the covenant that I made with their fathers in the day when I took them by the hand to lead them out of the land of Egypt; because they continued not in my covenant, and I regarded them not, says the Lord."[181] The day of the new covenant for both houses is yet to be fulfilled. It is the high holy day immediately following Trumpets.

A further description of the 144,000 is given in Revelation. "And I looked, and lo, a Lamb stood on the mount Sion, and with him a hundred and forty four thousand, having his Father's name written in their foreheads. These are they, which were not defiled with women; for they are virgins. These are they, which follow the Lamb wherever he goes. These were *redeemed from among men, being the first fruits* unto God and to the Lamb. And in their mouth was found no guile: for they are without fault before the throne of God."[182]

Many have assumed this to be a reference to the flesh, virgins, not defiled with women. If this were the case, there might be few men included in the 144,000. Straight women, it seems, would have a definite advantage, as would gay men. But the point here is spiritual in nature. The Greek word for defiled is *molyno*. It is a reference to those who keep themselves from sin, from following after false gods such as the Babylonian goddess of fertility and war, Ishtar. These 144,000 are those from the nations of Israel, which have followed "the Lamb wherever he goes."

The Greek word virgin used here in Revelation is *parthenos*. Used in its fleshly sense, it refers to a virgin woman or a maiden who is eligible for marriage, our current day morality notwithstanding. However, spiritually it is a reference to someone who has kept him or herself from idolatry, who is not impure religiously. It refers to someone who stops hijacking pagan holidays, someone who changes and stays true to the Word of God. It refers to someone who is worthy to be accepted for marriage with the Lamb in a spiritual sense.

Once we repent, are baptized, we are to leave behind the leaven of sin, and follow the path set out before us by God. We see that the spiritual fulfillment of the high holy days by Christ makes perfect sense to us, and puts into sharp contrast the falsity and error of "hijacking pagan holidays...for good reason, to influence the world with biblical worldview and culture." We can understand why Peter admonished the children of the House of Israel to "repent and be baptized…."

It should be quite clear that pagan holidays do not influence the world with a true Biblical worldview and culture. The pagan worldview and culture is not of God. It does not allow us to follow "the Lamb wherever he goes," but rather it takes us away from that path. This is the danger of these false holidays. "Enter you in at the straight gate: for wide is the gate, and broad is the way, that leads to destruction, and many there be which go in thereat. Because straight is the gate, and narrow is the way, which leads unto life, and few there be that find it. Beware of false prophets, which come to you in sheep's clothing, but inwardly they are ravening wolves."[183]

This being the case, then, do the many follow and participate in Christmas and Easter or the few? Quite obviously, it's the many as both these days are the most popular in Christendom. It may be difficult to understand this point on a visceral level, but both these days of pagan origin are wolves in sheep's clothing. Perhaps this is one reason why so few, only 144,000 of nearly two billion Christians will be sealed from the time of Jacob's trouble and the events thereafter. And "because they continued not in my covenant, and I regarded them not, says the Lord." It is food for thought for everyone serious about his or her Christian faith.

Let's look at a prophetic description of the "great day of his wrath." "*The great day of the LORD is near, it is near, and hastens greatly, even the voice of the day of the LORD: the mighty man shall cry there bitterly. That day is a day of wrath, a day of trouble and distress, a day of waste and desolation, a day of darkness and gloominess, a day of clouds and thick darkness, *day of the trumpet* and alarm against the fenced cities, and against the high towers. And I will bring distress upon men, that they shall walk like blind men, because they have sinned against the LORD: and their blood shall be poured out as dust, and their flesh as the dung. Neither their silver nor their gold shall be able to deliver them in *the day of the LORD'S wrath*; but the whole land shall be devoured by the fire of his jealousy: for he shall make even a speedy riddance of all them that dwell in the land."[184]

This particular description is found in Zephaniah, one of the twelve minor prophets of the Old Testament. His book is one of the two Babylonian period books along with that of Habakkuk. The prophecy of Zephaniah is just another example of the fact that the Bible is one book written to the same people. And as we'll see, Babylon the Great, the sixth empire, will be devoured by fire in the day of the last trumpet; in one hour, a speedy riddance for sure.

In the meantime, those of Jacob are also warned in the book of Isaiah, "*Howl; for *the day of the LORD is at hand; it shall come as a destruction* from the Almighty. Therefore shall all hands be faint, and every man's heart shall melt: And they shall be afraid: pangs and sorrows shall take hold of them; they shall be in pain as a woman that travails [*in labor before birth*]: they shall be amazed one at another; their faces shall be as flames. Behold, *the day of the LORD comes, cruel both with wrath and fierce anger*, to lay the land desolate: and he shall destroy the sinners thereof out of it.

"For the stars of heaven and the constellations thereof shall not give their light: the sun shall be darkened in his going forth, and the moon shall not cause her light to shine. And I will punish the world [*its inhabitants*] for their evil, and the wicked for their iniquity; and I will cause the arrogancy of the proud to cease, and will lay low the haughtiness of the terrible....Therefore I will shake the heavens, and the earth shall remove out of her place, in the wrath of the LORD of hosts, and in the day of his fierce anger....And Babylon, the glory of kingdoms, the beauty of the Chaldees' excellency, shall be as when God overthrew Sodom and Gomorrah."[185]

The context of Isaiah chapter thirteen is the destruction of Babylon. It is a prophecy and it has a dual application. It is a reference to the first head, of gold, of the great image, which was the Babylonian Empire. This was the empire that took the House of Judah into captivity due to their idolatry. Daniel, a son of Judah, while in captivity interpreted the king of Babylon, Nebuchadnezzar's dream concerning the great image. But he saw the great image only up through the first five empires. Empire number six, in the book of Revelation, is a reprise of sorts of the first empire, hence the distinguishing of the latter by use of the phrase "the Great."

Sir Isaac Newton in his "Observations Upon the Prophecies of Daniel and the Apocalypse of St John" [*the book of Revelation*] makes note of this relationship between the two books, "The Apocalypse of John is written in the same style and language with the Prophecies of Daniel, and has the same relation to them which they have to one another, so that all of them together make but one complete Prophecy; and in like manner it consists of two parts, an introductory Prophecy, and an Interpretation thereof."[186] The Biblical record is one book written to the same people.

As we've read, there is no shortage of warnings to the children of Israel. But when we've lost our identity, and lost track of the plan that God has set out before us, and walked off the narrow path, led astray by our vain reasoning, cheerfully defiling ourselves with hijacked deceits passed off as the real thing, God gets more than a little upset.

But because we don't know when this day will occur, and because it hasn't happened yet, it doesn't mean God is slack. As Peter wrote, "The Lord is not slack concerning his promise, as some men count slackness; but is longsuffering towards us, not willing that any should perish, but that all should come to repentance."[187] It's not too late to change our ways…yet. "But of the times and the seasons, brethren, you have no need that I write unto you," as Paul reminded the church in Thessalonica, "For yourselves know perfectly that *the day of the Lord* so comes as a thief in the night."[188]

The Day of Trumpets marks the beginning of the new civil year in the seventh month of the year, which is Tishri. This is our autumn and corresponds to our September/early October. Interestingly, September, which is the ninth month in our Gregorian calendar and is based on the Julian calendar of the Romans, means seventh month. This great day of the LORD, the time of Jacob's trouble occurs just prior to the Day of Trumpets or the first day of the seventh month of the prophetic calendar.

To recap so far, we have seen that the first five seals mentioned in Revelation chapter six, including those of the "Four Horsemen of the Apocalypse," have been occurring since Christ's first coming. The time between his first coming and his return on the Day of Trumpets is the period of the "last days." The sixth seal has yet to be opened. It is the great day of the LORD's wrath known as the time of Jacob's trouble. This leads us to the opening of the seventh, and final seal. Keep in mind, it is the Lamb, or Christ who opens all seven seals.

"And when he had opened the seventh seal, there was silence in heaven about the space of half an hour. And I saw the seven angels which stood before God; and to them were given seven trumpets."[189] This silence for half an hour in heaven is not exactly clear to us despite some suggesting this proves, to update an old cliché, there are no cell phones in heaven.

Matthew Henry in his commentary states, "A profound *silence in heaven for the space of half an hour*, which may be understood either, 1. Of the silence of peace, that for this time no complaints were sent up to the ear of the Lord God of sabaoth; all was quiet and well in the church, and therefore all silent in heaven, for whenever the church on earth cries, through oppression, that cry comes up to heaven and resounds there; or, 2. A silence of expectation; great things were upon the wheel of providence, and the church of God, both in heaven and earth, stood silent, as became them, to see what God was doing, according to that of Zec. 2:13, *Be silent, O all flesh, before the Lord, for he has risen up out of his holy habitation. And elsewhere, Be still, and know that I am God."*[190]

Also, there is a duality relating to the fall of Jericho by Joshua and the fall of Babylon the Great by Jesus. Remember both names have the same meaning, "Jehovah is salvation." "*And Joshua had commanded the people, saying, You shall not shout, nor make any noise with your voice, neither shall any word proceed out of your mouth, until the day I bid you shout; then shall you shout."[191]

In other words, there was silence. And what in the Old Testament immediately followed the silence? "*And seven priests bearing seven trumpets of rams' horns before the ark of the LORD went on continually, and blew with the trumpets."[192] And what in the New Testament immediately follows the half hour of silence in heaven? "And I saw the seven angels which stood before God; and to them were given *seven trumpets*."[193]

The fall of Jericho and Babylon the Great have another common feature as well. Esau sold his birthright to Jacob. Esau became Edom and Jacob became Israel. When Isaac passed along the birthright to Israel, part of that condition was that Israel was to be master over Edom. "*And Isaac answered and said unto Esau, Behold, I have made him your lord, and all his brethren have I given to him for servants...."[194] This has never sat well with Edom. Even at the time of Christ, those of Edom claimed never to have been in bondage to anyone.[195] In fact, at the time of the blessings by Isaac, Edom swore an oath to himself, "*And Esau hated Jacob because of the blessing wherewith his father blessed him: and Esau said in his heart, The days of mourning for my father are at hand; then will I slay my brother Jacob."[196]

This is a prophecy that began being fulfilled with Christ and the opening of the fifth seal. "*And of the ten horns that were in his head, and of the other which came up, and before whom three fell; even of that horn that had eyes, and a mouth that spoke very great things, whose look was more stout than his fellows. I beheld, and the same horn [*Edom*] made war with the saints and prevailed against them until the Ancient of days came…."[197] Thus it continues into our modern day. "And when he had opened the fifth seal, I saw under the altar the souls of them that were slain for the word of God, and for the testimony which they held."[198]

Isaac further told Edom, "*And by your sword shall you live, and shall serve your brother; and it shall come to pass when you shall have the dominion, that you shall break his yoke from off your neck.[199] When Edom finally accomplishes this, and they are getting quite close to it, it will mark the opening of the sixth seal, the beginning of the sixth empire, the sixth head of the great image that is 666 and will have dominion for forty-two months. It is the time of Jacob's trouble.

Needless to say, Edom has never wanted to acknowledge Israel's lordship over them. It was the descendants of Edom who were responsible for the death of Christ in the flesh at his first coming, not those descended from the House of Judah. And Edom will not give an inch to Israel and its Lord Jesus Christ, the Lamb it put to death at that Passover nearly 2000 years ago. In the end, the Edomite empire, Babylon the Great will be utterly destroyed. This destruction of Babylon the Great, and Christ returning establishing the kingdom of God, is heralded by the sounding of seven trumpets.

Matthew Henry makes a perceptive observation that is applicable to Edom as well. "Jericho resolves Israel *shall not* be its master, v. 1. It was *straitly shut up, because of the children of Israel*. It *did shut up, and it was shut up* (so it is in the margin); it *did shut up* itself, being strongly fortified both by art and nature, *and it was shut* up by the obstinacy and resolution of the inhabitants, who agreed never to surrender nor so much as sound a parley; none went out as deserters or to treat of peace, nor were any admitted in to offer peace. Thus were they infatuated, and their hearts hardened to their own destruction—*the miserable case and character of all those that strengthen themselves against the Almighty*, Job 15:25..." But it made no difference for "God resolves Israel *shall* be its master...."[200]

The obstinacy and resolve of Edom that Israel shall not be its master is evident throughout the Biblical record. As it was in the end with Jericho, so too shall it be with Babylon the Great. "And they burnt the city [*Jericho*] with fire, and all that was therein: only the silver, and the gold, and the vessels of brass and of iron, they put into the treasury of the house of the LORD."[201]

And what is to be the outcome of Babylon the Great? "But the day of the Lord will come as a thief in the night; in the which the heavens shall pass away with a great noise, and the elements shall melt with fervent heat, the earth also and the works that are therein shall be burned up."[202] "And [*the merchants*] cried when they saw the smoke of her burning, saying, What city is like unto this great city!"[203]

There is a duality with Jericho and Babylon the Great: there is silence, then blowing of seven trumpets and the finally the fall of the cities being burned with fire.

Let's examine the blowing of the seven trumpets that mark the return of Christ to Earth.

"And I saw the seven angels which stood before God; and to them were given seven trumpets. And another angel came and stood at the altar, having a golden censer; and there was given unto him much incense, that he should offer it with the prayers of all saints upon the golden altar which was before the throne. And the smoke of the incense, which came with the prayers of the saints, ascended up before God out of the angel's hand. And the angel took the censer, and filled it with fire of the altar, and cast it into the earth: and there were voices, and thunderings, and lightnings, and an earthquake. And the seven angels which had the seven trumpets prepared themselves to sound."[204]

This brings us to the threshold of the return of Christ, which shall be the end of the sixth empire. Like Jericho when the seven priests blew seven trumpets, seven angels shall blow seven trumpets. When the first angel sounds the first trumpet, it will mark the *beginning* of the fulfillment by Christ of the Day of Trumpets given to our ancestors nearly four thousand years ago.

But as we've just read, while this is a day looked forward to by Christians, it is preceded by Jacob's time of trouble. Thus any joy looking forward to Christ's return should be tempered by the sobering fact that the children of Israel once again have strayed from the straight and narrow set before us by God, and once again we will pay a very heavy price for being "stupid and foolish."

The primary purpose of the Day of Trumpets is the establishing of the kingdom of God here on Earth. It's not to take everybody to heaven to play harp music with the angels because we're nice people. This 'day' marks great death and devastation of the kingdoms of men in addition to the destruction witnessed by the previous opening of the sixth seal. Taking all this very seriously, anyone alive at the time of these events should be scared, very scared. And as we've read, they will be.

"The first angel sounded, and there followed hail and fire mingled with blood, and they were cast upon the earth: and the third part of trees was burnt up, and all green grass was burnt up.

"And the second angel sounded, and as it were a great mountain burning with fire was cast into the sea: and the third part of the sea became blood; And the third part of the creatures which were in the sea, and had life, died; and the third part of the ships were destroyed.

"And the third angel sounded, and there fell a great star from heaven, burning as it were a lamp, and it fell upon the third part of the rivers, and upon the fountains of waters; And the name of the star is called Wormwood: and the third part of the waters became wormwood; and many men died of the waters, because they were made bitter [*poisonous*].

"And the fourth angel sounded, and the third part of the sun was smitten, and the third part of the moon, and the third part of the stars; so as the third part of them was darkened, and the day shone not for a third part of it, and the night likewise. And I beheld, and heard an angel flying through the midst of heaven, saying with a loud voice, Woe, woe, woe, to the inhabiters of the earth by reason of the other voices of the trumpet of the three angels, which are yet to sound!"[205]

The scope and magnitude of this is beyond anything we can possibly imagine. Yet to put it into perspective, all we need do is look at it from our own individual point of view. This isn't something we will watch happen to others on the seven o'clock news. We will be the news. It will happen to all those not sealed by God. The only question remaining for anyone is, will we repent or change and step away from our errors as did the people of Nineveh when warned by Jonah?[206] We can't claim we weren't warned. Our only claim will be willful ignorance or defiance. And as we've just read and will continue to read, the fruits of this tree are catastrophic.

Regardless of the exact timing of these events in our future, the choice is ours today as to how we will live our lives. None of us may live to see the opening of the sixth seal or hear the first trumpet. Does that make a difference in our choices? Does it make a difference as to which path we choose? These are questions each of us needs to answer for ourselves. But we should realize that the best path through life is following the Word of God regardless of the timing of future events.

While the first four trumpets have brought death and destruction to a large part of Earth and its inhabitants, the level of intensity gets taken up another notch with the three woes that will be let loose upon the Earth.

"And the fifth angel sounded, and I saw a star fall from heaven unto the earth: and to him was given the key of the bottomless pit. And he opened the bottomless pit; and there arose a smoke out of the pit, as the smoke of a great furnace; and the sun and the air were darkened by reason of the smoke of the pit. And there came out of the smoke locusts upon the earth: and unto them was given power, as the scorpions of the earth have power.

"And it was commanded them that they should not hurt the grass of the earth, neither any green thing, neither any tree; but only those men which have not the seal of God in their foreheads.

"And to them it was given that they should not kill them, but that they should be tormented five months: and their torment was as the torment of a scorpion, when he strikes a man. And in those days shall men seek death, and shall not find it; and shall desire to die, and death shall flee from them.

"And the shapes of the locusts were like unto horses prepared unto battle; and on their heads were as it were crowns like gold, and their faces were as the faces of men. And they had hair as the hair of women, and their teeth were as the teeth of lions. And they had breastplates, as it were breastplates of iron; and the sound of their wings was as the sound of chariots of many horses running to battle. And they had tails like unto scorpions, and there were stings in their tails: and their power was to hurt men five months.

"And they had a king over them, which is the angel of the bottomless pit, whose name in the Hebrew tongue is Abaddon, but in the Greek tongue has his name Apollyon. One woe is past; behold, there come two woes more hereafter."[207]

The exact manifestation of these events remains to be seen. However, it is interesting to read how Matthew Henry in his commentary described it , "These locusts were of a monstrous size and shape, v. 7, 8, etc. They were equipped for their work like horses prepared to battle. (1.) They pretended to great authority, and seemed to be assured of victory: *They had crowns like gold on their heads*; it was not a true, but a counterfeit authority. (2.) They had the show of wisdom and sagacity, *the faces of men*, though the spirit of devils. (3.) They had all the allurements of seeming beauty, to ensnare and defile the minds of men—*hair like women*; their way of worship was very gaudy and ornamental. (4.) Though they appeared with the tenderness of women, they had *the teeth of lions*, were really cruel creatures. (5.) They had the defence and protection of earthly powers—*breastplates of iron*. (6.) They made a mighty noise in the world; they flew about from one country to another, and the noise of their motion was like that of an army with chariots and horses. (7.) Though at first they soothed and flattered men with a fair appearance, there was a sting in their tails; the cup of their abominations contained that which, though luscious at first, would at length bite like a serpent and sting like an adder. (8.) The king and commander of this hellish squadron is here described, [1.] As an angel; so he was by nature, an angel, once one of the angels of heaven. [2.] *The angel of the bottomless pit*; an angel still, but a fallen angel, fallen into the bottomless pit, vastly large, and out of which there is no recovery. [3.] In these infernal regions he is a sort of prince and governor, and has the powers of darkness under his rule and command. [4.] His true name is *Abaddon, Apollyon—a destroyer*, for that is his business, his design, and employment, to which he diligently attends, in which he is very successful, and takes a horrid hellish pleasure; it is about this destroying work that he sends out his emissaries and armies to destroy the souls of men. And now here we have the end of one woe; and where one ends another begins."[208]

A.R. Fausset in his commentary adds, "Abaddon--that is, *perdition or destruction* (Job 26:6 Pro 27:20). The locusts are supernatural instruments in the hands of Satan to torment, and yet not kill, the ungodly, under this fifth trumpet. Just as in the case of godly Job, Satan was allowed to torment with elephantiasis, but not to touch his *life*. In Rev 9:20 , these two woe-trumpets are expressly called "plagues." ANDREAS OF CAESAREA, A.D. 500, held, in his *Commentary on Revelation*, that the locusts mean *evil spirits* again permitted to come forth on earth and afflict men with various plagues."[209]

Up to this point, the trumpets have signaled the coming of destruction and death. The fifth trumpet, the first woe is torment, pain and suffering so fiercely terrible that men will seek to die, but will not be allowed to do so. And for those of you still trying to figure out a date, keep in mind that while the blowing of trumpets announces the advent of Christ, this fifth trumpet and first woe continues for a space of five months. The day and the hour of Christ's return are still an unknown even at this time. The moral is that our focal point in life is to be living by the Word of God each and every day true to our heritage.

The parable of the ten virgins makes this very point. "And five of them were wise, and five were foolish. They that were foolish took their lamps, and took no oil with them: But the wise took oil in their vessels with their lamps. And at midnight there was a cry made, Behold, the bridegroom comes; go you out to meet him. And the foolish said unto the wise, Give us of your oil; for our lamps are gone out. But the wise answered, saying, Not so; lest there be not enough for us and you: but go you rather to them that sell, and buy for yourselves. And while they went to buy, the bridegroom came; and they that were ready went in with him to the marriage: and the door was shut. Afterward came also the other virgins, saying, Lord, Lord, open to us. But he answered and said, Verily I say unto you, I know you not."[210]

We are reminded in all four of the gospels, "He that loves his life shall lose it; and he that hates his life in this world shall keep it unto life eternal. If any man serve me, let him follow me; and where I am, there shall also my servant be: if any man serve me, him will my Father honor."[211] In other words, we need to follow after Christ every day wherever it may lead.

"And the sixth angel sounded, and I heard a voice from the four horns of the golden altar which is before God, Saying to the sixth angel which had the trumpet, Loose the four angels which are bound in the great river Euphrates. And the four angels were loosed, which were prepared for an hour, and a day, and a month, and a year, for to slay the third part of men. And the number of the army of the horsemen were two hundred thousand thousand: and I heard the number of them. And thus I saw the horses in the vision, and them that sat on them, having breastplates of fire, and of jacinth, and brimstone: and the heads of the horses were as the heads of lions; and out of their mouths issued fire and smoke and brimstone.

"By these three was the third part of men killed, by the fire, and by the smoke, and by the brimstone, which issued out of their mouths. For their power is in their mouth, and in their tails: for their tails were like unto serpents, and had heads, and with them they do hurt. And the rest of the men which were not killed by these plagues yet repented not of the works of their hands, that they should not worship devils, and idols of gold, and silver, and brass, and stone, and of wood: which neither can see, nor hear, nor walk: Neither repented they of their murders, nor of their sorceries, nor of their fornication, nor of their thefts."[212]

The great river Euphrates is the historical site of the heart of the first Babylonian empire. Christ's return marks the destruction of Babylon the Great. It appears that this latter Babylonian empire will have a military of at least two hundred thousand thousand, which is to say two hundred million men under arms. This vast army will lose a third of them or more than sixty-six million killed. It may well be the single largest loss of human life since the foundation of the Earth. And this will take place over a year, one month one day and one hour. Yet despite this great defeat, we are told that those men of war not killed refused to change their ways. They continued in their idolatry. Remember, Ishtar is the Babylonian goddess of fertility and war.

The time of the blowing of the seven trumpets occurs after the beginning of the sixth empire. "And they worshipped the dragon which gave power unto the beast: and they worshipped the beast [*metaphorically, a brutal and savage man*], saying, Who is like unto the beast? who is able to make war with him?" The question is raised because for three and a half years, the dragon and the beast, the sixth empire of Edom, will be allowed to continue.

"And there was given unto him a mouth speaking great things and blasphemies; and power *was* given unto him to continue forty and two months. And he opened his mouth in blasphemy against God, to blaspheme his name, and his tabernacle, and them that dwell in heaven. And it was given unto him to make war with the saints, and to overcome them [*the time of Jacob's trouble*]: and power was given him over all kindreds, and tongues, and nations. And all that dwell upon the earth shall worship him, whose names are not written in the book of life of the Lamb slain from the foundation of the world."[213]

As all that dwell upon the Earth shall worship the beast, it can explain the vast number of the two hundred million man army. And it would explain the question, "Who is able to make war with him?" The answer would be in the sounding of the sixth trumpet, the first woe when the four angels of the Euphrates are let loose to make war with Babylon the Great for the specified amount of time.

After the sixth trumpet sounds another angel comes down from heaven. "But in the days of the voice of the seventh angel, when he shall begin to sound, the mystery of God should be finished, as he has declared to his servants the prophets. And he had in his hand a little book open: and he set his right foot upon the sea, and his left foot on the earth. And cried with a loud voice, as when a lion roars: and when he had cried, seven thunders uttered their voices. And when the seven thunders had uttered their voices, I was about to write: and I heard a voice from heaven saying unto me, Seal up those things which the seven thunders uttered, and write them not."[214]

We aren't told then what the seven thunders said. But whatever it was, at first it seemed sweet but turned to bitterness as hope turns to disappointment. "And I went unto the angel, and said unto him, Give me the little book. And he said unto me, Take it, and eat it up; and it shall make your belly bitter, but it shall be in your mouth sweet as honey."[215]

The second woe involves the two witnesses as described in the eleventh chapter of Revelation. "And there was given me a reed like unto a rod: and the angel stood, saying, Rise, and measure the temple of God, and the altar, and them that worship therein. But the court which is without the temple leave out, and measure it not; for it is given unto the Gentiles: and the holy city shall they tread under foot forty and two months."[216]

The sixth empire, the rule of Edom, the gentiles or heathen in this case, shall last for three and a half years or forty-two months. During that time they shall trample Jerusalem. But during this same time, the two witnesses shall have power to afflict the Earth from their place in Jerusalem. The events of the sixth seal and including the sounding of the sixth trumpet occur within this forty-two month period.

"And I will give power unto my two witnesses, and they shall prophesy a thousand two hundred and threescore days, clothed in sackcloth. These are the two olive trees, and the two candlesticks standing before the God of the earth. These have power to shut heaven, that it rain not in the days of their prophecy: and have power over waters to turn them to blood, and to smite the earth with all plagues, as often as they will. And when they shall have finished their testimony, the beast that ascends out of the bottomless pit shall make war against them, and shall overcome them, and kill them."[217]

The reference to the two candlesticks may be a reference to the fact that the witnesses here represent the House of Israel and the House of Judah. The reference also is that these two witnesses are the two olive trees, which Paul references by metaphor in Romans, "And if some of the branches be broken off, and you, being a wild olive tree [*House of Israel*], were grafted in among them, and with them partake of the root and fatness of the olive tree [*House of Judah*]...."[218]

This is a reference that while the House of Israel was divorced by God, leaving only the House of Judah as heir to the birthright, the roles were reversed by Christ at his first coming when the old covenant was put away. The House of Israel is the wild olive tree, being divorced, while the House of Judah was the olive tree. The House of Israel was grafted back into its place before God. But at the return of Christ, the two shall be as one once again.

"And their dead bodies shall lie in the street of the [great] city, which spiritually is called Sodom and Egypt, where also our Lord was crucified. And they of the people and kindreds and tongues and nations shall see their dead bodies three days and a half, and shall not allow their dead bodies to be put in graves. And they that dwell upon the earth shall rejoice over them, and make merry, and shall send gifts one to another; because these two prophets tormented them that dwell on the earth."[219]

The bodies of the two witnesses will lie in the streets of Jerusalem, which at this point is spiritually called Sodom and Egypt. It is compared to Sodom because of the great wickedness that is taking place during this three and a half years. And it is compared to Egypt for all Israel will be under the merciless rule to the beast of this sixth empire, under the foot of Edom who vowed to kill his brother Jacob except for those sealed by God. "And he had power to give life unto the image of the beast, that the image of the beast should both speak, and cause that as many as would not worship the image of the beast should be killed."[220]

"And after three days and a half the Spirit of life from God entered into them, and they stood upon their feet; and great fear fell upon them which saw them. And they heard a great voice from heaven saying unto them, Come up here. And they ascended up to heaven in a cloud; and their enemies beheld them. And the same hour was there a great earthquake, and the tenth part of the city fell, and in the earthquake were slain of men seven thousand: and the remnant were frightened, and gave glory to the God of heaven. The second woe is past; and, behold, the third woe comes quickly."[221]

The seventh angel sounds the seventh, or last trumpet. This signals the third woe and the imminent return of Christ when his foot shall touch down on the Mount of Olives. As the account in Matthew tells us, "And then shall appear the sign of the Son of man in heaven: and then shall all the tribes of the earth mourn, and they shall see the Son of man coming in the clouds of heaven with power and great glory. And he shall send his angels with a great sound of a trumpet, and they shall gather together his elect from the four winds, from one end of heaven to the other."[222]

In the Old Testament we read, "*And it shall come to pass in that day, that the LORD shall thresh from the channel of the river unto the stream of Egypt, and you shall be gathered one by one, O you *children of Israel*. And it shall come to pass *in that day*, the *great trumpet shall be blown*, and they shall come which were ready to perish in the land of Assyria [*the House of Israel*], and the outcasts in the land of Egypt, and shall worship the LORD in the holy mount at Jerusalem."[223]

Remember, it was the Assyrians that took captive the children of the House of Israel first from the land of Galilee when they were cut off from God and his promises. Also, the children of Israel were the outcasts in the land of Egypt. The blowing of the seventh trumpet marks the gathering of the children of Israel by Christ at his second coming. This rings true with what Christ said about his first coming. "I am not sent except to the lost sheep of the House of Israel."

"And the seventh angel sounded; and there were great voices in heaven, saying, The kingdoms of this world are become the kingdoms of our Lord, and of his Christ; and he shall reign for ever and ever."[224]

"For the Lord himself shall descend from heaven with a shout, with the voice of the archangel, and with the trump[et] of God...."[225] The fall of both Jericho and Babylon the Great are preceded by a shout, then the blowing of trumpets.

"And the nations were angry, and your wrath is come, and the time of the dead, that they should be judged, and that you should give reward unto your servants the prophets, and to the saints, and them that fear your name, small and great; and should destroy them which destroy the earth."[226]

This also marks the first resurrection. "And I saw thrones, and they sat upon them, and judgment was given unto them: and I saw the souls of them that were beheaded for the witness of Jesus, and for the word of God, and which had not worshipped the beast, neither his image, neither had received his mark upon their foreheads, or in their hands; and they lived and reigned with Christ a thousand years. But the rest of the dead lived not again until the thousand years were finished. This is the first resurrection. Blessed and holy is he that has part in the first resurrection: on such the second death has no power, but they shall be priests of God and of Christ, and shall reign with him a thousand years."[227]

The disciples asked about the events marking the day of Christ's return, "And as he sat upon the mount of Olives, the disciples came unto him privately, saying, Tell us, when shall these things be? and what shall be the sign of your coming, and of the end of the world?"[228]

Then in the book of Acts, "And when he had spoken these things, while they beheld, he was taken up; and a cloud received him out of their sight. And while they looked steadfastly toward heaven as he went up, behold, two men stood by them in white apparel. Which also said, You men of Galilee, why stand you gazing up into heaven? this same Jesus, which is taken up from you into heaven, shall so come in like manner as you have seen him go into heaven. Then returned they unto Jerusalem from the mount called Olivet, which is from Jerusalem a sabbath day's journey."[229]

We find in the Old Testament, that on the day of Christ's return, "*And his feet shall stand in that day upon the mount of Olives, which is before Jerusalem on the east, and the mount of Olives shall cleave in the midst thereof toward the east and toward the west, and there shall be a very great valley; and half of the mountain shall remove toward the north, and half of it toward the south."[230]

As we can see from these references in both the Old and New Testaments, that the Biblical record is truly one book written to the same people. When Christ was asked about the sign of his second coming, it was done so on the Mount of Olives. Forty days after Christ's resurrection, and upon his ascension into heaven, this too takes place on the Mount of Olives. And when Christ returns at his second coming, once again it is to the same place according to an Old Testament prophecy, the Mount of Olives. His second coming will usher in a thousand years of peace. And even today, the olive branch is the symbol of peace.

"But I would not have you to be ignorant, brethren, concerning them which are asleep, that you sorrow not, even as others which have no hope. For if we believe that Jesus died and rose again, even so them also which sleep in Jesus will God bring with him. For this we say unto you by the word of the Lord, that we which are alive and remain unto the coming of the Lord shall not prevent them which are asleep...and the dead in Christ shall rise first: Then we which are alive and remain shall be caught up together with them in the clouds, to meet the Lord in the air: and so shall we ever be with the Lord."[231]

"In a moment, in the twinkling of an eye, at the last [*seventh*] trump: for *the trumpet shall sound*, and the dead shall be raised incorruptible, and we shall be changed. For this corruptible must put on incorruption, and this mortal must put on immortality. Therefore, my beloved brethren, be you steadfast, unmovable, always abounding in the work of the Lord, forasmuch as you know that your labor is not in vain in the Lord."[232]

"And I saw another sign in heaven, great and marvelous, seven angels having the seven last plagues; for in them is filled up the wrath of God. And I saw as it were a sea of glass mingled with fire: and them that had gotten the victory over the beast, and over his image, and over his mark, and over the number of his name, stand on the sea of glass, having the harps of God. And *they sing the song of Moses* the servant of God, and the song of the Lamb, saying, Great and marvelous are your works, Lord God Almighty; just and true are your ways, you King of saints. Who shall not fear you, O Lord, and glorify your name? for you only are holy: for all nations shall come and worship before you; for your judgments are made manifest."[233]

"Who would not fear you, O King?" from Jeremiah ten sounds a lot like "Who shall not fear you, O Lord?" in Revelation. If you recall, in the warning the House of Israel receives about Christmas and the tree, this question was asked. So now here is the fulfillment of that future Day of Trumpets by Christ at his second coming, preceded by the apocalypse, the time of Jacob's, all Israel's, trouble and the same question again is being asked of Israel. It's probably safe to assume that the answer will be different after the events here in Revelation than it is today.

However, the correct answer to this question posed in the New Testament book of Revelation is answered in the Old Testament book of Kings, "*But the LORD, who brought you up out of the land of Egypt with great power and a stretched out arm, him shall you fear, and him shall you worship...."[234]

In this account here in the New Testament Book of Revelation, those who had gotten victory over the beast, the Edomite sixth empire, *sing the song of Moses*.[235] All Israel was brought out of the land of Egypt by the hand of God and his servant Moses. To whom were the ordinances of the holy days given? Moses. "*And the LORD spoke unto Moses, saying, Speak unto the children of Israel, saying, In the seventh month, in the first day of the month, shall you have a sabbath, a memorial of blowing of trumpets, an holy convocation."[236]

And what is this event fulfilling? The high holy Day of Trumpets, which marks the beginning of the civil new year as recorded in the book of Leviticus. And it is as we read in the beginning of chapter eleven in Revelation, "The kingdoms of this world are become the kingdoms of our Lord, and of his Christ; and he shall reign for ever and ever."[237]

This fulfilling of Trumpets denotes a civil new year, one that establishes the kingdom or government of God on Earth closing the book on the era of the kingdoms of men. As it was written in chapter nine of Isaiah, "For unto us a child is born, unto us a son is given: and the government shall be upon his shoulder...."

"And I saw heaven opened, and behold a white horse; and he that sat upon him was called Faithful and True, and in righteousness he does judge and make war. His eyes were as a flame of fire, and on his head were many crowns; and he had a name written, that no man knew, but he himself. And he was clothed with a vesture dipped in blood: and his name is called The Word of God.

And the armies, which were in heaven followed him upon white horses, clothed in fine linen, white and clean.

"And out of his mouth goes a sharp sword, that with it he should smite the nations: and he shall rule them with a rod of iron: and he treads the winepress of the fierceness and wrath of Almighty God. And he has on his vesture and on his thigh a name written, KING OF KINGS, AND LORD OF LORDS.

"And I saw an angel standing in the sun; and he cried with a loud voice, saying to all the fowls that fly in the midst of heaven, Come and gather yourselves together unto the supper of the great God; That you may eat the flesh of kings, and the flesh of captains, and the flesh of mighty men, and the flesh of horses, and of them that sit on them, and the flesh of all men, both free and bond, both small and great.

"And I saw the beast, and the kings of the earth, and their armies, gathered together to make war against him that sat on the horse, and against his army. And the beast was taken, and with him the false prophet that wrought miracles before him, with which he deceived them that had received the mark of the beast, and them that worshipped his image. These both were cast alive into a lake of fire burning with brimstone. And the remnant were slain with the sword of him that sat upon the horse, which sword proceeded out of his mouth: and all the fowls were filled with their flesh."[238]

"And after these things I saw another angel come down from heaven, having great power; and the earth was lightened with his glory. And he cried mightily with a strong voice, saying, Babylon the great is fallen, is fallen, and is become the habitation of devils, and the hold of every foul spirit, and a cage of every unclean and hateful bird.

"For all nations have drunk of the wine of the wrath of her fornication, and the kings of the earth have committed fornication with her, and the merchants of the earth are waxed rich through the abundance of her delicacies. And I heard another voice from heaven, saying, Come out of her, my people, that you be not partakers of her sins, and that you receive not of her plagues. For her sins have reached unto heaven, and God has remembered her iniquities...How much she has glorified herself, and lived deliciously, so much torment and sorrow give her: for she says in her heart, I sit a queen, and am no widow, and shall see no sorrow.

"Therefore shall her plagues come in one day, death, and mourning, and famine; and she shall be utterly burned with fire: for strong is the Lord God who judges her...And a mighty angel took up a stone like a great millstone, and cast it into the sea, saying, Thus with violence shall that great city Babylon be thrown down, and shall be found no more at all."[239]

The seventh angel has seven vials to pour out on the Earth. Remember there are seven seals, seven trumpets and then seven vials containing the seven last plagues. These plagues shall come in one day.

"And after that I looked, and, behold, the temple of the tabernacle of the testimony in heaven was opened: And the seven angels came out of the temple, having *the seven plagues*, clothed in pure and white linen, and having their breasts girded with golden girdles. And one of the four beasts gave unto the seven angels seven golden vials full of the wrath of God, who lives forever and ever. And the temple was filled with smoke from the glory of God, and from his power; and no man was able to enter into the temple, till the seven plagues of the seven angels were fulfilled."[240]

"And I heard a great voice out of the temple saying to the seven angels, Go your ways, and pour out the vials of the wrath of God upon the earth. And the first went, and poured out his vial upon the earth; and there fell a noisome and grievous sore upon the men, which had the mark of the beast, and upon them, which worshipped his image.

"And the second angel poured out his vial upon the sea; and it became as the blood of a dead man: and every living soul died in the sea.

"And the third angel poured out his vial upon the rivers and fountains of waters; and they became blood. And I heard the angel of the waters say, Thou art righteous, O Lord, which is, and was, and shall be, because you hast judged thus. For they have shed the blood of saints and prophets, and you hast given them blood to drink; for they are worthy. And I heard another out of the altar say, Even so, Lord God Almighty, true and righteous are your judgments.

"And the fourth angel poured out his vial upon the sun; and power was given unto him to scorch men with fire. And men were scorched with great heat, and blasphemed the name of God, which has power over these plagues: and they repented not to give him glory.

"And the fifth angel poured out his vial upon the seat of the beast; and his kingdom was full of darkness; and they gnawed their tongues for pain, And blasphemed the God of heaven because of their pains and their sores, and repented not of their deeds.

"And the sixth angel poured out his vial upon the great river Euphrates; and the water thereof was dried up, that the way of the kings of the east might be prepared. And I saw three unclean spirits like frogs come out of the mouth of the dragon, and out of the mouth of the beast, and out of the mouth of the false prophet. For they are the spirits of devils, working miracles, which go forth unto the kings of the earth and of the whole world, to gather them to the battle of that great day of God Almighty. Behold, I come as a thief. Blessed is he that watches, and keeps his garments, lest he walk naked, and they see his shame. And he gathered them together into a place called in the Hebrew tongue Armageddon.

"And the seventh angel poured out his vial into the air; and there came a great voice out of the temple of heaven, from the throne, saying, It is done. And there were voices, and thunders, and lightnings; and there was a great earthquake, such as was not since men were upon the earth, so mighty an earthquake, and so great. And the great city was divided into three parts, and the cities of the nations fell: and great Babylon came in remembrance before God, to give unto her the cup of the wine of the fierceness of his wrath.

"And every island fled away, and the mountains were not found." This is a difference from what we read of the time of Jacob's trouble upon opening of the sixth seal. There the islands and the mountains were moved out of their place. Here they disappear altogether.

"And there fell upon men a great hail out of heaven, every stone about the weight of a talent [*about sixty pounds or twenty-seven kilos*]: and men blasphemed God because of the plague of the hail; for the plague thereof was exceeding great."[241]

At the beginning of this chapter we began with Christ sitting on the Mount of Olives with his disciples who were asking Christ about these events and the timing of his return just as many do today. "And as he sat upon the Mount of Olives over against the temple, Peter and James and John and Andrew asked him privately, Tell us, when shall these things be? And what shall be the sign when all these things shall be fulfilled?"

Christ answered them, "For many shall come in my name, saying, I am Christ; and shall deceive many. And when you shall hear of wars and rumors of wars [*as we have again with the Middle East recently*], be you not troubled: for such things must need be; but the end shall not be yet. For nation shall rise against nation, and kingdom against kingdom: and there shall be earthquakes in diverse places, and there shall be famines and troubles: these are the *beginnings of sorrows*.[242] But take heed to yourselves: for they shall deliver you up to councils; and in the synagogues you shall be beaten: and you shall be brought before rulers and kings for my sake, for a testimony against them."[243]

Christ was outlining to his apostles the first five seals found in Revelation that we read about in the beginning of this chapter. He was telling them that these things need to take place, but are not harbingers of the day of his coming. We've read about the seven trumpets that mark the beginning of the events leading up to the last trump, which marks the first resurrection of the first fruits and Christ's return.

"For in those days shall be affliction, such as was not from the beginning of the creation which God created unto this time, neither shall be. And except that the Lord had shortened those days, no flesh should be saved: but for the elect's sake, whom he has chosen, he has shortened the days."[244]

This cascade of events fulfill the Day of Trumpets by Christ, first observed by our ancestors as a high holy day upon their coming out of bondage in Egypt. This day ties together the days of the Old Testament and the kingdoms of men to the New Testament and the ushering in not only a new civil year, but a new era of government established by the kingdom of God. It is a day looked forward to by Christianity because Christians, whether or not we realize it, are the lost sheep of the House of Israel.

To review, Christ opened the first five seals just after his first coming. They are the beginning of sorrows and continue today. As he said, "I am not come to send peace, but a sword." The sixth seal has yet to be opened by Christ. It is the time of Jacob's trouble when Edom shall gain dominion. Isaac spoke this prophecy nearly four thousand years ago. It has yet come to pass, but it is near. "*And by the sword shall you [*Esau/Edom*] live and you shall serve your brother [*Jacob/Israel*]; and it shall come to pass when you shall have the dominion that you shall break his yoke from off your neck." Then Esau said in his heart, "I will slay my brother Jacob."[245]

The seven trumpets will sound, and at the sounding of the seventh trumpet or last trump, Babylon the Great, the sixth empire will be destroyed in one day and then Christ will return to set foot on the Mount of Olives.

The duality of the Day of Trumpets should be very clear. It is the next high holy day to be fulfilled by Christ. The hijacked pagan festivals, Christmas, with Santa and the tree, as well as the Easter bunny, Ishtar, the Babylonian goddess of fertility and war [or the sword], are obvious fakes. They serve no purpose other than to put us off the straight and narrow path that the high holy days were designed to keep us on. When considering the direction of Christianity and our circumstances today, it is not surprising that these fakes are very firmly entrenched and are becoming more so each year.

Not knowing who we are, thinking that Christ came to save the gentiles of the world rather than the lost sheep of the House of Israel has blinded us. We are blind to the deceits that will lead us into our time of trouble. Yet we are given fair warning. As we just read, "Come out of her, my people, that you be not partakers of her sins, and that you receive not of her plagues. For her sins have reached unto heaven, and God has remembered her iniquities."[246]

This is a reference to that spiritual Babylon, the perpetrator of hijacked pagan festivals, the sixth empire, our brother Edom who seeks to kill us. All theses events in Revelation have their roots in the book of Genesis. The characters in Genesis are here in Revelation. The Biblical record is one story written to the same people. And those people are the children of Israel, all Israel "who drank of that spiritual rock, and that Rock was Christ."

Whether or not we know the date of Christ's return, in one sense is irrelevant for us as Christians. Our faith is to be our way of life, everyday. It is not something that is done once a week and on special occasions a couple times a year, falsely honoring the hijacked elephant.

Chapter Six
Christ and the Duality of Atonement

The previous chapter was about the return of Christ marked by the Day of Trumpets. It marks the beginning of the new civil year, the first day of the seventh month in the autumn. The Passover signaled the beginning of the sacred year in the spring. The high holy day that follows Trumpets is the Day of Atonement. It is the most solemn of the high holy days. The Day of Atonement is national in scope, unlike Pentecost, which is personal in nature. It is a future national day of reconciliation, yet to be fulfilled for Jacob, both the House of Israel and the House of Judah that will result in a new covenant, our redemption set in motion by Christ's death and resurrection.

"For if that first covenant had been faultless, then should no place have been sought for the second. For finding fault with them, he said, Behold, the days come, says the Lord, when I will make a new covenant with the House of Israel and with the House of Judah: Not according to the covenant that I made with their fathers in the day when I took them by the hand to lead them out of the land of Egypt; because they continued not in my covenant, and I regarded them not, said the Lord."[247] This quote is from the New Testament.

"*Behold, the days come, says the LORD, that I will make a new covenant with the House of Israel, and with the House of Judah: Not according to the covenant that I made with their fathers in the day that I took them by the hand to bring them out of the land of Egypt; which my covenant they broke, although I was an husband unto them, says the LORD …."[248] This quote is from the Old Testament book of Jeremiah.

These two quotes are virtually identical. The New Testament writer, most likely the apostle Paul, was quoting from Jeremiah in the Old Testament. And they both refer to a reconciling on a national level. This is to take place just after the return of Christ on that future Day of Trumpets. But prior to this, from Christ's first coming up to our current day, we've read that on a personal level the first fruits of the House of Israel are reconciled through repentance, baptism and the receiving of the Holy Spirit marked by the day of Pentecost nearly 2000 years ago.

"For this is the covenant that I will make with the *House of Israel* after those days, says the Lord; I will put my laws into their mind, and write them in their hearts: and I will be to them a God, and they shall be to me a people: And they shall not teach every man his neighbor, and every man his brother, saying, Know the Lord: for all shall know me, from the least to the greatest. For I will be merciful to their unrighteousness, and their sins and their iniquities will I remember no more. In that he says, A new [*covenant*], he has made the first old. Now that which decays and waxes old is ready to vanish away."[249] This is in the New Testament.

"*But this shall be the covenant that I will make with the *House of Israel*; After those days, says the LORD, I will put my law in their inward parts, and write it in their hearts; and will be their God, and they shall be my people. And they shall teach no more every man his neighbor, and every man his brother, saying, Know the LORD: for they shall all know me, from the least of them unto the greatest of them, says the LORD: for I will forgive their iniquity, and I will remember their sin no more."[250] This is in the Old Testament.

Please notice that this second reference to this particular aspect of the new covenant is only for the House of Israel. Christ very plainly said, "I am not sent except to the lost sheep of the House of Israel." On that Pentecost day nearly 2000 years ago, Peter said, "Therefore let all the *House of Israel* know assuredly, that God has made that same Jesus, whom you have crucified, both Lord and Christ."[251] "I will put my law in their inward parts, and write it in their hearts" refers to the Comforter,[252] the Holy Spirit sent on that Pentecost day fulfilled by Christ. Christ is that "shoelace" that ties together both the Old and the New Testaments.

Christ's death disannulled the first covenant for both the House of Israel and the House of Judah. This paved the way for the new covenant. Initially the new covenant is made with individuals of the House of Israel, and then on a national level on this future Day of Atonement. The days of Passover, Unleavened Bread and Pentecost have been fulfilled. Christ has established a better covenant, a new covenant that is spiritual in nature rather than physical. "Now of the things which we have spoken this is the sum: We have such an high priest, who is set on the right hand of the throne of the Majesty in the heavens; But now has he obtained a more excellent ministry, by how much also he is the mediator of a better covenant, which was established upon better promises."[253]

We see that Christ "is set on the right hand of the throne of the Majesty in the heavens" and that "he is the mediator of a better covenant," present tense, which "was," past tense, "established upon better promises." At his second coming, the established new covenant will be officially made on a *national* basis with both the House of Israel and the House of Judah. This will be the time of atonement or reconciliation.

Until his return on the Day of Trumpets, and subsequently, the

Day of Atonement, it is "the covenant that I will make with the House of Israel after those days, says the Lord; I will put my laws into their mind, and write them in their hearts..."[254] that is being fulfilled now. This is the smaller, summer harvest, the time between Pentecost and this Day of Atonement. It is the time of the personal, sacred new year as opposed to the national, civil new year establishing the kingdom of God on Earth at Christ's return. It is "church and state." Church was Christ's first coming. State is his second coming.[255] Again we see that the spiritual takes precedence over the royal or governmental. Christ is our savior first and then will return as a king.

"Then said he, Lo, I come to do your will, O God. He takes away the first [*old covenant*] that he may establish the second by which we are sanctified through the offering of the body of Jesus Christ once. And every priest stands daily ministering and offering oftentimes the same sacrifices, which can never take away sins: But this man, after he had offered *one sacrifice for sins for ever*, sat down on the right hand of God; from henceforth expecting till his enemies be made his footstool."[256]

This is reference to this time between the establishing the new covenant, the time of "church," until Christ's enemies are made his footstool or put under his foot. Then, upon his return, the new covenant will be established with the "state." It is individual reconciliation first, then national atonement.

"For by *one offering he has perfected for ever* them that are sanctified. The Holy Spirit also is a witness to us: for after that he had said before, This is the covenant that I will make with them after those days, says the Lord, I will put my laws into their hearts, and in their minds will I write them; And their sins and iniquities will I remember no more. Now where remission of these is, there is no more offering for sin."²⁵⁷

The one offering of Christ, compared to daily sacrifices under the old covenant, has established a new covenant, for both the first fruits individually and then, at a date in our future, for the nations. We've seen mentioned three times here the difference between the national promises of the new covenant with the House of Israel and the House of Judah and those individuals led by the Holy Spirit beginning on the fulfillment of the day of Pentecost made at this time with the "lost sheep" of the House of Israel. On the fulfillment of the Day of Atonement, the national promises of the new covenant established by Christ will take effect.

First, we have seen the *reconciliation* to God through Christ as the mediator for the lost sheep of the House of Israel. "And for this cause he is the mediator of the new testament, that by means of death, for the redemption of the transgressions that were under the first testament, they which are called might receive the promise of eternal inheritance."²⁵⁸ Those under the first testament were all Israel. Initially however, from Pentecost until Trumpets, the application of the new testament is for the first fruits, individuals of the House of Israel. It is a new life.²⁵⁹

"*Therefore, from now on, we regard no one according to*²⁶⁰ the flesh: yea, though we have known Christ after the flesh, yet now henceforth know we him no more. Therefore if any man be in Christ, he is a new creature: old things are passed away; behold, all things are become new. And all things are of God, who has *reconciled* us to himself by Jesus Christ, and has given to us the ministry of *reconciliation*; To wit, that God was in Christ, *reconciling* the world [Greek, *kosmos*] unto himself, not imputing their trespasses unto them; and has committed unto us the word of *reconciliation*. Now then we are ambassadors for Christ, as though God did beseech you by us: we pray in Christ's stead, be you *reconciled* to God. For he has made him to be sin for us, who knew no sin; that we might be made the righteousness of God in him."[261]

"For if, when we were enemies [*the divorced state of the House of Israel, the lost sheep*], we were *reconciled* to God by the death of his Son, much more, being reconciled, we shall be saved by his life. And not only so, but we also joy in God through our Lord Jesus Christ, by whom we have now received the *atonement*. Wherefore, as by one man sin entered into the world, and death by sin; and so death passed upon all men, for that all have sinned...."[262]

We see that from Christ's first coming until Trumpets and the Day of Atonement, the children of the House of Israel are reconciled. We have received the personal atonement through repentance, baptism and receiving of the Holy Spirit emerging as a new creature or creation. Our mortal life is now of the Spirit of God rather than the spirit of man. The principle of reconciliation therefore has come to those called and chosen by God in this time since the fulfilling of Pentecost. The national reconciliation will come for all Israel on the Day of Atonement.

Now might be a good time to define atonement and reconciliation. The Hebrew verb, *kaphar* means to cover, to purge, make atonement, reconciliation. It is a covering of the sins of Israel both on a personal level and as a nation. Once again we see a duality.

In the New Testament Greek, reconciliation is the noun *katallage* meaning an exchange as with moneychangers. It is the adjustment of difference, a restoration as when you reconcile your checkbook with your bank account statements. You make corrections to adjust any differences to restore your account with the proper balance.

The common New Testament Greek verb meaning to reconcile is *apokatallass*, which means to reconcile back to a former state of harmony, hence our redemption. In our discussion then, this is to say a new covenant will restore a former state of harmony [*kosmos*], but this time it is no longer of the flesh and the law, but of the Spirit. Christ is the mediator of a better covenant. As we read above, "To wit, that God was in Christ, reconciling the world [*kosmos*] unto himself...."

The Greek word *kosmos*, translated as world, means a harmonious, ordered arrangement, implying governance. This is the new covenant of the Spirit. The old law covenant or harmonious arrangement was external in its physical governance. Its terms of agreement were broken in that no one was perfect under the law; everyone violated it. Christ has fulfilled the physical terms of that old covenant by his death on our behalf.

The new covenant is spiritual in its governance. It is the love of Christ in us through the Spirit, rather than the lusts of the flesh, that provides motivation in our daily lives, though not without a battle between the two as we still have our duality in that we are alive in the flesh. The terms of the new harmonious arrangement came first to individuals of the House of Israel; then to all the nations of Israel when the Day of Atonement is fulfilled spiritually. Once again we have a duality in the high holy days.

"And, having made peace through the blood of his cross, by him to *reconcile* all things unto himself; by him, I say, whether they be things in earth, or things in heaven. And you, that were sometime alienated and enemies in your mind by wicked works, yet now has he reconciled in the body of his flesh through death, to present you holy and unblameable and unreproveable [*unable to speak disapprovingly of*] in his sight...."[263]

Another Greek verb is *hilaskomai* means to be propitious or to appease. It is translated once in the New Testament KJV as reconciliation.

"Forasmuch then as the children are partakers of flesh and blood, he also himself likewise took part of the same; that through death he might destroy him that had the power of death, that is, the devil;[264] And deliver them who through fear of death were all their lifetime subject to bondage. For verily he took not on him the nature of angels; but he took on him the seed of Abraham. Wherefore in all things that were owed in debt he was made like unto his brethren, that he might be a merciful and faithful high priest in things pertaining to God, to make *reconciliation* for the sins of the people. For in that he himself has suffered being tempted, he is able to succor them that are tempted."[265]

Christ became human flesh as the seed of Abraham, that through his death, as a sin offering, he paid our debt having appeased the penalty of the law on our behalf. This applies to both the personal and the national debt we had to the law that death has no more power over us.

It should be pointed out again that this particular high holy day was the most solemn of the year for all Israel. In the scholarly commentary, Jamieson, Fausset and Brown, it states in regard to the Day of Atonement, "The Jewish writers suppose it to have a spiritual signification. Now at the beginning of the year they were called by this sound of trumpet to shake off their spiritual drowsiness, to search and try their ways, and to amend them: the day of atonement was the ninth day after this; and thus they were awakened to prepare for that day, by sincere and serious repentance, that it might be indeed to them a day of atonement. And they say, 'The devout Jews exercised themselves more in good works between the Day of Trumpets and the day of expiation than at any other time of the year'... This day of annual expiation for all the sins, irreverences, and impurities of all classes in Israel during the previous year, was to be observed as a solemn fast, in which "they were to afflict their souls"; it was reckoned a sabbath, kept as a season of "holy convocation," or, assembling for religious purposes. All persons who performed any labor were subject to the penalty of death (Exd 31:14, 15 35:2). It took place on the tenth day of the seventh month, corresponding to our third of October [*note: it varies year to year with our solar calendar*]; and this chapter, together with Lev 23:27-32 , as containing special allusion to the observances of the day, was publicly read. The rehearsal of these passages appointing the solemn ceremonial was very appropriate, and the details of the successive parts of it (above all the spectacle of the public departure of the scapegoat under the care of its leader) must have produced salutary impressions both of sin and of duty that would not be soon effaced."[266]

Let's go back now and read what ordinances were for the original Day of Atonement.

The High Holy Day of Atonement Remembrance: "*And the LORD spoke unto Moses, saying, Also on the tenth day of this seventh month there shall be a day of atonement: it shall be an holy convocation unto you; and you shall afflict your souls, and offer an offering made by fire unto the LORD. And you shall do no work in that same day: for it is a day of atonement, to make an atonement for you before the LORD your God. For whatsoever soul it be that shall not be afflicted in that same day, he shall be cut off from among his people. And whatsoever soul it be that does any work in that same day, the same soul will I destroy from among his people. You shall do no manner of work: it shall be a statute for ever throughout your generations in all your dwellings. It shall be unto you a sabbath of rest, and you shall afflict your souls: in the ninth day of the month at even, from even unto even, shall you celebrate your sabbath."[267]

"*It shall be unto you a sabbath of rest, and you shall afflict your souls: in the ninth day of the month at even, from even unto even, shall you celebrate your Sabbath. But you shall offer a burnt offering unto the LORD for a sweet savor; one young bullock, one ram, and seven lambs of the first year; they shall be unto you without blemish: And their meat offering shall be of flour mingled with oil, three tenth deals to a bullock, and two tenth deals to one ram, A several tenth deal for one lamb, throughout the seven lambs: One kid of the goats for a sin offering; beside the sin offering of atonement, and the continual burnt offering, and the meat offering of it, and their drink offerings."[268]

"*And this shall be a statute for ever unto you: that in the seventh month, on the tenth day of the month, you shall afflict your souls, and do no work at all, whether it be one of your own country, or a stranger that sojourns among you: For on that day shall the priest make an atonement for you, to cleanse you, that you may be clean from all your sins before the LORD. It shall be a sabbath of rest unto you, and you shall afflict your souls, by a statute for ever. And the priest, whom he shall anoint, and whom he shall consecrate to minister in the priest's office in his father's stead, shall make the atonement, and shall put on the linen clothes, even the holy garments: And he shall make an atonement for the holy sanctuary, and he shall make an atonement for the tabernacle of the congregation, and for the altar, and he shall make an atonement for the priests, and for all the people of the congregation. And this shall be an everlasting statute unto you, to make an atonement for the children of Israel for all their sins once a year. And he did as the LORD commanded Moses."[269]

Matthew Henry in his commentary from the very early 18th century points out the key aspects of the Atonement for the old covenant observation of this day. "They must on this day rest from all manner of work, and not only from servile works as on other annual festivals; it must be as strict a rest as that of the weekly sabbath, v. 28, 30, 31. The reason is: *For it is a day of atonement*. Note, The humbling of our souls for sin, and the making of our peace with God, is work that requires the whole man, and the closest application of mind imaginable, and all little enough. He that would do the work of a day of atonement in its day, as it should be done, had need lay aside the thoughts of every thing else. On that day God *spoke peace unto his people, and unto his saints*; and therefore they must lay aside all their worldly business, that they might the more clearly and the more reverently hear that voice of joy and gladness. Fasting days should be days of rest.

"2. They must afflict their souls, and this upon pain of being cut off by the hand of God, v. 27, 29, 32. They must mortify the body, and deny the appetites of it, in token of their sorrow for the sins they had committed, and the mortifying of their indwelling corruptions. Every soul must be afflicted, because every soul was polluted, and guilty before God; while none have fulfilled the law of innocency none are exempt from the law of repentance, besides that every man must sigh and cry for the *abominations of the land.*

"3. The entire day must be observed: *From even to even you shall afflict your souls* (v. 32), that is, "You shall begin your fast, and the expressions of your humiliation, in the *ninth* day of the month at even." They were to leave off all their worldly labor, and compose themselves to the work of the day approaching, some time before sun-set on the ninth day, and not to take any food (except children and sick people) till after sun-set on the tenth day. Note, The eves of solemn days ought to be employed in solemn preparation. When work for God and our souls is to be done, we should not straiten ourselves in time for the doing of it; for how can we spend our time better? Of this sabbath the rule here given is to be understood: From even unto even shall you celebrate your sabbath."[270]

The duality of the Day of Atonement, both of the old covenant, the flesh and the new covenant, the Spirit, is referred to in the New Testament book of Acts. "But those things, which God before had showed by the mouth of all his prophets, that Christ should suffer, he has so *fulfilled*. Repent you therefore, and be converted, that your sins may be blotted out, *when the times of refreshing shall come* from the presence of the Lord; And he shall send Jesus Christ [*the second time*] which before was preached unto you…."[271]

"But those things, which God before had showed by the mouth of all his prophets [*in the Old Testament*], that Christ should suffer, *he has so fulfilled*" refers to the first three high holy days already fulfilled by Christ. The two days of Unleavened Bread and the day of Pentecost.

"The times of refreshing *shall come*" is a future reference to the

Day of Atonement to be fulfilled by Christ. In other words, the Day of Atonement would have a spiritual fulfillment and it was spoken of by the prophets in the Old Testament. As you should have come to fully see by now, both the Old Testament and the New, the entire Biblical record is one book written for the same people. Christ is the central character in both. He ties them both together. This is the point made here in the book of Acts, most likely written by Luke in the early 60's of the first century.

Luke continues in Acts, "*Whom the heaven must receive until the times of restitution of all things, which God has spoken by the mouth of all his holy prophets since the world [age] began. For Moses truly said unto the fathers, A prophet shall the Lord your God raise up unto you of your brethren, like unto me; him shall you hear in all things whatsoever he shall say unto you.*"[272] Remember, the physical ordinances of the high holy days were given to Moses for the children of Israel including the high holy Day of Atonement.

The times of refreshing, the times of restitution is a specific reference to the fulfillment of the Day of Atonement in which all things will be reconciled to Christ. It is the national reconciliation of both the House of Israel and the House of Judah. And it is part of the story that has been told throughout pages of the Biblical record since the world [*age or eon*] began.

The commentary of Jamieson, Faussett, Brown points out that this turns upon the national reconciliation of Israel. "*...when the times of refreshing shall come*--rather, in order that the times of refreshing may come; that long period of repose, prosperity and joy, which all the prophets hold forth to the distracted Church and this miserable world, as eventually to come, and which is here, as in all the prophets, made to turn upon the national conversion of Israel."²⁷³ The church, again, is a reference to individuals, who should be the first fruits, though as the commentary states even in the late 19th century, they were, and we are more so now, distracted, walking off the paths the prophets and apostles set before us.

The national conversion of Israel is the fulfilling of the future Day of Atonement. There is a prophecy in the book of Isaiah that refers to this future fulfillment of the Day of Atonement by Christ. "*Thus says the LORD, the Redeemer of Israel [*Christ*], his Holy One, to him whom man despises, to him whom the nation abhors, to a servant of rulers, Kings shall see and arise, princes also shall worship, because of the LORD that is faithful, and the Holy One of Israel, and he shall choose you.

"*Thus says the LORD, In *an acceptable time* have I heard you, and in *a day of salvation* have I helped you: and I will preserve you, and give you for a covenant of the people, to establish the earth, to cause to inherit the desolate heritages [*our abandoned Genesis Birthright*]; That you may say to the prisoners, Go forth; to them that are in darkness, Show yourselves.

"*They shall feed in the ways, and their pastures shall be in all high places. They shall not hunger nor thirst; neither shall the heat nor sun smite them: for he that has mercy on them shall lead them, even by the springs of water shall he guide them. And I will make all my mountains a way, and my highways shall be exalted. Behold, these shall come from far: and, lo, these from the north and from the west; and these from the land of Sinim. Sing, O heavens; and be joyful, O earth; and break forth into singing, O mountains: for the LORD has comforted his people, and will have mercy upon his *afflicted*."²⁷⁴

The Day of Atonement was a day in which Israel was to afflict themselves before God in consideration of the seriousness and solemnity of what this day portrayed for them on a national scale. And indeed, the events preceding this future day, the time of Jacob's trouble, will greatly afflict Israel. While we have forgotten the ways our LORD has given us, Christ will not forget Israel though it may appear that way to the survivors of those days.

"*But Zion [*Jerusalem*] said, The LORD has forsaken me, and my LORD has forgotten me. Can a woman forget her sucking child, that she should not have compassion on the son of her womb? Yes, they may forget, yet will I not forget you. Behold, I have graven you upon the palms of my hands [*referring to Christ's death by crucifixion*]; your walls are continually before me...And I will feed them that oppress you with their own flesh; and they shall be drunken with their own blood, as with sweet wine: and all flesh shall know that I am the LORD your Savior and your Redeemer, the mighty One of Jacob."[275]

This quote from Isaiah is similar to what we find in Revelation concerning the national atonement. "And I saw an angel standing in the sun; and he cried with a loud voice, saying to all the fowls that fly in the midst of heaven, Come and gather yourselves together unto the supper of the great God; That you may eat the flesh of kings, and the flesh of captains, and the flesh of mighty men, and the flesh of horses, and of them that sit on them, and the flesh of all [men, both] free and bond, both small and great."[276]

In the book of Malachi, one of the prophetic restoration books written after the Babylonian captivity about 400 BCE, it says, "*And I will come near to you to judgment; and I will be a swift witness against the sorcerers, and against the adulterers, and against false swearers, and against those that oppress the hireling in his wages, the widow, and the fatherless, and that turn aside the stranger, and fear not me, says the LORD of hosts. For I am the LORD, I change not; therefore you sons of Jacob are not consumed. Even from the days of your fathers you are gone away from mine ordinances, and have not kept them. Return unto me, and I will return unto you, says the LORD of hosts. But you said, Wherein shall we return?"[277]

Today, hijacked holidays have blinded us to the fact we've left. However, Jeremiah provides the answer to our question. "*In those days, and in that time, says the LORD, *the children of Israel shall come, they and the children of Judah together*, going and weeping: they shall go, and seek the LORD their God. They shall ask the way to Zion [*Jerusalem*] with their faces towards there, saying, Come, and *let us join ourselves to the LORD in a perpetual covenant that shall not be forgotten*. My people have been lost sheep: their shepherds have caused them to go astray, they have turned them away on the mountains: they have gone from mountain to hill, they have forgotten their resting place [*the high holy day sabbaths, days of rest*]. All that found them have devoured them: and their adversaries said, We offend not, because they have sinned against the LORD, the habitation of justice, even the LORD, the hope of their fathers."[278]

Even though Jeremiah lived at the time of the first Babylonian empire, this is a prophecy. Both the children of Israel and of Judah will be joined again, this time in a perpetual covenant that shall not be forgotten as they forgot the first. Obviously, this has not occurred in the past 2400 or so years since Jeremiah wrote it.

According to the Biblical text, the reason Israel were lost sheep is that their shepherds caused them to go astray. As Jeremiah pointed out in chapter ten, the chapter warning the House of Israel concerning the Christmas tree and its celebration, their "pastors are become stupid and have not sought the LORD."²⁷⁹

This is a pretty strong statement. The reason they have "caused them to go astray" is simply assuming, wrongly that "We have every right to take these things and spin them with the goodness of the Lord as part of the Great Commission…We take something bad and make it good." This deceitful line of reasoning is similar to what Eve was told in the garden of Eden by Satan. "But of the fruit of the tree which is in the midst of the garden, God has said, You shall not eat of it, neither shall you touch it, lest you die. And the serpent said unto the woman, You shall not surely die…." Taking pagan based festivals and shuffling them into Christianity justifying it on the basis that it is done for good reason for God's commission is stupid…and deadly. That's the hijacked elephant.

Jeremiah also pointed out as we just read, "*All that found them have devoured them [*all the children of Israel*]: and their adversaries said, We offend not, because they have sinned against the LORD, the habitation of justice, even the LORD, the hope of their fathers." Of course, it's easy to be devoured when we have no idea who we are or what days we should be mindful of. The excuse offered by our adversaries sounds very much like Edom, the sixth empire, who will have dominion over Israel for three and a half years. Yet, it is no excuse to justify their actions according to God. In other words, Christ will deal with us. No outsiders can justify their interference in a family matter. To do so, they proceed at their own peril.

Our LORD warns them, "*You should not have entered into the gate of my people in the day of their calamity [*time of Jacob's trouble*]; yes, you should not have looked on their affliction, in the day of their calamity, nor have laid hands on their substance in the day of their calamity...But *upon mount Zion shall be deliverance*, and there shall be holiness; and the house of Jacob shall possess their possessions."[280] Edom, in other words, will not get the birthright.

"And I looked, and, lo, *a Lamb stood on the mount Sion, and with him an hundred forty and four thousand*, having his Father's name written in their foreheads."[281] These are the children of Israel, the House of Jacob who have been sealed.

It is after events of the Day of Trumpets, after the day when those sealed stand on mount Sion that the Day of Atonement will be fulfilled by Christ. "And after these things I heard a great voice of much people in heaven, saying, Alleluia; Salvation, and glory, and honor, and power, unto the Lord our God: For true and righteous are his judgments: for he has judged the great whore, which did corrupt the earth with her fornication, and has avenged the blood of his servants at her hand. And again they said, Alleluia. And her smoke rose up for ever and ever. And the four and twenty elders and the four beasts fell down and worshipped God that sat on the throne, saying, Amen; Alleluia And a voice came out of the throne, saying, Praise our God, all you his servants, and you that fear him, both small and great. And I heard as it were the voice of a great multitude, and as the voice of many waters, and as the voice of mighty thunderings, saying, Alleluia: for the Lord God omnipotent reigns."[282] This marks the fulfillment of Trumpets. The events that follow mark the Day of Atonement or national reconciliation.

"Let us be glad and rejoice, and give honor to him: *for the marriage of the Lamb is come, and his wife has made herself ready*. And to her was granted that she should be *arrayed in fine linen*, clean and white: for the fine linen is the righteousness of saints. And he said unto me, Write, Blessed are they, which are called unto the marriage supper of the Lamb. And he said unto me, These are the true sayings of God. And I fell at his feet to worship him. And he said unto me, See you do it not: I am your fellow servant, and of your brethren that have the testimony of Jesus: worship God: for the testimony of Jesus is the spirit of prophecy."[283]

The marriage of the Lamb is the Day of Atonement. We find another duality in the high holy days. "*And the priest, whom he shall anoint, and whom he shall consecrate to minister in the priest's office in his father's stead, shall make the atonement, and shall put on the linen clothes, the holy garments: And he *shall make an atonement* for the holy sanctuary, and he shall make an atonement for the tabernacle of the congregation, and for the altar, and he shall *make an atonement* for the priests, and for all the people of the congregation. And this shall be an everlasting statute unto you, to *make an atonement* for the children of Israel for all their sins once a year. And he did as the LORD commanded Moses." [284]

The high priest, on behalf of the children of Israel, wore linen garments when atoning for their sins. And on the future Day of Atonement for all the children of Israel, they shall wear fine linen, too, spiritually symbolic of the righteousness of the saints when they stand before Christ, their high priest. The duality of the flesh and of the Spirit began in the flesh about 4000 years ago when Christ, "the LORD, spoke unto Moses, saying, Also on the tenth day of this seventh month there shall be a day of atonement...." It is a day of reconciliation between the House of Israel and the House of Judah, all Israel, which will come full circle in the Spirit with the marriage of the Lamb, Christ.

While Israel has forsaken the covenant that God made with them in that day when they were delivered out of Egypt from slavery and hardship and brought into the promised land by Joshua, Christ, who has loved Israel and was that Spiritual Rock that Israel drank from on their sojourn out of Egypt, shall make a new covenant with them this day. It is portrayed as a wedding day, a solemn occasion, when Israel will take their vows, not with a fleshly covenant, but a new perpetual covenant entered into in the Spirit, and with the laws of love and peace written in their hearts.

When Christ was asked by the Pharisees, "Why don't your disciples fast?" as the Day of Atonement is a day of fasting and represents the marriage of the Lamb, he said, "Can the children of the bridechamber mourn, as long as the bridegroom is with them? but the days will come, when the bridegroom shall be taken from them, and then shall they fast."[285] And as Christ was taken from them, so shall he return, fulfilling the fast, the affliction of this Day of Atonement as the bridegroom.

Recall, the House of Israel so thoroughly violated the original agreement, their vows, that they were literally divorced, "*...my covenant they broke, although *I was a husband unto them*, says the LORD ...." The House of Judah was no better, but because of the promises of Christ to Israel and David, they were not put away, but were taken into captivity for 70 years in Babylon. "*And I saw, when for all the causes whereby backsliding Israel committed adultery I had put her away, and given her a bill of divorce; yet her treacherous sister Judah feared not, but went and played the harlot also."[286]

Yet Christ so loved Israel, that he took the form of Abraham's seed, that is, he became flesh, and as the Son of God, paid the penalty of death so that he could, on this day once again, be the bridegroom, the husband of all Israel.

The covenant with House of Judah ended with Christ's death, as do all marriages when one spouse dies. The House of Judah legally then became a widow. This is the point Paul is making in the book of Romans. "What then? Israel has not obtained that which he seeks for; but the election has obtained it, and the rest were blinded."[287] Up to Christ's first coming only the House of Judah, of all the nations of Israel, was still in a covenant or marriage relationship.

But that changed as Paul tells us. "I say then, Have they [*the House of Judah*] stumbled that they should fall? God forbid: but rather through their fall salvation is come unto the nations [*of the House of Israel*], for to provoke them to jealousy... For if the *first fruit* be holy, the lump is also: and if the root be holy, so are the branches. Will you say then, The branches [*the House of Judah*] were broken off, that I might be grafted in. Well because of unbelief they were broken off, and you stand by faith. Be not high-minded, but fear: For if God spared not the natural branches, take heed lest he also spare not you...For I would not, brethren, that you should be ignorant of this mystery, lest you should be wise in your own conceits; that blindness in part is happened to Israel [*the House of Judah part*], until the fullness of the nations [*of the House of Israel*] be come in."[288]

The fullness refers to the harvest of the first fruits of the House of Israel, as Peter stated, that began at Pentecost nearly 2000 years ago and comes to fruition at the sounding of the last trumpet. Then the national blindness of Judah will be lifted and a new covenant will be made with the nations of Judah and Israel.

At Christ's first coming, the covenant relationship with the House of Judah was ended. A new covenant was established with the individuals, the election or those chosen, of the House of Israel. This is what Christianity commonly refers to as "the church." Paul's reference to the election is that of the first fruits of the House of Israel. It is the time of the priesthood, in the sacred year before the reconciling of all the nations of Israel in the civil year marked by Christ's return.

Because of Christ's abiding love for Judah too, all these millennia later, the nations of the Houses of Israel and Judah will be reconciled, free to marry again. "For God so loved the world, that he gave his only begotten Son, that whosoever believes in him should not perish, but have everlasting life...that the world through him might be saved."[289] The word world is *kosmos*, which means the *harmonious arrangement*. It will be the perpetual new covenant that once again reconciles all Israel to Christ their LORD with the marriage vows made on this future Day of Atonement.

"As the Father has loved me, so have I loved you: continue you in my love. If you keep my commandments, you shall abide in my love; even as I have kept my Father's commandments, and abide in his love. *These things have I spoken unto you, that my joy might remain in you, and that your joy might be full*. This is my commandment, That you love one another, as I have loved you. Greater love has no man than this, that a man lay down his life for his friends."[290]

"For if, when we were enemies, we were *reconciled* to God by the death of his Son, much more, being reconciled, we shall be saved by his life. And not only so, but we also joy in God through our Lord Jesus Christ, by whom we have now received the *atonement*."[291] The first fruits beginning with Pentecost nearly

2000 years ago were reconciled by the receiving of the Holy Spirit. The national reconciliation or atonement occurs on this coming Day of Atonement.

The Son of God became mortal and gave his life, that he will become the bridegroom to those whom he has loved. It is written "...Jacob have I loved, but Esau have I hated."[292] It all started back in the book of Genesis with these two brothers. However, Esau/Edom, having sold the birthright, would not be allowed to take Israel's place. Edom is jealous of Israel being Christ's bride. Edom is doing everything in their power to kill us off in order to take our place. But no amount of effort and conniving on the part of Edom would have made Christ forsake his love for Israel. Even though, the unfaithful wife, Israel treated the first covenant disdainfully.

Some people say the Biblical record is just a collection of stories that are suitable for Sunday school and those a little weak in the gray matter. They have no relevance to our world today. Edom has been trying to convince Israel of this for thousands of years. Edom has sworn to kill us in hope of getting back the birthright. And were it not for Christ's love for Israel, Edom may well succeed. The story contained in the pages of the Biblical record is the greatest love story in history. It's all there for us to see. But even today, the House of Israel is mostly blinded to this. We believe we honor our bridegroom, our Savior, once again by following after the same false lovers that Israel has loved in the past.

Take a step back for a moment and reflect: the major holidays espoused by Christianity, supposedly honoring our Savior Christ, have as their star attractions Santa Claus and the Easter bunny. Not only has Christianity abandoned the days given to us by

Christ, the holy days that provide meaning in our daily lives, but in our self-proclaimed enlightenment, we've turned our backs on Christ's great love, to merrily run after Santa Claus and the Easter bunny!

Is it any wonder then the prophecies tell us he is *fiercely angry* with us? Is it any wonder when Christ opens the sixth seal and he unleashes the events of the apocalypse on our deep-sixed derrieres that when we cry out for his help, we are told he will firmly tell us, "But where are Santa Claus and the Easter bunny, the gods you have made yourselves? Let them rise and save you if they can in *your time of trouble*." How blind and stupid have we become?

We have allowed Christmas and Easter to hijack us from the truth. They do not honor Christ; they dishonor him. And even after his sacrifice to redeem us, giving his life for us, we repay our debt by reverting back to the same old stupidity and foolishness that has plagued our forefathers. We thoughtlessly run around buying up trees in December teaching our children that they better be nice or Santa Claus won't slide down the chimney and bring them presents. Come spring, stupidly we color eggs, and buy chocolate bunnies unendingly giving our children the gift of spiritual blindness. And with bundles of justifications ready at hand, our pastors lead the way. It's time we stand up for our heritage and put an end to this nonsense!

Christ is so angry with us, that he will open the sixth seal, the time of Jacob's trouble, the apocalypse, that for three and a half years, he will allow the anti-Christ to brutalize us. When it's all said and done, Christ will seal up 12,000 each from the twelve nations of Israel who have kept themselves from giving their hearts to false lovers, worshipping the beast. More than likely each and every Christian probably believes in his or her heart that they will not worship the anti-Christ when the time comes, yet we are already doing so every spring and every December.

"Every tree that brings not forth good fruit is hewn down, and cast into the fire. Wherefore by their fruits you shall know them. Not every one that says unto me, Lord, Lord, shall enter into the kingdom of heaven; but he that *does* the will of my Father which is in heaven. *Many* will say to me in that day, Lord, Lord, have we not prophesied in your name? and in your name have cast out devils? and in your name done many wonderful works? And then will I profess unto them, I never knew you: depart from me, you that work iniquity."[293] Do the many or the few celebrate Christmas and Easter?

The advice we are given now, both as individuals and as the nations of Israel, is the same. "Enter you in at the straight gate: for wide is the gate, and broad is the way, that leads to destruction, and many there be which go in thereat: Because straight is the gate, and narrow is the way, which leads unto life, few there be that find it."[294] For the time being, individually, we can choose to run with the herd or not.

It's not until the future Day of Atonement that the nations of Israel and Judah will join into a new covenant, a new *kosmos*, a harmonious arrangement with Christ. But only after great sorrow and near extinction after suffering through the time of Jacob's trouble will we fully realize our recklessness.

To summarize events for us: The ordinances of the Old Testament were given to Moses for the children of Israel. This covenant formed the agreement between Christ and Israel. If you haven't realized it yet, Christ is the LORD God of the Old Testament. As the apostle John has told us, "No man has seen God [*the Father*] at any time; only the begotten Son, which is in the bosom of the Father, he has declared him."[295]

Yet there are more than thirty verses in the Biblical record in which we are told that the LORD God appeared...to Abraham, to Moses, to David and to Solomon. "And when Abram was ninety years old and nine, the LORD appeared to Abram, and said unto him, I am the Almighty God; walk before me, and be you perfect."[296] This is a reference to Christ as no man has seen God the Father.

The House of Israel, we know, did not remember their covenant obligations, to the point they were divorced from our LORD, Christ, seven hundred years before his first coming. Only the House of Judah remained in the covenant agreement up to that point. Christ is the central character of both the Old and the New Testaments. Recall from the preface, Shakespeare's "cynical character Jacques stated in <u>As You Like It</u>, 'All the world's a stage... and one man in his time plays many parts....' He might have been more insightful than he realized." Christ has played many roles in our history, and will again in the future of all Israel.

At Christ's first coming, "he was sent only to the lost sheep of the House of Israel." His death marked the end of the first covenant or harmonious agreement. This officially ended the first covenant with House of Judah as Paul explains in Romans chapter eleven. The new covenant established at Christ's resurrection, resulted in individuals of the previously divorced House of Israel no longer being under the schoolmaster of the law represented by the fulfilling of the days of Unleavened Bread. Reconciliation attained through repentance, baptism and receiving of the Holy Spirit, was fulfilled by Christ on the day of Pentecost. This is the time of the gathering the first fruits prior to Christ's return. This is where we are today in God's plan for Israel, the first five seals have been opened.

Next up for us in real time is the opening of the sixth seal, the time of Jacob's trouble, both individually and nationally. Edom, the sixth empire and beast described in Revelation will have power for forty-two months over Jacob or all Israel excepted for those sealed. Then the seven trumpets will sound, marking the fulfillment of the Day of Trumpets by Christ. Babylon the Great, the sixth empire will fall. At the seventh trumpet, the 144,000 sealed from all Israel will stand on Mt Sion with Christ, marking the first resurrection. Shortly thereafter is the most solemn high holy day, when the Day of Atonement will be fulfilled by Christ. It is a day of national reconciliation for both the House of Israel and the House of Judah when our LORD will make a new covenant with them both. It is the marriage of the Lamb, the bridegroom, who once again will be a husband to Israel, but with a better, perpetual covenant of the Spirit rather than of the flesh.

The duality of the Old Testament and the New Testament should be clear. Christ is fulfilling the high holy days of the Old Testament. He is the central character of both testaments, tying the two together. There is a plan for us. That plan is not manifest in either of the duplicitous Christmas or Easter observances. That plan is manifest when we sincerely and seriously examine our heritage contained within the high holy days given to us. The counterfeits are deceits intended to betray our relationship with our Savior. They take us off the straight and narrow path given to us to walk on. While all Israel will be saved, there lies before us a terrible time if we continue in our willful ignorance. Will we stand up and follow where our Savior leads us, or will we continue to blindly follow the paths that lead to destruction?

The coming Day of Atonement will be a somber time of reflection and understanding for those few remaining of Israel. Yet, it is also is a day of great joy as it heralds a beginning, a new harmonious agreement, and a new marriage for Israel. And as with most weddings, there is the honeymoon as well. This "honeymoon," a thousand years of peace and harmony, is depicted by the next high holy day.

Chapter Seven
Christianity & The Duality of the Autumn Harvest Feast

There are a total of seven high holy days throughout the year. Three of them take place during the sacred year beginning in the first month, which is Nisan. The final four take place in the new civil year marking the kingdom of God on Earth beginning on the first day of the seventh month. In fact, the final four high holy days all occur in the seventh month of Tishri. It is no accident that these days were given to the children of Israel for observance as they outline God's plan. Contained in all of them is the duality of the physical observance by Israel, and Christ's fulfillment of them.

"*Wherefore I caused them to go forth out of the land of Egypt, and brought them into the wilderness. And I gave them my statutes, and showed them my judgments, which if a man do, he shall even live in them. Moreover also I gave them my Sabbaths [*holy days*], to be a sign between me and them, that they might know that I am the LORD that sanctify them [*set them apart as holy*]."[297]

The point made to us about these high holy days, the sabbaths, is that they were given to the children of Israel as a sign between our LORD, Jesus Christ and the children of Israel. Christ is now fulfilling these sabbath days. *These days represent every major theological event in Christianity found in the New Testament*. Of this, there is no doubt. The indigenous Christian nations of the world today are the nations of Israel. As we read earlier, "*And Jacob [*Israel*] called unto his [*twelve*] sons, and said, Gather yourselves together, that I may tell you that which shall befall you in the last days."²⁹⁸

Remember, we talked about our waypoints, the signs that lead us on the path in which we need to be walking? Christmas and Easter are not signs between our LORD and us. They are deceits made to take us away from where we need to be. Thinking that these high holy days in the Old Testament are only for one son of Israel, "the Jews," those descended from Judah, misleads us.

Why do we think this? Because Christians erroneously have been taught to believe we are an anomalous group of "gentiles" having nothing to do with Israel. But as we have seen, nothing could be further from the truth. Christ is fulfilling these days on a spiritual level for Christians, who are the lost sheep of the House of Israel exactly as he said. This is what the original text tells us as delivered by those who walked and talked and were taught by Christ in the first century.

The high holy day sabbaths occur in two seasons of the year. The first three high holy days occur in spring. Pentecost, however, while occurring in late spring marks the beginning of the summer harvest. Then the final four occur in autumn, the time of the larger fall harvest. Notice that none of these days occur in the "dead" season of winter when Christmas is celebrated. As mentioned in *The Blind Man's Elephant*, there are many indications that Christ was born in late summer.

"*Three times in a year shall all your males appear before the LORD your God in the place which he shall choose; in the feast of unleavened bread, and in the feast of weeks [*Pentecost*], and in the feast of tabernacles: and they shall not appear before the LORD empty: Every man shall give as he is able, according to the blessing of the LORD your God which he has given you."²⁹⁹ The males of Israel were to go to the site of the temple in Jerusalem at these three times. Christ did this as well during his time here on Earth. "And when he was twelve years old, they went up to Jerusalem after the custom of the feast."[300] There are other examples of his apostles and Christ doing this as well as we'll read.

Matthew Henry in his commentary states, "The general commands concerning them are, 1. That all the males must then make their personal appearance before God, that by their frequent meeting to worship God, at the same place, and by the same rule, they might be kept faithful and constant to that holy religion which was established among them. 2. That none must appear before God empty, but every man must bring some offering or other, in token of a dependence upon God and gratitude to him. And God was not unreasonable in his demands; let every man but give as he was able, and no more was expected. The same is still the rule of charity, (1 Cor. 16:2) Those that give to their power shall be accepted, but those that give beyond their power are accounted worthy of double honour (2 Cor 8:3), as the poor widow that gave *all she had*, (Luke 21:4)"[301]

The high holy day after Atonement is the feast of Tabernacles, or booths. It is different than the other high holy feast days in that the children of Israel were to live in temporary dwellings made from branches and boughs of trees for a period of seven days. It marks the largess of the autumn harvest, a time of joy and peace at the end of the agricultural harvest cycle. While it is a solemn feast, it is a time of rejoicing. It, too, is a remembrance for the time of the children of Israel coming out of Egypt.

The Holy Day Remembrance: "*Speak unto the children of Israel, saying, The fifteenth day of this seventh month shall be the *feast* *of tabernacles for seven days* unto the LORD. On the first day shall be a holy convocation: you shall do no servile work. Seven days you shall offer an offering made by fire unto the LORD: *on the eighth day shall be an holy convocation unto you*; and you shall offer an offering made by fire unto the LORD: it is a solemn assembly; and you shall do no servile work. These are the feasts of the LORD, which you shall proclaim to be holy convocations, to offer an offering made by fire unto the LORD, a burnt offering, and a meat offering, a sacrifice, and drink offerings, every thing upon his day: Beside the sabbaths of the LORD, and beside your gifts, and beside all your vows, and beside all your freewill offerings, which you give unto the LORD."[302]

The eighth day mentioned above is a separate high holy day, the seventh of the year, and is observed after the seventh day of the Feast of Tabernacles. It is the last day, or high holy day of the year, and is referred to as the great day. We'll see why in the next chapter.

"*Also in the fifteenth day of the seventh month, when you have gathered in the fruit of the land, you shall keep a feast unto the LORD *seven days*: on the first day shall be a sabbath, and on the eighth day shall be a sabbath. And you shall take you on the first day the boughs of goodly trees, branches of palm trees, and the boughs of thick trees, and willows of the brook; and you shall rejoice before the LORD your God seven days. And you shall keep it a feast unto the LORD seven days in the year. It shall be a statute for ever in your generations: you shall celebrate it in the seventh month. You shall dwell in booths seven days; all that are Israelites born shall dwell in booths: That your generations may know that I made the children of Israel to dwell in booths, when I brought them out of the land of Egypt: I am the LORD your God. *And Moses declared unto the children of Israel the feasts of the LORD.*"[303]

"*You shall observe the feast of tabernacles seven days, after that you have gathered in your corn and your wine: And you shall rejoice in your feast, you, and your son, and your daughter, and your manservant, and your maidservant, and the Levite, the stranger, and the fatherless, and the widow, that are within your gates. Seven days shall you keep a solemn feast unto the LORD your God in the place, which the LORD shall choose: because the LORD your God shall bless thee in all your increase, and in all the works of your hands, therefore you shall surely rejoice. And you shall rejoice in your feast, you, and your son, and your daughter, and your manservant, and your maidservant, and the Levite, the stranger, and the fatherless, and the widow, that are within your gates. Seven days shall you keep a solemn feast unto the LORD your God in the place which the LORD shall choose: because the LORD your God shall bless you in all your increase, and in all the works of your hands, therefore you shall surely rejoice."[304]

The New Testament mention of the feast of Tabernacles is found in the gospel of John. The word Jews' used in John's gospel in reference to the feast of Tabernacles is not a noun meaning a Jewish person or persons, but rather it is an adjective, [*Greek, Ioudaios*] descriptive of belonging to a country, in this case the national high holy day of Israel as given by Moses. "Now the Jews' feast of tabernacles was at hand."[305] Christ told his disciples to go up to Jerusalem. "You go up unto this feast: I go not up yet unto this feast; for my time is not yet full come. When he had said these words unto them, he abode still in Galilee. But when his brethren were gone up, then went he also up unto the feast, not openly, but as it were in secret. Then the Jews sought him at the feast, and said, Where is he? Now about the midst of the feast Jesus went up into the temple, and taught."[306]

The feast of Tabernacles has a duality to it like all the other high holy days. The physical observance was to commemorate the time that Israel spent living in *temporary* dwellings, or booths made from branches. They had come out of their bondage in Egypt but had not yet entered into the land promised them as their inheritance from Abraham and Jacob. So while they had their freedom, they had not yet received the fullness of the promises.

Christ's fulfilling of the feast day, the high holy day of Tabernacles will usher in a period of a thousand years of peace, free from the bondage to sin and evil in the world. It begins just after Babylon the Great is destroyed, Satan is bound for a thousand years, the first fruits are gathered at the first resurrection, and Christ is the bridegroom of Israel, both the Houses of Israel and Judah will have entered into a new covenant, a new and harmonious marriage arrangement. It is a "honeymoon" for all the children of Israel.

"And he laid hold on the dragon, that old serpent, which is the Devil, and Satan, and bound him a thousand years. And cast him into the bottomless pit, and shut him up, and set a seal upon him, that he should deceive the nations no more, till the thousand years should be fulfilled: and after that he must be loosed a little season. And I saw thrones, and they sat upon them, and judgment was given unto them: and I saw the souls of them that were beheaded for the witness of Jesus, and for the word of God, and which had not worshipped the beast, neither his image, neither had received his mark upon their foreheads, or in their hands; and they lived and reigned with Christ a thousand years. But the rest of the dead lived not again until the thousand years were finished. This is the first resurrection. Blessed and holy is he that has part in the first resurrection: on such the second death has no power, but they shall be priests of God and of Christ, and shall reign with him a thousand years."³⁰⁷

"*In that day shall you not be ashamed for all your doings, wherein you have transgressed against me: for then I will take away out of the midst of you them that rejoice in your pride, and you shall no more be haughty because of my holy mountain. I will also leave in the midst of you an afflicted and poor people, and they shall trust in the name of the LORD. The *remnant* of Israel shall not do iniquity, nor speak lies; neither shall a deceitful tongue be found in their mouth: for they shall feed and lie down, and none shall make them afraid."³⁰⁸

Recall that the Day of Atonement, which precedes the feast of Tabernacles was a day of affliction. And all Israel [Jacob] was afflicted in their time of trouble noted by the sixth seal. The thousand years of the feast of Tabernacles is a time of peace when the truth will prevail among men. They shall live a bounteous life in peace so that even in their sleep there will be no reason to fear.

And while not everyone on Earth will have died during the events heralded by the seven trumpets, the three woes and seven last plagues, those who are left alive of other nations besides Israel will have an annual obligation as did the males of Israel when they were to appear before the LORD in Jerusalem. The remnant of Israel will live in the area created by Christ when the Mount of Olives is opened north and south at his second coming. The rest of the Earth, whatever condition it will be in then, will be home to those who are left alive.

"*And it shall come to pass, that every one that is left of all the nations which came against Jerusalem shall even go up from year to year to worship the King, the LORD of hosts, and to keep the feast of tabernacles. And it shall be, that whoso will not come up of all the families of the earth unto Jerusalem to worship the King, the LORD of hosts, even upon them shall be no rain. And if the family of Egypt go not up, and come not, that have no rain; there shall be the plague, wherewith the LORD will smite the heathen that come not up to keep the feast of tabernacles.

"*This shall be the punishment of Egypt, and the punishment of all nations that come not up to keep the feast of tabernacles. In that day shall there be upon the bells of the horses, HOLINESS UNTO THE LORD; and the pots in the LORD'S house shall be like the bowls before the altar. Yes, every pot [*everyone's own house*] in Jerusalem and in Judah [*historically the area that had belonged to the House of Judah*] shall be holiness unto the LORD of hosts: and all they that sacrifice shall come and take of them, and seethe [*cook by boiling*] therein: and in that day there shall be no more the Canaanite in the house of the LORD of hosts."309

The reference to 'no more Canaanite in the house of the LORD" means there will be no ungodly person there. Remember, when the Israelites were wandering in the wilderness, before they were come into the promised land, they were told,"*And it shall be when the LORD shall bring you into the land of the Canaanites, and the Hittites, and the Amorites, and the Hivites, and the Jebusites, which he swore unto your fathers to give you, a land flowing with milk and honey, that you shall keep this service in this month."310

And once they had left the wilderness, led by Joshua, Israel was told "*And Joshua said, Hereby you shall know that the living God is among you, and that he will without fail drive out from before you the Canaanites, and the Hittites, and the Hivites, and the Perizzites, and the Girgashites, and the Amorites, and the

Jebusites. Behold, the ark of the covenant of the Lord of all the earth passes over before you into Jordan."[311]

We have another duality here. When Israel arrived in the promise land, the ungodly, the Canaanites and others, were driven out of the land promised to Israel by God. And in the future fulfillment of this day by Christ, "in that day there shall be no more the Canaanite in the house of the LORD of hosts" meaning spiritually speaking, ungodliness will not be found among the children of Israel, a new covenant with both the House of Israel and the House of Judah will pass over before them. That new covenant will have been made before on that day of reconciliation, the Day of Atonement.

Beginning with the Day of Trumpets, Christ returns to Earth establishing the kingdom of God in power and in might. We are wise as Christians, then, if we don't get lulled into a false sense of who Christ really is. He is not a helpless baby in a manger or dead on a cross. He is very much the living Son of God and will rule the nations of the Earth. "And out of his mouth goes a *sharp sword*, that with it he should smite the nations: and he shall rule them with a rod of iron: and he treads the winepress of the *fierceness and wrath of Almighty God*."[312] This is just a little bit different than Christianity's symbolism of his first coming, isn't it? In terms of mental images, Christians would be smart to look forward in this regard rather than looking backward.

The period of time, the thousand years, or millennium, will be a wonderful time for Israel even though during the time of Jacob's trouble it certainly won't have been so. But for those who do survive that time and are alive to see the fulfillment of the feast of Tabernacles by Christ, they shall be greatly blessed.

"*The wilderness and the solitary place shall be glad for them; and the desert shall rejoice, and blossom as the rose. It shall blossom abundantly, and rejoice even with joy and singing: the glory of Lebanon shall be given unto it, the excellency of Carmel and Sharon, they shall see the glory of the LORD, and the excellency of our God. Strengthen you the weak hands, and confirm the feeble knees. Say to them that are of a fearful heart, Be strong, fear not: behold, your God will come with vengeance, even God with a recompense [*a commitment to Israel again*]; he will come and save you."[313]

The reference to Sharon and Carmel goes back to Israel of the past. Carmel was known for its beauty while Sharon was a fertile agricultural area. In other words, even areas that were desert shall be made beautiful and bounteous. "*And Sharon shall be a fold of flocks, and the valley of Achor a place for the herds to lie down in, for my people that have sought me."[314] And in the poetic book of Songs, "*I am the rose of Sharon, and the lily of the valleys."[315]

Matthew Henry in his commentary explains, "What pleased to compare himself to; and he condescends very much in the comparison. He that is the Son of the Highest, the bright and morning star, calls and owns himself *the rose of Sharon, and the lily of the valleys*, to express his presence with his people in this world, the easiness of their access to him, and the beauty and sweetness which they find in him, and to teach them to adorn themselves with him, as shepherds and shepherdesses, when they appeared gay [*light-hearted and merry*], were decked with roses and lilies, garlands and chaplets of flowers.

"*The rose*, for beauty and fragrance, is the chief of flowers, and our Savior prefers the clothing of *the lily* before that of *Solomon in all his glory*. Christ is *the rose of Sharon*, where probably the best roses grew and in most plenty, *the rose of the field* (so some), denoting that the gospel salvation is a common salvation; it lies open to all; whoever will may come and gather the rose-buds of privileges and comforts that grow in the covenant of grace. He is not a rose locked up in a garden, but all may come and receive benefit by him and comfort in him. He is a *lily* for whiteness, a *lily of the valleys* for sweetness, for those, which we call so yield a strong perfume. He is a *lily of the valleys*, or *low places*, in his humiliation, exposed to injury. Humble souls see most beauty in him. Whatever he is to others, to those that are in the *valleys* he is a *lily*. He is the rose, the lily; there is none besides. Whatever excellence is in Christ, it is in him singularly and in the highest degree."[316]

The blessings to Israel at the time of the feast of Tabernacles are further expressed in Isaiah, "*Then the eyes of the blind shall be opened, and the ears of the deaf shall be unstopped. Then shall the lame leap as a hart, and the tongue of the dumb sing: for in the wilderness shall waters break out, and streams in the desert. And the parched ground shall become a pool, and the thirsty land springs of water: in the habitation of dragons, where each lay, shall be grass with reeds and rushes. And a highway shall be there, and a way, and it shall be called The way of holiness; the unclean shall not pass over it; but it shall be for those: the wayfaring men, though fools, shall not err therein. No lion shall be there, nor any ravenous beast shall go up thereon, it shall not be found there; but the redeemed shall walk there And the ransomed of the LORD shall return, and come to Zion with songs and everlasting joy upon their heads: they shall obtain joy and gladness, and sorrow and sighing shall flee away."[317] And it shall be so for a thousand years.

And this joyous time for Israel will be as Christ promised the apostles when he told them during the Passover supper he had with them; they shall be kings sitting on thrones judging the twelve nations of Israel. "But I say unto you, I will not drink henceforth of this fruit of the vine [*wine, not grape juice*], until that day when I drink it new with you in my Father's kingdom."*318* The fulfillment of the feast of Tabernacles by Christ will be that day. For when he appeared to the apostles in the flesh after his resurrection, and ate with them, Christ did not drink wine.

"And he said unto them, Why are you troubled? And why do thoughts arise in your hearts? Behold my hands and my feet, that it is I myself: handle me, and see; for a spirit has not flesh and bones, as you see me have. And when he had thus spoken, he showed them his hands and his feet. And while they yet believed not for joy, and wondered, he said unto them, Have you here any meat? And they gave him a piece of a broiled fish, and of a honeycomb. And he took it, and did eat before them... And he led them out as far as to Bethany, and he lifted up his hands, and blessed them. And it came to pass, while he blessed them, he was parted from them, and carried up into heaven. And they worshipped him, and returned to Jerusalem with great joy: And were continually in the temple, praising and blessing God. Amen."*319*

We have a further description of this time of peace when the feast of Tabernacles is fulfilled. "*The wolf also shall dwell with the lamb, and the leopard shall lie down with the kid; and the calf and the young lion and the fatling together; and a little child shall lead them. And the cow and the bear shall feed; their young ones shall lie down together: and the lion shall eat straw like the ox. And the sucking child shall play on the hole of the asp, and the weaned child shall put his hand on the cockatrice [*viper*] den.

They shall not hurt nor destroy in all my holy mountain: for the earth shall be full of the knowledge of the LORD, as the waters cover the sea.

"*And in that day there shall be a root of Jesse [*Christ*], which shall stand for an ensign of the people; to it shall the nations seek: and his rest [*the thousand years of peace*] shall be glorious. And it shall come to pass in that day, that the Lord shall set his hand again the second time to recover the remnant of his people [*after the sixth seal, the time of Jacob's trouble as pictured by the Day of Atonement*], which shall be left, from Assyria, and from Egypt, and from Pathros, and from Cush, and from Elam, and from Shinar, and from Hamath, and from the islands of the sea. And he shall set up an ensign for the nations, and shall assemble the outcasts of Israel, and gather together the dispersed of Judah from the four corners of the earth. The envy also of Ephraim [*the House of Israel*] shall depart, and the adversaries of Judah [*the House of Judah*] shall be cut off: Ephraim shall not envy Judah, and Judah shall not vex Ephraim."[320]

A.R. Fausset remarks in his commentary, concerning the envying and vexing, Ephraim and Judah have a long history. "...envy . . . of Ephraim . . . Judah--which began as early as the time (Jdg 8:1 12:1 , &c.). Joshua had sprung from, and resided among the Ephraimites (Num 13:9 Jos 19:50); the sanctuary was with them for a time (Jos 18:1). The jealousy increased subsequently (2Sa 2:8 , &c. 19:41 20:2 3:10); and even before David's time (1Sa 11:8 15:4), they had appropriated to themselves the national name Israel. It ended in disruption. (1Ki 11:26 , &c. 1Ki 12:1-33 ; compare 2Ki 14:9 Psa 78:56-71)."[321]

Recall that Ephraim is the kingly line of the House of Israel, who were the divorced outcasts and Judah is the House of Judah, the natural branches broken off. They will be gathered together. A new covenant will be made with them both on that future Day of atonement.

"*At that time they shall call Jerusalem the throne of the LORD; and all the nations shall be gathered unto it, to the name of the LORD, to Jerusalem: neither shall they walk any more after the imagination of their evil heart. In those days the House of Judah shall walk with the House of Israel, and they shall come together out of the land of the north to the land that I have given for an inheritance unto your fathers."³²²

"And so all Israel shall be saved: as it is written, There shall come out of Sion [*Jerusalem*] the Deliverer, and shall turn away ungodliness from Jacob: For this is my covenant unto them, when I shall take away their sins. As concerning the gospel, [Judah are] enemies [*vexing Ephraim or the House of Israel*] for your sakes: but as touching the election, [*Judah is*] beloved for the fathers' sakes [*and therefore the envy of Ephraim will be removed*]."³²³ This was the period when the bonds of brotherhood between the House of Israel, Ephraim, and the House of Judah were broken beginning at the first coming of Christ. And this condition exists today as well. However, the day of reconciliation comes when their brotherhood will be restored just prior to the feast of Tabernacles on the day of national atonement.

"*Moreover, you son of man, take you one stick, and write upon it, For Judah, and for the children of Israel his companions: then take another stick, and write upon it, For Joseph, the stick of Ephraim, and for all the House of Israel his companions: And join them one to another into one stick; and they shall become one in your hand. And when the children of your people shall speak unto you, saying, Will you not show us what you mean by these?

Say unto them, Thus says the Lord GOD; Behold, I will take the stick of Joseph, which is in the hand of Ephraim, and the tribes of [*House of*] Israel his fellows, and will put them with him, even with the stick of Judah, and make them one stick, and they shall be one in mine hand. And the sticks whereon you wrote shall be in your hand before their eyes."[324] Take note that it is Judah and the House of Israel being rejoined, not gentiles.

This is coming back full circle from the prophecy in Zechariah, the breaking of the bands between Ephraim and Judah at Christ's first coming when the terms of the old covenant were fulfilled by Christ's death. "*And I will feed the flock of slaughter, even you, O poor of the flock. And I took unto me two staves; the one I called Beauty, and the other I called Bands; and I fed the flock. And I took my staff, Beauty, and cut it asunder, that I might break my covenant, which I had made with all the people. And it was broken in that day: and so the poor of the flock that waited upon me knew that it was the word of the LORD...Then I cut asunder mine other staff, Bands, that I [Christ] might break the brotherhood between Judah and Israel."[325]

While the houses are divided now, once the Day of Atonement is fulfilled, they shall be joined as one again during this time of a thousand years of peace of the feast of temporary dwellings.

In the Preface to the book we talked about how all the world's a stage, a point made by Shakespeare. And just like the temporary stage that many Shakespearean plays are presented upon, our Earth, this blue globe that we call home, it too is a temporary stage. Nothing lasts forever as it is said. And the thousand years of peace that we just read about is temporary in nature.

The original feast of Tabernacles as delivered to the children of

Israel was made to commemorate their leaving Egypt. And as they wandered in the wilderness for forty years, they lived in temporary dwellings the entire time. But they had peace and their every need was taken care of by the spiritual Rock that they drank from, Christ as Paul has told us. "*And the children of Israel did eat manna forty years, until they came to a land inhabited; they did eat manna, until they came unto the borders of the land of Canaan. And the House of Israel called the name thereof Manna: and it was like coriander seed, white; and the taste of it was like wafers made with honey."*326*

The point here is that the daily needs of the children of Israel were provided for by our LORD Christ. However, the wandering in the wilderness and living in temporary dwellings was just that, temporary. And so, too, the time marked by the fulfillment of the coming feast of Tabernacles, one thousand years, will be temporary, though there will be peace on Earth as there never has been up to that time.

As we will come to realize, this Earth was made to be a temporary dwelling as were our mortal bodies. We are the spiritual experiencing the physical. And it is so not only for Israel, but for everyone living on the Earth during that period of a thousand years. As we'll discover, it is not the final circumstance of Israel or mankind. These events are represented by the eighth day, the final high holy day given to Israel by Moses. Our story that began in Genesis is coming to its final chapter in the book of Revelation. All our characters are still here.

The feast of Tabernacles was observed physically for the seven days by living in temporary booths. The fulfillment of the eighth day, or the last high holy day of the year will take place at the end of the thousand years. This eighth day's fulfillment will signal the end of the thousand years of peace on Earth. And it will result in a dramatic change in circumstances that will culminate in the second resurrection, the resurrection of all those who have lived upon Earth for it signals the great day of judgment.

Let's go to the final chapter in mankind's history on this Earth, which is the final chapter of this book.

Chapter Eight
The Last Great Day: Fulfillment of the Spiritual-Physical Duality

The last of the high holy days is the eighth day of the feast of Tabernacles, and is referred to by the apostle John in his gospel as "the last, the great day of the feast." "In the last day, that great day of the feast, Jesus stood and cried, saying, If any man thirst, let him come unto me, and drink. He that believes on me, as the scripture has said, out of his belly shall flow *rivers of living water*. (But *this spoke he of the Spirit*, which they that believe on him should receive: for the Holy Spirit was not yet given; because that Jesus was not yet glorified)."[327]

In the Book of Revelation, John wrote, "And I said unto him, Sir, you know. And he said to me, These are they, which came out of great tribulation, and have washed their robes, and made them white in the blood of the Lamb. Therefore are they before the throne of God, and serve him day and night in his temple: and he that sits on the throne shall dwell among them. For the Lamb which is in the midst of the throne shall feed them, and *shall lead them unto living fountains of waters*: and God shall wipe away all tears from their eyes."[328]

Recall Acts chapter two, Peter said on the day of Pentecost when the Holy Spirit was given, "Therefore let all the House of Israel know assuredly, that God has made that same Jesus, whom you have crucified, both Lord and Christ. Now when they heard this, they were pricked in their heart, and said unto Peter and to the rest of the apostles, Men and brethren, what shall we do? Then Peter said unto them, Repent, and be baptized every one of you in the name of Jesus Christ for the remission of sins, and you shall receive the gift of the Holy Spirit."

We are baptized physically by immersion into water, yet we rise out of the water spiritually immersed in the Holy Spirit by the laying on of hands, that is, the river of living water. It is the anointing that dwells in us of which John tells us.[329]

The quote in Revelation, "These are they which came out of great tribulation..." immediately follows the sealing of 12,000 from each of the nations of Israel. The Holy Spirit was sent to the children of the House of Israel initially on that Pentecost nearly 2000 years ago that they would be lead "unto living fountains of waters: and God shall wipe away all tears from their eyes."

This last great day was observed on the twenty-third day of the seventh month. In terms of our life, this day marks the end of the temporary, the physical and ushers in the day of the permanent, the spiritual. The stage we live our mortal lives on, the Earth, is temporary or transitional. It is like the temporary Shakespearean summer stock theatre stage taken down after the last act of the last performance. As we'll see, this metaphor applies to our life here on this blue marble planet.

The first high holy day of the feast of Tabernacles commemorates when the children of Israel dwelled in temporary booths made of tree branches and boughs, when Israel lived in the wilderness after leaving Egypt. The last great day in contrast marks the time when in the promised land, led by Joshua, not by Moses, the children of Israel would dwell in permanent houses. As we'll discover in this chapter discussing the last, great day, there are two temporary dwellings that will be changed into permanent ones.

The Last Great Day: Fulfillment of the Spiritual-Physical Duality

But first, let's read what Moses told the children of Israel concerning the old covenant observance for this last great day.

The High Holy Day Remembrance: "*On the eighth day you shall have a solemn assembly: you shall do no servile work therein: But you shall offer a burnt offering, a sacrifice made by fire, of a sweet savor unto the LORD: one bullock, one ram, seven lambs of the first year without blemish: Their meat offering and their drink offerings for the bullock, for the ram, and for the lambs, shall be according to their number, after the manner: And one goat for a sin offering; beside the continual burnt offering, and his meat offering, and his drink offering. These things you shall do unto the LORD in your set feasts, beside your vows, and your freewill offerings, for your burnt offerings, and for your meat offerings, and for your drink offerings, and for your peace offerings. And Moses told the children of Israel according to all that the LORD commanded Moses."[330]

This is very similar to the requirements given to the children of Israel for the physical observance of all the high holy days. And no doubt by now you should be able to recognize some symbolism. There are seven high holy days and seven lambs of the first year as a sweet savor unto the LORD offered. And they had to be without blemish as Christ, our Passover Lamb was without blemish. And you should also know by now that Christ is the LORD of the Old Testament as no man has seen nor spoken to the Father.

This eighth day, the last, the great day of Tabernacles, is a great day of change. It is the day that marks the change in two physical dwellings into the spiritual. First, it marks the great resurrection, the day of resurrection when all who have ever lived shall be raised up from the dead to be judged. Those found worthy will have eternal life, transformed into the spirit.

"Behold, I show you a mystery...For this corruptible must put on incorruption, and this mortal must put on immortality So when this corruptible shall have put on incorruption, and this mortal shall have put on immortality, then shall be brought to pass the saying that is written, Death is swallowed up in victory. O death, where is your sting? O grave, where is your victory? The sting of death is sin; and the strength of sin is the law. But thanks to God, which gives us the victory through our Lord Jesus Christ. Therefore, my beloved brethren, be you steadfast, unmovable, always abounding in the work of the Lord, forasmuch as you know that your labor is not in vain in the Lord."[331]

"But is now made manifest by the appearing of our Savior Jesus Christ, who has abolished death, and has brought life and immortality to light through the gospel...."[332]

This day is fulfilled, as we can read in the book of Revelation, following the seven days of Tabernacles. However, Daniel wrote of the same event in the Old Testament.

"*I beheld till the thrones were cast down, and the Ancient of days did sit, whose garment was white as snow, and the hair of his head like the pure wool: his throne was like the fiery flame, and his wheels as burning fire. A fiery stream issued and came forth from before him: thousand thousands ministered unto him, and ten thousand times ten thousand stood before him: the judgment was set, and the books were opened. I beheld then because of the voice of the great words which the horn spoke: I beheld till the beast was slain, and his body destroyed, and given to the burning flame."[333]

The Last Great Day: Fulfillment of the Spiritual-Physical Duality

In the book of Revelation it reads, "His head and his hairs were white like wool, as white as snow; and his eyes were as a flame of fire; And his feet like unto fine brass, as if they burned in a furnace; and his voice as the sound of many waters."[334]

"And when the thousand years are expired, Satan shall be loosed out of his prison. And shall go out to deceive the nations which are in the four quarters of the earth, Gog and Magog, to gather them together to battle: the number of whom is as the sand of the sea. And they went up on the breadth of the earth, and compassed the camp of the saints about, and the beloved city: and fire came down from God out of heaven, and devoured them.

"And the devil that deceived them was cast into the lake of fire and brimstone, where the beast and the false prophet are, and shall be tormented day and night for ever and ever. And I saw a great white throne, and him that sat on it, from whose face the earth and the heaven fled away; and there was found no place for them.

"And I saw the dead, small and great, stand before God; and the books were opened: and another book was opened, which is the book of life: and the dead were judged out of those things which were written in the books, according to their works. And the sea gave up the dead, which were in it; and death and hell delivered up the dead, which were in them: and they were judged every man according to their works. And death and hell were cast into the lake of fire. This is the second death. And whosoever was not found written in the book of life was cast into the lake of fire."[335]

This is the resurrection event that most Christians are familiar with although not within the context of the holy days. It is the great judgment day when every man will be judged according to his works. However, it should be pointed out that no one will be scorched for ever and ever. The lake of fire will burn up who and whatever is thrown into it. Immortality is eternal life. Eternal death is of the lake of fire. Those not found in the book of life will be cast into the lake of fire to be consumed. They will no longer exist despite Dante's popular fourteenth century allegorical work to the contrary.

These references are to the great judgment day when those who are not cast into the lake of fire will become immortal, that is they will have eternal life. We do not now, meaning in the flesh, have an "immortal soul." As we have just read, however, we do have the potential for immortality. And when this potential is fulfilled in us as pictured by this high holy day, we will have put off the temporal, our temporary fleshly bodies which we lived in, and will now put on the incorruptible, having eternal life in the spirit.

But remember, there are two temporary dwellings that will be changed here. The first is the fleshly body given to Adam, the first man. The second one is the temporary dwelling, that summer stock theatre stage if you will, that we call heaven and Earth. And just like the temporary stage that comes down after the last performance, the temporary stage of our current heaven and Earth will come down at the last high holy day. Our temporary stage was put up back at the beginning as we can read in Genesis, chapter one, verse one. "In the beginning God created the heaven and the Earth."

For spirit beings will not dwell on this temporary, physical Earth. Our habitat shall change. Our story, written in the pages of the Biblical record, will have come to an end.

The Last Great Day:
Fulfillment of the Spiritual-Physical Duality

And recall as we said from the beginning, the Biblical record is one book written to the same people. It is one story. The characters and events that were there in the book of Genesis are present here at the end as well. So first let's read from the Old Testament, that "Jewish Bible" written for all Israel, and then from the New concerning our new home.

The prophet Isaiah wrote of this day, "*For, behold, I create new heavens and a new earth: and the former shall not be remembered, nor come into mind. But be you glad and rejoice for ever in that which I create: for, behold, I create Jerusalem a rejoicing, and her people a joy. And I will rejoice in Jerusalem, and joy in my people: and the voice of weeping shall be no more heard in her, nor the voice of crying. There shall be no more thence an infant of days, nor an old man that has not filled his days: for the child shall die an hundred years old; but the sinner being an hundred years old shall be accursed. And they shall build houses, and inhabit them; and they shall plant vineyards, and eat the fruit of them. They shall not build, and another inhabit; they shall not plant, and another eat: for as the days of a tree are the days of my people, and mine elect shall long enjoy the work of their hands. They shall not labor in vain, nor bring forth for trouble; for they are the seed of the blessed of the LORD, and their offspring with them. And it shall come to pass, that before they call, I will answer; and while they are yet speaking, I will hear. The wolf and the lamb shall feed together, and the lion shall eat straw like the bullock: and dust shall be the serpent's meat. They shall not hurt nor destroy in all my holy mountain, says the LORD."[336]

The apostle Peter also commented concerning this day. "Looking for and hasting unto the coming of the day of God, wherein the heavens being on fire shall be dissolved, and the elements shall melt with fervent heat? Nevertheless, we, according to his promise, look for *new heavens and a new earth*, wherein dwells righteousness."[337]

Then as we read in the book of Revelation, "And I saw a *new heaven and a new earth*: for the first heaven and the first earth were passed away; and there was no more sea. And I John saw the holy city, new Jerusalem, coming down from God out of heaven, prepared as a bride adorned for her husband. And I heard a great voice out of heaven saying, Behold, *the tabernacle of God is with men, and he will dwell with them, and they shall be his people, and God himself shall be with them, and be their God*. And God shall wipe away all tears from their eyes; and there shall be no more death, neither sorrow, nor crying, neither shall there be any more pain: for the former things are passed away.

"And he that sat upon the throne said, Behold, I make all things new. And he said unto me, Write: for these words are true and faithful. And he said unto me, It is done. I am Alpha and Omega, the beginning and the end. I will give unto him that is athirst of the fountain of the water of life freely. He that overcomes shall inherit all things; and I will be his God, and he shall be my son. But the fearful, and unbelieving, and the abominable, and murderers, and whoremongers, and sorcerers, and idolaters, and all liars, shall have their part in the lake, which burns with fire and brimstone: which is the second *death*.

"And there came unto me one of the seven angels which had the seven vials full of the seven last plagues, and talked with me, saying, Come hither, I will show you the bride, the Lamb's wife. And he carried me away in the spirit to a great and high mountain, and showed me that great city, the holy Jerusalem, descending out of heaven from God, Having the glory of God: and her light was like unto a stone most precious, even like a jasper stone, clear as crystal; And had a wall great and high, and had twelve gates, and at the gates twelve angels, and names written thereon, which are *the names of the twelve tribes of the children of Israel*: On the east three gates; on the north three gates; on the south three gates; and on the west three gates.[338]

"And the wall of the city had twelve foundations, and in them the names of the twelve apostles of the Lamb. And he that talked with me had a golden reed to measure the city, and the gates thereof, and the wall thereof. And the city lies foursquare, and the length is as large as the breadth: and he measured the city with the reed, twelve thousand furlongs. [*1500 miles or 2400 kilometers*] The length and the breadth and the height of it are equal. And he measured the wall thereof, an hundred and forty and four cubits [or nearly 220 feet or 66 meters], according to the measure of a man, that is, of the angel.

"And the building of the wall of it was of jasper: and the city was pure gold, like unto clear glass. And the foundations of the wall of the city were garnished with all manner of precious stones. The first foundation was jasper; the second, sapphire; the third, a chalcedony; the fourth, an emerald; The fifth, sardonyx; the sixth, sardius; the seventh, chrysolite; the eighth, beryl; the ninth, a topaz; the tenth, a chrysoprasus; the eleventh, a jacinth; the twelfth, an amethyst. And the twelve gates were twelve pearls; every several gate was of one pearl: and the street of the city was pure gold, as it was transparent glass.

"And I saw no temple therein: for the Lord God Almighty and the Lamb are the temple of it. And the city had no need of the sun, neither of the moon, to shine in it: for the glory of God did lighten it, and the Lamb is the light thereof. And the nations of them, which are saved shall walk in the light of it: and the kings of the earth do bring their glory and honor into it. And the gates of it shall not be shut at all by day: for there shall be no night there. And they shall bring the glory and honor of the nations into it. And there shall in no wise enter into it any thing that defiles, neither whatsoever works abomination, or makes a lie: but they which are written in the Lamb's book of life."[339]

"And he showed me a *pure river of water of life*, clear as crystal, *proceeding out of the throne of God and of the Lamb*.[340] In the midst of the street of it, and on either side of the river, was there the tree of life, which bare twelve manner of fruits, and yielded her fruit every month: and the leaves of the tree were for the healing of the nations. And there shall be no more curse: but the throne of God and of the Lamb shall be in it; and his servants shall serve him: And they shall see his face; and his name shall be in their foreheads. And there shall be no night there; and they need no candle, neither light of the sun; for the Lord God gives them light: and they shall reign for ever and ever. And he said unto me, These sayings are faithful and true: and the Lord God of the holy prophets sent his angel to show unto his servants the things which must shortly be done. Behold, I come quickly: blessed is he that keeps the sayings of the prophecy of this book."[341]

The second dwelling that shall be changed and made permanent is the new heaven and new Earth. And it is a dwelling where God shall be. We are not going to be living in heaven with harp playing angels. Rather God will be dwelling on this new Earth with those people who have a new spiritual dwelling, who are now immortal. Consequently, at the end of the feast of Tabernacles, the feast of temporary booths or dwellings, we have a high holy day that points us to the culmination of God's plan for us. It is a plan that

The Last Great Day: Fulfillment of the Spiritual-Physical Duality

was delivered in type from Christ to Moses in the Old Testament for all Israel and has its fulfillment in Christ pictured by this high holy day, the last, great day more than a thousand years into our future. Our bodies and physical life, and our physical universe and Earth turn out to be temporary. It is the spiritual that is permanent.

Recall again, the Biblical record is tied together by the physical portraying the spiritual fulfillment. And so it is with the duality of this day as well. Let's jump back to God's dwelling on Earth before this day is fulfilled. God's physical dwelling in the Old Testament was in the Ark of the Covenant. King David had wanted a "permanent" residence to honor God. So he petitioned God to allow him to build a temple for this purpose since the ark had never had its own dwelling since the time Moses was commanded to build the ark.

"*And the LORD spoke unto Moses, saying,... And they shall make an ark of shittim [*likely a species of acacia*] wood: two cubits and a half shall be the length thereof, and a cubit and a half the breadth thereof, and a cubit and a half the height thereof. And you shall overlay it with pure gold, within and without shall you overlay it, and shall make upon it a crown of gold round about. And you shall cast four rings of gold for it, and put them in the four corners thereof; and two rings shall be in the one side of it, and two rings in the other side of it. And you shall make staves of shittim wood, and overlay them with gold. And you shall put the staves into the rings by the sides of the ark that the ark may be borne with them. The staves shall be in the rings of the ark: they shall not be taken from it.

"*And you shall put into the ark the testimony which I shall give you. And you shall make a mercy seat of pure gold: two cubits and a half shall be the length thereof, and a cubit and a half the breadth thereof. And you shall make two cherubims of gold, of beaten work shall you make them, in the two ends of the mercy seat. And make one cherub on the one end, and the other cherub on the other end: even of the mercy seat shall you make the cherubims on the two ends thereof. And the cherubims shall stretch forth their wings on high, covering the mercy seat with their wings, and their faces shall look one to another; toward the mercy seat shall the faces of the cherubims be. And you shall put the mercy seat above upon the ark; and in the ark you shall put the testimony that I shall give you. And there I will meet with you, and I will commune with you from above the mercy seat, from between the two cherubims which are upon the ark of the testimony, of all things which I will give you in commandment unto the children of Israel."[342]

"*Again, David gathered together all the chosen men of Israel, thirty thousand. And David arose, and went with all the people that were with him from Baale of Judah, to bring up from there the ark of God, whose name is called by the name of the LORD of hosts that dwells between the cherubims. And they set the ark of God upon a new cart, and brought it out of the house of Abinadab that was in Gibeah: and Uzzah and Ahio, the sons of Abinadab, drave the new cart. And they brought it out of the house of Abinadab which was at Gibeah, accompanying the ark of God: and Ahio went before the ark.

"*And David and all the house of Israel played before the LORD on all manner of instruments made of fir wood, even on harps, and on psalteries, and on timbrels, and on cornets, and on cymbals. And when they came to Nachon's threshingfloor, Uzzah put forth his hand to the ark of God, and took hold of it; for the oxen shook it. And the anger of the LORD was kindled against Uzzah; and

The Last Great Day: Fulfillment of the Spiritual-Physical Duality

God smote him there for his error; and there he died by the ark of God.

"*And David was displeased, because the LORD had made a breach upon Uzzah: and he called the name of the place Perezuzzah to this day. And David was afraid of the LORD that day, and said, How shall the ark of the LORD come to me? So David would not remove the ark of the LORD unto him into the city of David: but David carried it aside into the house of Obededom the Gittite. And the ark of the LORD continued in the house of Obededom the Gittite three months: and the LORD blessed Obededom, and all his household. And it was told king David, saying, The LORD has blessed the house of Obededom, and all that pertains unto him, because of the ark of God. So David went and brought up the ark of God from the house of Obededom into the city of David with gladness."[343]

However, God did not allow David to build the temple wherein the ark would reside. That task was given to his son, Solomon. "*And it came to pass in the four hundred and eightieth year after the children of Israel were come out of the land of Egypt, in the fourth year of Solomon's reign over Israel, in the month Zif, which is the second month, that he began to build the house of the LORD.

"*And the house which king Solomon built for the LORD, the length thereof was threescore cubits, and the breadth thereof twenty cubits, and the height thereof thirty cubits...Concerning this house which you are building, if you will walk in my statutes, and execute my judgments, and keep all my commandments to walk in them; then will I perform my word with you, which I spoke unto David your father: And I will dwell among the children of Israel, and will not forsake my people Israel. So Solomon built the house, and finished it."[344]

The Ark of the Covenant was placed in the Holy of Holies, or the most sacred place within the temple wherein only the high priest could enter only at prescribed times. When the temple Solomon built was destroyed by the Babylonians, the Ark of the Covenant, the presence of God, ceased to be there any longer. While the first temple housed the Ark of the Covenant, the second temple, the Herodian [*Edomite*] building never had the ark. No one has ever found the ark despite Indiana Jones' movie heroics and real life archeologists who have sought it.

We discover its location, however, in the book of Revelation. "And the nations were angry, and your wrath is come, and the time of the dead, that they should be judged, and that you should give reward unto your servants the prophets, and to the saints, and them that fear your name, small and great; and should destroy them which destroy the earth. And the temple of God was opened in heaven, and *there was seen in his temple the ark of his testament* [*covenant*]: and there were lightnings, and voices, and thunderings, and an earthquake, and great hail."[345]

Until the time the Babylonians destroyed the temple in Jerusalem, the Ark of the Covenant in that temple was the dwelling place of our LORD on Earth.[346] And as we have been mentioning all along, the Biblical record is rife with dualities concerning the high holy days physically observed by the children of Israel and their spiritual fulfillment by Christ. The duality between God's first dwelling on Earth, the temple built by Solomon housing the ark of the covenant and the new heaven and new Earth where God shall dwell among his people, are connected by the physical observance of the eighth day of Tabernacles which is the last great day and then by the spiritual fulfillment of the last great day.

The Last Great Day:
Fulfillment of the Spiritual-Physical Duality

We have a link between Solomon's temple and the new heaven and new Earth associated with this day. And this link is not as oblique as some might think. Recall, this last great day was to be observed by the children of Israel on *the twenty-third day of the seventh month*. On what day, then, was the physical temple, God's dwelling on Earth, that housed the ark of the covenant built by Solomon completed?

"*And in the eighth day they made a solemn assembly: for they kept the dedication of the altar seven days, and the feast seven days. And *on the three and twentieth day of the seventh month* he sent the people away into their tents, glad and merry in heart for the goodness that the LORD had showed unto David, and to Solomon, and to Israel his people. Thus *Solomon finished the house of the LORD*, and the king's house: and all that came into Solomon's heart to make in the house of the LORD, and in his own house, he prosperously effected."[347]

Both the Old Testament "permanent" residence of the ark of the covenant in Solomon's temple in Jerusalem, and the New Testament reference to the residence of the ark in the new Jerusalem both take place on the last great day, the final high holy day originally set forth to all the children of Israel by Moses more than three thousand years ago.

The dualities between the Old Covenant high holy days and the New Testament spiritual fulfillment by Christ are unmistakable. These are the days of which we should be mindful. For all the major events of Christianity are contained within them. God's feelings concerning these days should be amply clear as should his feelings concerning the hijacked festivals Christians have very ignorantly chosen to follow. Wise in our own deceits, we're behaving as "silly twits, willy-nilly wandering off the path" that leads to life.

As it's been mentioned many times previously, the Biblical record is one book written to the same people. The characters introduced in Genesis are here in Revelation. The Alpha and the Omega. It's one story.

In Conclusion

Every major theological event in Christianity found in the New Testament is the fulfillment of the archetypical high holy days found in the Old Testament.

This is the first statement in the beginning of the book. Now, having finished reading the book, its authenticity should ring clear and true.

The Biblical record is one book written to the same people. And Jesus Christ is the central character to both testaments. However, in the Old Testament he is referred to primarily as our LORD. This, too, should be apparent after reading about the duality of the seven high holy days.

From the Christian point of view, we've discovered that the high holy days are not an irrelevant collection of days delivered only to the nation of Judah, "the Jews," by Moses, a Levite. They were ordinances, days of observance given to all the children of Israel, *all twelve nations*, as signs between Christ and his people. While the days were emblematic of events experienced by Israel leaving Egypt, upon which their physical observances were based, Christ has, and is spiritually fulfilling them on our behalf.

As such they lay out our LORD's plan for his people from the time they left Egypt until there is a new heaven and a new Earth. The duality of days is central to this plan. And we have a duality of "elephants" too. We have the truth delivered to us by those who walked, talked and learned from Christ first hand; those men chosen by him to write down and canonize that text for us so we can rediscover the original elephant. And then we have the hijacked elephant, those "hijacked pagan holidays" espoused by most Christian religions today.

However, the words spoken by Christ, which were written down and canonized for us by his apostles and lastly the apostle John at the end of the first century, enable us to discern the truth of Christ's teachings. "But the Comforter, which is the Holy Spirit, whom the Father will send in my name, shall teach you all things, and *bring all things to your remembrance*, whatsoever I [Christ] have said unto you."[348] This is one reason why no other books can be included in the New Testament canon. They are the record of what Christ spoke to his apostles, which in turn, are now spoken to us millennia later.

In regards to what you've read here in this book, we should, as the apostle Paul admonished the church at Thessalonica, "Prove all things. Hold fast that which is good." Study these things and prove them for yourselves. Don't take my word for it. As Paul advised Timothy, "Study to show yourself approved unto God, a workman that needs not to be ashamed, rightly dividing the word of truth."

In this regard, this book is like a sign posted on a path, i.e., "Extreme Danger: Avalanche Area. Do Not Ski Beyond This Point." You can ignore it completely or you can heed it. There is no point in arguing with it. Prove it one way or the other yourself, and then make your own personal decision. If you think the information in this book is total BS, then forget it, and go on with your life. On the other hand, if you discover it has merit, then stand up and make the necessary changes. One day everyone will know with certainly which was the correct course of action.

Let's recap "the original elephant," the dualities as delivered to us by those who experienced it first hand.

Passover: A day of preparation, not a high holy day. It is the sacrifice of the LORD 's passover, who passed over the houses of the children of Israel in Egypt, and delivered their houses and their first born from death when he spared not the Egyptians.

Christ was the Passover lamb, the first born of God, who became the sacrificial lamb for the sins of Israel granting us victory over death.

Days of Unleavened Bread: The children of Israel left Egypt so quickly in one day that they took only unleavened bread. Both Egypt and leavening equate with sin metaphorically. Therefore these days pictured coming out of sin.

Christ's death ended the old covenant by which sin was imputed. The fulfilling of these days by Christ paid the penalty of sin, death, once for the sins of the children of Israel. Sin is the transgression of the law, "...but sin is not imputed when there is no law."[349] Therefore, the sins of Israel were covered, in one day, by Christ's death. His day of resurrection, in between these two high holy days, marked the beginning of the new covenant.

Pentecost: This was a day of remembrance for the children of Israel when they were to offer up the first fruits of their summer harvest unto God.

Christ sent the Holy Spirit to those called and chosen, that they will be the first fruits of his harvest, the first resurrection, marked by his second coming. It was the first official day of Christianity ushering in the period of *personal reconciliation*.

Christ has fulfilled these three high holy days. We are now living in the time between the fulfillment of Pentecost and the return of

Christ when he will fulfill the four remaining high holy days.

Day of Trumpets: The high holy day that heralds the beginning of the new civil year for the children of Israel, the first day of the seventh month, marked by the blowing of trumpets.

Christ will return on this day marked by a blowing of seven trumpets, the seventh instituting the kingdom of God on Earth preceded by the time of Jacob's trouble, the sixth seal.

Day of Atonement: This was the most solemn high holy day for the nation of Israel. It was a day marked by fasting that pictured a forgiveness of sins of the nation and their reconciliation to God.

Christ will fulfill this day when a new covenant is made with the House of Israel and the House of Judah, *a national day of reconciliation*. They shall be joined again as one in the hand of God. However, they will both have been greatly afflicted during the time of Jacob's trouble leading to this day.

Feast of Tabernacles: Or the festival of booths as it was known. The people of Israel were to live in temporary dwellings made of tree branches and boughs to represent the time when, after coming out of Egypt, they lived in the wilderness. All during this time our LORD watched over them, "And did all drink the same spiritual drink: for they drank of that spiritual Rock that followed them: and that Rock was Christ."*350*

Christ will fulfill this day, which will mark the beginning of the thousand years of peace, the millennium, when Israel will enjoy the spiritual blessings of the promises given to Abraham. The other nations of the world at that time will have to make an

In Conclusion

appearance each year before the LORD on this day. However, this Earth, as well as our mortal bodies are temporary dwellings.

The Last Great Day: The last high holy day of the year immediately follows the feast of temporary dwellings. It was on this eighth day, that Solomon finished the temple, the house of the LORD containing the Ark of the Covenant, which no longer had a temporary dwelling place in the physical sense.

This day will be fulfilled with the great day of judgment which is the resurrection day of all who have lived and culminates when the temporary heavens and Earth we inhabit now will pass away on this day, along with our mortal bodies, with the creation of a new heaven and new Earth which will be God's dwelling place.

The dark and deceitful counterfeits of Christmas and Easter, among others, which lead us nowhere except to our own confusion, are derisory by comparison to the days God set aside for us that light the way along our destined path. In the darkness, we have lost sight of our identity and our direction. Christmas and Easter are nothing more than "Detour" signs that direct us down the wrong path. The result? The elephant has been hijacked.

We can do better than the imposters. But do we want better? Do we really want to make a difference now? One would think so, at least for anyone who seriously considers himself or herself a Christian. As Christians, the Biblical record forms the foundation of our faith. In this case, Christ is telling us that the very people he was sent to redeem, are the very ones that he is angry with over the tree and the Christmas celebration. He tells us we are stupid and foolish for doing this. Do not Christmas and the tree pertain to him? Then why would we not listen to him?

He is fiercely angry, we are told, so much so that he will shake the Earth mightily that the mountains and islands will move off their foundations. The light of the Sun and the Moon will cease. Yet, I doubt most people will react to this…until it happens. Our "top of the ninth" home run winning mentality has made us lukewarm in our day-to-day faith.

I suspect some others will dismiss all this as mere folklore, or hyperbole designed to scare us. Whatever the excuses may be, however, the next four high holy days to be fulfilled by Christ are statements of future fact.

Therefore, we would be wise to consider that in the Book of Daniel, our LORD told us about five world empires that would succeed one another over an exact period of 2520 years beginning in 602 BCE.[351] He gave us exacting details about each one. And he brought it to pass exactly as he said, despite the fact that scientists tell us man cannot know the future because of the way the universe and we are created. We live in a world of probabilities. God does not. He brings all things to pass. This is the theological arrow of time. The evidence is there for us to see if we are not blind. That which we call the apocalypse, the opening of the sixth seal, the ushering in of the sixth empire, is no exception.

The holidays celebrated by most Christians are sweetened falsehoods with the specific anti-Christ intent to keep us away from our birthright and true identity as Christians. Do we settle, then, for inferior knowledge because we are blind, naked and poor as our LORD has told us when all along we wrongly think we are rich and increased with goods? Or are we more blasé in our thinking, "What's the harm in having family over and exchange some gifts set under a tree? It's fun and we don't worship the tree. We celebrate Christmas for good reason."

Christ gives Christians living in this time some very good advice, by way of metaphor, in the book of Revelation concerning our attitude towards the destitute holidays we blindly follow.

"So then because you are lukewarm, and neither cold nor hot, I will spit you out of my mouth. Because you say, I am rich, and increased with goods, and have need of nothing; and know not that you are wretched, and miserable, and poor, and blind, and naked: I counsel you to buy of me gold tried in the fire, that you may be rich; and white raiment, that you may be clothed, and that the shame of your nakedness do not appear; and anoint your eyes with eye salve, that you may see.

"As many as I love, I rebuke and chasten: be zealous therefore, and repent, Behold, I stand at the door, and knock: if any man hear my voice, and open the door, I will come in to him, and will sup with him, and he with me. To him that overcomes will I grant to sit with me in my throne, even as I also overcame, and am set down with my Father in his throne."[352]

Along these same lines, Christ also gave us this sage advice, "Enter you in at the straight gate: for wide is the gate, and broad is the way, that leads to destruction, and many there be which go in thereat: Because straight is the gate, and narrow is the way, which leads unto life, and few there be that find it."

"Beware of false prophets, which come to you in sheep's clothing, but inwardly they are ravening wolves. You shall know them by their fruits. Do men gather grapes of thorns, or figs of thistles? Even so every good tree brings forth good fruit; but a corrupt tree brings forth evil fruit. A good tree cannot bring forth evil fruit; neither can a corrupt tree bring forth good fruit. Every tree that brings not forth good fruit is hewn down, and cast into the fire." [353]

We have explored the seven high holy days in their physical and spiritual dualities. They are signs, lampposts that light our way into the past and into our future. Their light of discernment shines only on one path before us. The other path is darkness, spiritual blindness. The path we choose to follow will define our lives and, ultimately our destiny.

"*For the LORD [*Christ*] gives wisdom: out of his mouth comes knowledge and understanding. He lays up sound wisdom for the righteous: a defender to them that walk uprightly. He keeps the paths of judgment, and preserves the way of his saints. Then shall you understand righteousness, and judgment, and equity; yes, every good path.

"Then wisdom enters into your heart, and knowledge is pleasant to your soul; Discretion shall preserve you, understanding shall keep you: to deliver you from the way of the evil, from the man that speaks contrary things; who leave the paths of uprightness, to walk in the ways of darkness;

"Which forsake the guide of her youth, and forgets the covenant of her God. For her house inclines unto death, and her paths unto the dead. None that go unto her return again, neither take they hold of the paths of life. *That you may walk in the way of good, and keep the paths of the righteous* for the upright shall dwell in the land, and the perfect shall remain in it. But the wicked shall be cut off from the earth, and the transgressors shall be rooted out of it."[354]

The "guide of her youth" here refers to our LORD, the spiritual Rock and husband of Israel when the covenant [*Israel's marriage arrangement*] was first established through Moses. Now in the end times, Christ has established a new covenant, not of the flesh and the law, but of the Spirit and the promises. Christ is fulfilling the high holy days.

But we are blind to all this. We have followed false prophets and walked off the path of righteousness, delivered to us by the apostles, our first century forefathers, once again. Why have we done this? Because we think we know better. "When the church hijacked these pagan holidays it was for good reason, to influence the world with biblical worldview and culture. We have every right to take these things and spin them with the goodness of the Lord as part of the Great Commission… We take something bad and make it good." These hijacked pagan holidays, in terms of our faith and destiny, are unusable; they're worthless, nothing more than errors that have been introduced into Christianity over the past two millennia. And as we just read, Christ said "A corrupt tree *cannot* bring forth good fruit."

Most people say they want to know the truth. But in fact, most people want a comfortable, i.e., lukewarm, version of the truth which ceases to be the truth. The truth is we have no power or authority to take that which is "bad and make it good." The truth is we have no right to take false pagan holidays and spin them with the "goodness of the LORD." The truth is we don't need to hijack pagan holidays.

What we need to do is understand who we Christians really are, acknowledge our heritage, and get back on the paths of righteousness knowing our LORD Jesus Christ is fulfilling his promises to us. As it is now, the Houses of Israel and Judah are following the path that leads to the opening of the sixth seal, the apocalypse, the time of Jacob's trouble.

The opportunity to make a choice is present still. Which path will we choose? The path whose light shines before us, or the path of persistent darkness? Be honest with yourself and choose wisely.

For "*The way of the wicked is as darkness: they know not at what they stumble. But the path of the just is as the shining light, that shines more and more unto the perfect day."*355*

Appendix One: Lists

Names

Abram became **Abraham** and had a son, Isaac

Isaac had two sons, Esau and Jacob

Esau became **Edom**, sold the birthright to his younger, non-identical twin brother Jacob

Jacob became **Israel** and had 12 sons

Twelve sons of Israel: Reuben, Simeon, Levi, Judah [Jews], Zebulun, Issachar, Dan, Gad, Asher, Naphtali, Joseph, and Benjamin.

Israel's wife Leah gave birth to **Reuben, Simeon, Levi, Judah, Issachar and Zebulon.**
Leah's handmaid, Zilpah, **became wife to Israel** and gave birth to **Gad and Asher.**
Israel's wife Rachel gave birth to **Joseph and Benjamin.**
Rachel's handmaid, Bilhah, **became wife to Israel** and gave birth to **Dan and Naphtali.**

Moses, and his brother **Aaron** were descendants of **Levi**, which became the priesthood of God for Israel. Therefore, Moses was not Jewish or a descendent of Judah. Moses was a descendant of Israel however.

Joshua, a descendant of **Joseph** and Ephraim, led the children of Israel across the Jordan river into the land promised to Abraham.

Initial **king of all Israel** was **Saul** who was a descendant of **Benjamin**. The kingship was taken away from the nation of Benjamin and given to **David**, descendant of **Judah**, then to his son, **Solomon**, and then Israel was split into two houses.

Israel split: **House of Israel** [*10 nations plus priesthood*] Later, they were divorced and no longer partakers of the covenant. None of them are Jews or descendants of the House of Judah.

House of Judah [*1 nation plus priesthood*] **Edom** legally incorporated into Judah by time of Christ. They are the Jews.

House of Israel kingly line is of **Joseph**, who had two sons **Manasseh**, and **Ephraim**, although the younger brother, Ephraim became the kingly line of the House of Israel.

House of Judah kingly line is of **David**.

Christ, a physical descendant of **David**, was "sent only to the **lost sheep of the House of Israel**."

High Holy Days

The high holy days are the archetype of every major theological event in Christianity found in the New Testament.

*"*Three times you shall keep a feast unto me in the year.*

[1] "You shall keep the feast of unleavened bread: (you shalt eat unleavened bread seven days, as I commanded thee, in the time appointed of the month Abib [Nisan]; for in it you came out from Egypt: and none shall appear before me empty:)

Passover [preparation day] Death of Christ ends the first covenant.

First and last **Days of Unleavened Bread**. Sin taken away by Christ.

[2] "And the feast of harvest, the first fruits of your labors, which you have sown in the field:

Pentecost First day of Christianity through receiving of the Holy Spirit.

Christ has fulfilled these first three days.

[3] "and the feast of ingathering, which is in the end of the year, when you have gathered in your labors out of the field. Exodus 23:14-16.

Day of Trumpets Return of Christ.

Day of Atonement New covenant with House of Israel and House of Judah.

Feast of Tabernacles Millennium, thousand years of peace.

Last Great Day Great day of resurrection, new heaven and new Earth.

Book abbreviations and names

Old Testament

Gen	Genesis
Exd	Exodus
Lev	Levitcus
Num	Numbers
Deu	Deuteronomy
Jos	Joshua
Ki	Kings
Chr	Chronicles
Psa	Psalms
Pro	Proverbs
Isa	Isaiah
Jer	Jeremiah
Ezk	Ezekiel
Dan	Daniel
Has	Hosea
Oba	Obadiah
Jon	Jonah
Zph	Zephaniah
Zec	Zechariah
Mal	Malachi

New Testament

Mat	Matthew
Mrk	Mark
Luk	Luke
Jhn	John
Rom	Romans
Cor	Corinthians
Gal	Galatians
Col	Colossians
Phi	Philemon
Ths	Thessalonians
Tim	Timothy
Heb	Hebrews
Jms	James
Ptr	Peter
Rev	Revelation

Most Old Testament authors were not Jewish

It is likely that most Christians, who think of the Old Testament [OT] as being for the Jews and therefore written by the Jews, would be surprised to discover that most of the OT was not written by Jews, or those descended from the House of Judah. In fact, those of Levi wrote most of the OT for all twelve sons of Israel. "And I [God], behold, I have taken the Levites from among the children of Israel instead of all the firstborn that opens the matrix among the children of Israel: therefore the Levites shall be mine...." Num 3:12

Levi became the priesthood under Aaron from the times of Moses. The Pentateuch, the Law, the first division of the OT, originated with Moses. Moses was not Jewish either, but a Levite.

Those who are descendants of the one son of Israel, Judah, are those who are Jews in the literal sense of the word. It is genealogy rather than religion. Daniel, for example, was a descendant of Judah. Although modern scholars discount that the book of Daniel was written by Daniel due to the accuracy of the prophecies contained therein by 165 BCE. If this premise is taken to its logical conclusion, the book of Daniel could not have been written until the early twentieth century. See chapter five of *The Blind Man's Elephant*.

It should be noted that we do not have specific lineage information about many OT authors. As Moses and the priesthood were of Levi, it is likely that the books in the Prophet division were written by them as well, which, by definition, would exclude those descended from Judah.

Jeremiah and Ezekiel were Levites. Samuel, born into an Ephraimite family, is thought to be of Levi ancestry too. It is possible he may have written the book of Ruth as well. While Isaiah traditionally has been linked to royalty, no Biblical record of this can be supported.

However, many of the royal books, such as Psalms, Proverbs, Ecclesiastes, etc., were most like written by those descended from Judah, specifically David and Solomon. Others like Ezra and Nehemiah were Levitical.

Also, the exact identity, in terms of ancestry, of the 12 minor prophets cannot be established. It is likely, therefore, that most of these books, too, were Levitical.

Ezra organized the OT canon as we know it today. Therefore, the majority of the books of the OT very likely were not written by Jews, but more than likely were written by the descendants of Levi for all the sons of Israel.

Appendix One: List

*Original Order of Books**

The Old Testament: 3 Divisions, 22 Books

The Law: Genesis
Exodus
Leviticus
Numbers
Deuteronomy

The Prophets: *The Former Prophets:* Joshua-Judges
Samuel-Kings

The Latter Prophets:
<u>The Major Prophets:</u> Isaiah
Jeremiah
Ezekiel
<u>The Minor Prophets:</u> The Twelve
[Hosea-Malachi]

The Writings: *The Poetic Books:* Psalms
Proverbs
Job

The Festival Books: Song of Songs
Ruth
Lamentations
Ecclesiastes
Esther

The Restoration Books: Daniel
Ezra-Nehemiah
Chronicles

The New Testament: 3 Divisions, 27 Books

Gospels & Acts: *The Gospels:*   Matthew
　　　　　　　　　　　　　　　　　　Mark
　　　　　　　　　　　　　　　　　　Luke
　　　　　　　　　　　　　　　　　　John

　　　　　　　　　　Acts:　　　　　Acts

Epistles: *Universal:*   1, 2 Peter
　　　　　　　　　　　　　　　　James
　　　　　　　　　　　　　　　　1, 2, 3 John
　　　　　　　　　　　　　　　　Jude

　　　　　Paul's: <u>Seven Churches:</u>   Romans
　　　　　　　　　　　　　　　　　　　　　1, 2 Corinthians
　　　　　　　　　　　　　　　　　　　　　Galatians
　　　　　　　　　　　　　　　　　　　　　Ephesians
　　　　　　　　　　　　　　　　　　　　　Philippians
　　　　　　　　　　　　　　　　　　　　　Colossians
　　　　　　　　　　　　　　　　　　　　　1, 2 Thessalonians

　　　　　　　　　　<u>General:</u>   Hebrews

　　　　　　　　　　<u>Pastoral:</u>   1, 2 Timothy
　　　　　　　　　　　　　　　　　Titus
　　　　　　　　　　　　　　　　　Philemon

Prophetic:　　　　　　　　　　　　Revelation

The Biblical record has 2 Testaments, 6 divisions, and 49 books
*Restoring The Original Bible, Ernest L. Martin, 1994

Appendix Two: Endnotes

Endnotes

Preface

[1] The content of Chapter Five in The Blind Man's Elephant is verification of this point.

[2] www.askelm.com

Chapter One

[3] See Exd 13:21, 22; 14:21; 16:32. For a full understanding of how it was that the House of Israel became "gentiles," see footnote 4.

[4] For a full explanation read *The Blind Man's Elephant*, in particular Chapter Six, *The Genesis Birthright*.2008, Michael J. Miller

[5] Ecc 3:19-22

[6] The Blind Man's Elephant, Chapter Six, Michael J. Miller

[7] Gen 49:22-26

[8] Dan 2:44

[9] Heb 13:8

[10] Hebrew word, ets, meaning tree, stock, wood, etc.

[11] Jer 10:1-13

[12] 2 Ptr 2:1-22

[13] Isa 13:10,13

[14] www.salon.com, "Global boiling", December 12, 2008, Kirsten Weir

[15] For an interesting fictional account of the methane hydrate scenario read, *The Swarm* by German author Frank Schätzing. There are, from time to time, programs on the Discovery, History and National Geographic Channels that deal with these scenarios. The Shoemaker-Levy comet collision with Jupiter in 1994 demonstrates the validity of human extermination with such an impact.

[16] http://blog.wired.com/wiredscience/2008/05/could-methane-t.html

[17] Rev 6:12-17

[18] Isa 56:1,2

[19] Eze 20:13

[20] Jer 2:26ff

[21] 1Ki 11:4

[22] 1Ki 11:5ff

[23] Jhn 20:1

[24] Mat 12:39,40

[25] Jhn 19:38-42

[26] Jhn 19:31

[27] Mat 15:18

[28] Jer 7:18 JFB commentary, A.R. Fausset. "Cakes were made of honey, fine flour, &c., in a round flat shape to resemble the disc of *the moon*, to which they were offered. Others read as *Margin*, "the frame of heaven," that is, the planets generally; so the *Septuagint* here; but elsewhere the *Septuagint* translates, "queen of heaven." The Phoenicians called the moon *Ashtoreth* or *Astarte*: the wife of Baal or Moloch, the *king* of heaven."

[29] Jer 7:19

[30] Jer 7:20

[31] 2 Tim 3:16

[32] 1 Cor 14:33

Chapter Two

[33] Mat 15:24

[34] If you need a fuller understanding of this, once again please read *The Blind Man's Elephant* particularly Chapter Six, <u>The Genesis Birthright</u>.

[35] Rom 9:7; Acts 3:13

[36] Zec 11:7,14

[37] Jer 3:8; Isa 50:1

[38] Heb 9:16, 17; Rom 11:21

[39] Heb 8:8, 9

[40] 1 Cor 10:1-4

[41] Gal 3:24

[42] Heb 9:15

[43] 1 Cor 6:19

[44] The significance of this for mankind is covered in *The Blind Man's Elephant*, Chapter One.

[45] Gal 3:24,29

[46] Gen 12:1-3

[47] Gen 13:15,16

[48] Gen 16:2

[49] Gen 17:4-8

[50] Gen 17:16

[51] Gen 17:19-21

[52] Gen 18:12-15

[53] Gen 22:2

[54] Gen 22:6-10

[55] Gen 22:12

[56] Gen 22:14

Appendix Two: Endnotes

[57] Gen 22:16-18

[58] 2 Chr 3:1

[59] Gal 3:1-19

[60] Deut 12:1-3

[61] Lev 23:1-36, 39-44

[62] Lev 23:37,38

[63] Jos 1:1,2

[64] Gal 2:15

[65] Heb 9:16-28

[66] Heb 8:5; Phi 3:20

[67] 1 Cor 10:4

[68] Heb 8:8; Jer 31:31

[69] *The Blind Man's Elephant*, Chapter Six, Michael J. Miller

Chapter Three

[70] Exd 12:15ff

[71] Exd 13:3ff

[72] Acts 7:9-37

[73] Heb 9:11

[74] Jhn 1:17

[75] Exd 1:13

[76] Exd 2:23,24

[77] Exd 3:20

[78] Exd 8:21ff

[79] Exd 9:8ff

[80] Exd 9:15ff

[81] Exd 9:21

[82] Exd 12:23, 24

[83] Exd 12:21-31

[84] Heb 10:1-10

[85] Mrk 14:12-17. It should be noted that the observance of the Passover and the high holy Days of Unleavened Bread collectively had come to be known as the Days of Unleavened Bread even though the Passover was the day before the first day of unleavened bread.

[86] Luk 22:29, 30

[87] Luk 22:15, 20

[88] 1 Cor 11:20-29

[89] Luk 24:41-44

[90] Exd 12:1, 2

[91] Exd 12:33ff

[92] JFB (Jamieson, Faussett, Brown, 1871) commentary, Exodus Chapter 12, Robert Jamieson

[93] Exd12:33ff

[94] 1 Cor 5:6-8

[95] Rom11:26, 27

[96] Gal 5:1

[97] Gal 5:2

[98] Gal 5:7, 8

[99] Gal 5:13-18, 25

[100] 1 Jhn 3:4 Think of it this way. If you drive through an intersection where no STOP sign is posted, can you get a ticket for not stopping? Of, course not. But if a legal STOP sign is posted, then yes you can. It's the law.

Chapter Four

[101] Mat 15:24

[102] Lev 23:10-22

[103] Redeemed: here used by Peter is *lytroo* in Greek. It means to release on receipt of a ransom. This is what one would pay kidnappers to get someone back. On a lesser note, it is the same

principle as buying back your watch from the pawnshop. You've bought back something that belonged to you. You've redeemed it. In either case, it implies buying back something that previously was yours for a payment.

In Christianity, Christ is called the Redeemer. However, if Christians are merely a group of gentiles that believe in Christ, he could be their savior, but he could hardly be their redeemer. For a redeemer can only buy back that which previously belonged to him. Gentiles would hardly qualify on this count. The children of Israel, however, were in a covenant relationship, which, at least metaphorically, was a marriage. Thus, Christ could buy back his bride with payment of a ransom, in this case his death and resurrection for the lost sheep of the House of Israel.

Even though Christians often sing hymns referring to Christ as their Redeemer, we still consider ourselves to be gentiles rather than descendants of Israel. We miss the forest for the trees. www.hymns.me.uk/there-is-a-redeemer-favorite-hymn.htm

[104] 1 Ptr 1:18-20

[105] Rom 8:29

[106] Lev 23:15, 16

[107] Lev 23:22

[108] Mat 15:22-28

[109] Jhn 14:24

[110] Acts 2:5,6

[111] Acts 2:7,8

Appendix Two: Endnotes

[112] Acts 2:16

[113] Rom 9:26; Mat 4:14-17

[114] Hsa 1:10; 2:23

[115] JFB commentary, Romans Chapter Nine, David Brown

[116] 1 Jhn 2:12

[117] Matthew Henry Commentary, c.1706, Acts Chapter Two

[118] Acts 2:17-21

[119] Acts 2:22-25

[120] Acts 2:36, 38

[121] Rom 8:1

[122] Rom 8:2ff

[123] 1 Jhn 3:1-11

[124] Rev 20:5.6

[125] Rev 20:12

[126] Gal 3:16

[127] Gal 3:25

[128] 1 Cor 15: 20-23

[129] Rom 8:29

[130] Jhn 15:26

[131] Rom 8:13

[132] Change times: It states in Daniel 7:25 "And he [*the antichrist*] shall speak great words against the most High, and shall wear out the saints of the most High, and *think* to change times and laws: and they [*Israel*] shall be given into his [*Edom's*] hand until a time and times and the dividing of time." This is a reference to the 42 moons or months of Jacob's time of trouble known as the apocalypse. A time is a year. Times is two years and the dividing of time is six months. This will be the sixth empire led by Edom. We'll read more about this in chapter five.

A.R. Fausset makes a perceptive observation in reference to this verse in Daniel, "...*change times*--the prerogative of God alone (Dan 2:21 *see below*); blasphemously assumed by Antichrist. The "times and laws" here meant *are those of religious ordinance; stated times of feasts* [MAURER]." [A.R.Fausset, JFB, Daniel chapter 7] Christmas and Easter are changed times.

Of course, this entire book is an examination of those original religious ordinances, the *"stated times of feasts"* in contrast to the hijacked pagan festivals that have taken Christianity away from its birthright. Beware of false prophets Christ warned. Instead, Christianity has embraced them. And what is perhaps most amazing is that Christianity today thinks they are doing this to honor Christ completely oblivious to who they really are serving.

"Daniel answered and said, Blessed be the name of God for ever and ever: for wisdom and might are his: And he [*God*] changes the times and the seasons: he removes kings, and sets up kings: he gives wisdom unto the wise, and knowledge to them that know understanding: He reveals the deep and secret things: he knows what is in the darkness, and the light dwells with him." [Dan 2:21-22]

The other point made in Daniel is that "they [*Israel*] shall be given into his [*Edom's*] hand until a time and times and the dividing of time." This is the opening of the sixth seal. And who is it that delivers Israel into Edom's hand? Christ. And to whom does the doctrine of the Christmas tree pertain? Christ. "And I beheld when he had opened the sixth seal, and, lo, there was a great earthquake; and the sun became black as sackcloth of hair, and the moon became as blood... For *the great day of his wrath is come; and who shall be able to stand?*"

And what are we told about those to whom Christ said he was sent because they were following after changed times and laws, no longer cognizant of the days set forth by Christ for his children? "But the LORD is the true God, he is the living God, and an everlasting king: at *his wrath the earth shall tremble, and the nations* [of Israel] *shall not be able to abide his indignation.*" [Jer10:10]

The antichrist of the apocalypse has already changed the *stated times of feasts*, and replaced them with hijacked pagan festivals which Christianity has whole-heartedly accepted. The church, prior to the opening of the sixth seal, is told we are poor and blind. We are told we are stupid and foolish. The doctrine of the tree is vanity, or theologically, nothing more than "hot air" to put it in today's vernacular.

[133] Mat 25:13

[134] Rom 8:23

[135] James 1:18

[136] Col 2:1-20

[137] "Ezra also changed the names of the calendar months from the old names (i.e., Abib is the first Hebrew month) to the common names then in use in the international Aramaic language, (i.e., Abib became Nisan, etc.). This further distinguished the Jewish calendar and its official holyday system from that of the Samaritans." *Restoring the Original Bible*, Chapter 6, page 92, Ernest L. Martin.

[138] Jhn 12:15

[139] Zec 9:9

[140] Zec 9:10

Chapter Five

[141] see *The Blind Man's Elephant*, Chapter Five, Michael J. Miller. It is Heisenberg's Uncertainty Principle.

[142] Mat 24:2, 3

[143] Acts 2:36

[144] Lev 23:23-25

[145] Num 29:1-6

[146] Num 10:10

[147] JFB commentary Lev 23:24, Num 10:10, Robert Jamieson

[148] Mat 24:44

Appendix Two: Endnotes

[149] Jms 1:25

[150] JFB commentary, Numbers Chapter Ten, Robert Jamieson

[151] Num 10:8

[152] Num 10:9

[153] Num 31:6

[154] 2 Chr 13:12-16

[155] Rev 3:17-19

[156] Jos 6:1-21

[157] Rev 6:12

[158] Rev 13:5

[159] Gen 27:41

[160] Acts 2:20

[161] Rev 6:12

[162] Jer 10:10-12, 14-16, 21

[163] Jer 31:10,11

[164] Gen 25:23

[165] Mrk 10:45

[166] Rev 6:1-11

[167] 2 Cor 11:4, 13,14

[168] Mat 7:15-19

[169] Ptr 2:1

[170] Jhn 4:1-3

[171] Mat 10:34

[172] Matthew Henry Commentary, Revelation, Chapter Six

[173] Rev 6:12-17

[174] Jer 30:7

[175] Deu 31:15-21

[176] JFB commentary, Deuteronomy, Robert Jamieson

[177] Rom 9:27-29

[178] Gen 2:1

[179] ibid

[180] Rev 7:1-4

[181] Heb 8:9

[182] Rev 14:4,5; see also Phi 2:15, 1 Th 5:23

[183] Mat 7:13-15

[184] Zph 1:14-18

[185] Isa 13:6-11, 13,19

[186] Isaac Newton, 1733

[187] 2 Ptr 3:9

[188] 1 Ths 5:1,2

[189] Rev 8:1,2

[190] Matthew Henry Commentary, Revelation, Chapter Eight

[191] Jos 6:10

[192] Jos 6:13

[193] Rev 8:2

[194] Gen 27:37

[195] Jhn 8:33

[196] Gen 27:41

[197] Dan 7:20-22; also see *The Blind Man's Elephant*, Chapter Six; and *The Gulag Archipelago* I & II, Aleksandr I. Solzhenitsyn regarding Joseph Stalin, nee Jughashvili, "...the other great holocaust of our century." [NY Times book review, June 16, 1974, Stephen F. Cohen]. http://www.bbc.co.uk/history/historic_figures/stalin_joseph.shtml

[198] Rev 6:9

[199] Gen 27:40; for an in depth look, see *The Blind Man's Elephant*, Chapter Six, Michael J. Miller

[200] Matthew Henry Commentary, Joshua, Chapter Six

[201] Jos 6:24

[202] 2 Ptr 3:10

[203] Rev 18:18, The sixth century BCE Ishtar gate still stands at the ancient site of Bablyon though many of the gate's decorative dragons, or sirrush, were vandalized during the latest Iraqi war.

[204] Rev 8:2-6

[205] Rev 8:7-13

[206] Jon 3:10 "And God saw their works, that they turned from their evil way; and God repented of the evil, that he had said that he would do unto them; and he did it not."

[207] Rev 9:1-12

[208] Matthew Henry Commentary, Revelation, Chapter Nine

[209] JFB commentary, Revelation, Chapter Nine, A.R. Fausset

[210] Mat. 24:1-12

[211] Jhn 12:25,26 Related to this is the principle, we find in John, chapter three, "The wind blows where it desires, and you hear the sound thereof, but can not tell from where it comes, and where it goes: so is every one that is born of the Spirit."

[212] Rev 9:13-21

[213] Rev 13:4-8

Appendix Two: Endnotes

[214] Rev 10:2-4

[215] Rev 10:9

[216] Rev 11:1,2

[217] Rev 11:3-7

[218] Rom 11:17

[219] Rev11:8-10

[220] Rev 13:5

[221] Rev 11:11-14

[222] Mat 24:30, 31

[223] Isa 27:12, 13

[224] Rev 11:15

[225] 1Ths 14:16,17

[226] Rev 11:18

[227] Rev 20:4-6

[228] Mat 24:3

[229] Act 1:9-12; Sabbath's day journey is about one kilometer.

[230] Zec. 14:4

[231] 1 Ths 4:13-15

232 1 Cor 15:52, 53, 58

233 Rev 15:1-4

234 2Ki 17:36"

235 Deu 31:19-23

236 Lev 23:24

237 Rev 18:2-5

238 Rev 19:11-21

239 Rev 18: 2-5, 7, 8, 21

240 Rev 15:1-8; Dan 12:7

241 Rev 16:1-21

242 The 535 CE eruption of just one volcano, Krakatoa, whose worldwide effects lasted for more than a decade, provides us a *tiny* example of what lies ahead. "The sun began to go dark, rain poured red, as if tinted by blood. Clouds of dust enveloped the earth... Yellow dust rained down like snow. It could be scooped up in handfuls," according to The Nan Shi Ancient Chronicle of Southern China, describing weather there in late 535. See http://ezinearticles.com/?Days-of-Darkness-(AD-535-AD-546)&id=202540

243 Mrk 13:3-9

244 Mrk 12:19-20

245 Gen 27: 40,41

[246] Rev 18:4

Chapter Six

[247] Heb 8:7, 8

[248] Jer 31:31

[249] Heb 8:10-13

[250] Jer 31:33,34

[251] Acts 2:36

[252] Jhn 14:26

[253] Heb 8:1,6

[254] Heb 8:10

[255] This order of spiritual or sacred first and physical or royalty second is the same ranking found in the Old Testament books. The Law and the Prophets precede the Writings or royal books. "The prophets had greater rank than the kings." "*Restoring the Original Bible*, p.94, Ernest L. Martin. Within the duality of our lives, we learn from the Biblical record that our insight concerning life is greater the closer we come to living spiritually through the Spirit of God rather than with a focus on the physical through the spirit of man. Hence the apostle Peter's admonition to the House of Israel to "change, be baptized, every one of you in the name of Jesus Christ for the remission of sins, and you shall receive the gift of the Holy Spirit."

[256] Heb 10:9-13

[257] Heb 10:14-18

[258] Heb 9:15

[259] Read Rom 8:5-17

[260] Italics from New King James Version

[261] 2Cor 5:16-21

[262] Rom 5:10-12

[263] Col1:20-22

[264] Read Gen 3:1-4

[265] Heb 2:14-18

[266] JFB commentary Book of Numbers, and Leviticus Chapter Sixteen, Robert Jamieson

[267] Lev 23:23-32

[268] Num 29:7-11

[269] Lev 16:29-34

[270] Matthew Henry Commentary, Leviticus, Chapter Sixteen

[271] Acts 3:18-20

[272] Acts 3:21,22

[273] JFB commentary, Book of Acts, Chapter Three, David Brown

[274] Isa 49:7-16

[275] Isa 49:14, 15, 26

[276] Rev 19:17,18

[277] Mal 3:5-7

[278] Jer 50:4-7

[279] Jer 10:21

[280] Oba verses 13,17

[281] Rev 14:1

[282] Rev 19:1-6; Dan 12:7

[283] Rev 19: 8-10

[284] Lev 16:32-34

[285] Mat 9:15

[286] Jer 3:8

[287] Rom 11:7

[288] Rom 11:8-21, 25

[289] Jhn 3:16,17

[290] Jhn 15:9-13

[291] Rom 5:10,11

[292] Rom 9:13

[293] Mat 7:19-23

[294] Mat 7:14

[295] Jhn 1:18

[296] Gen 17:1

Chapter Seven

[297] Ezek 20:9-11

[298] Gen 49:1

[299] Deu 16:16

[300] Luke 2:42

[301] Matthew Henry Commentary, Deuteronomy, Chapter 16

[302] Lev 23:34-38

[303] Lev.23:39-44

[304] Deut 16:13-15

[305]"Now the Jews' feast of tabernacles was at hand." At the time this was occurring in the early first century, the House of Judah, the Jews, were the only repository of these days given to all Israel. The other nations of Israel were still in their divorced state with regard to the first covenant. Thus the observance to this day would be referred to as the Jews' feast. To take it as implying that this high holy day is, historically, for the Jews only, and not

for all Israel, would be incorrect.

[306] Jhn 7:2ff

[307] Rev 20:2-6

[308] Zep 3:11-13

[309] Zec 14:16-21

[310] Ex. 13:5

[311] Jos 3:10,11

[312] Rev 19:15

[313] Isa 35:1-4

[314] Isa 65:10

[315] Songs 2:1

[316] Matthew Henry Commentary, Song of Songs, Chapter Two

[317] Isa 35:5-10

[318] Mt 26:29

[319] Luke 24:41-43, 50-53

[320] Isa 11:6-13

[321] JFB Commentary, Isaiah, Chapter Eleven, A. R. Fausset

[322] Jer 3:17,18

[323] Rom 11:26-28

[324] Ezek 37: 16-20

[325] Zech 11:10-12,14

[326] Ex 16:35,31

Chapter Eight

[327] Jhn 7:37-39

[328] Rev 7:14-17

[329] 1 Jhn 2:27

[330] Num 29:35-40

[331] 1 Cor 14:52-58

[332] 2 Tim 1:10

[333] Dan 7:9-10

[334] Rev 1:14,15

[335] Rev 20: 7-15

[336] Isa 65:17-25

[337] 2 Ptr 3:12, 13

[338]"And *your seed* shall be as the dust of the earth, and you shall spread abroad to the west, and to the east, and to the north, and to the south: and in you and in your seed shall all the families

of the earth be blessed." Gen 28:14 Prophetic promise made to Abraham.

[339] Rev 21:1-27

[340] See John 7:37-39

[341] Rev 22:1-7

[342] Ex 25:1,10-22

[343] 2 Sam 6:1-12

[344] 1Kings 6:1, 2, 11-14

[345] Rev 11:18,19

[346] It is interesting to note that when the Babylonian's destroyed the temple built by Solomon, the ark of the covenant is not seen again until Christ, the temple of the new heaven and Earth, has destroyed Babylon the Great.

[347] 2 Ch 7:9-11

In Conclusion

[348] John 14:26

[349] Rom 5:13

[350] 1 Cor 10:4

[351] *The Blind Man's Elephant*, Chapter Five, Michael J. Miller

[352] Rev 3:16-21

[353] Mat 7:13-19

[354] Pro 2:6-13, 17-22

[355] Pro 4:19,18

About the author, Michael J. Miller

The author has written numerous articles for newspapers and magazines, as well as television documentaries and award winning educational films on varied topics including local, national and international politics, economics, medicine, history, the marine environment and theology among others. He has degrees in political science, history and theology. He is the author of "The Blind Man's Elephant."

www.ingramcontent.com/pod-product-compliance
Lightning Source LLC
LaVergne TN
LVHW051823080426
835512LV00018B/2702